THE
MODERN PUSHTU
INSTRUCTOR

THE
MODERN PUSHTU
INSTRUCTOR

QAZI RAHIMULLAH KHAN

دا یوﮦ قطرﮦ په مثل دَ باران کړی | اللهی دَ خپل حبیب دَ برکت
پهراوری یی بوستان اوګلستان کړی | پر خیرازﮦ دَ چمن وارﮦ غنچی کړی

EDITED BY
H. L. OGDEN

ASIAN EDUCATIONAL SERVICES
NEW DELHI ★ CHENNAI ★ 2005

ASIAN EDUCATIONAL SERVICES

* 31, HAUZ KHAS VILLAGE, NEW DELHI - 110016
  Tel : 2656-0187, 2656-8594   Fax : 011-2649-4946, 2685-5499
  e-mail : asian_jj@vsnl.com / aes_publications@yahoo.co.in

* 5, SRIPURAM FIRST STREET, CHENNAI - 600 014
  Tel : 2811-5040   Fax : 044-2811-1291
  e-mail : asianeds@md3.vsnl.net.in

  www.asianeds.com

Printed and Hand-bound in India

Price : Rs. 495
First Published : Peshawar, 1938
AES First Reprint : New Delhi, 1992
AES Second Reprint : New Delhi, 2001
AES Third Reprint : New Delhi, 2005
ISBN : 81-206-0584-5

Published by J. Jetley
For ASIAN EDUCATIONAL SERVICES
31, Hauz Khas Village, New Delhi - 110 016.
Processed by AES Publications Pvt. Ltd., New Delhi-110016

CONTENTS.

Part I.

GRAMMAR.

Part II.

PROSE COMPOSITION.

CONTENTS

Part I

GRAMMAR

AUTHORS PREFACE.

The need for a new Pushtu hand-book has become imperative since the Board of Examiners has raised the standard of Military Examinations in this language and the N. W. F. P. has achieved the dignity of a province.

The previous manuals and grammars, good as they were in their day, do not fulfil modern requirements.

The grammar, syntax rules, and exercises in this Manual are entirely original and have been designed to ensure that the student should gain a knowledge of Pushtu as spoken by genuine Pathans.

In a work of this kind where for the first time a Pathan born and bred has attempted to codify his mother tongue, it is inevitable that some errors, or at least weaknesses, should occur.

I shall be most grateful to any of my brother Munshis who may point out to me such things or make suggestions for improvements in future editions.

I dedicate this work, which has largely been a labour of love, to all future students of Pushtu.

QAZI RAHIMULLAH, Khalil,

ACKNOWLEDGEMENT.

I am most grateful to the many friends who have helped me in compiling this Manual and in particular to Maulana Abdul Qadir Khan, M. A., LLB., B. T., (Honours in Arabic), Headmaster, Islamia Collegiate School, Peshawar, and member of the Text-book Committee, Department of Education, N. W. F. P. Peshawar.

I should also like to mention Major F. J. Dillon M.C. R.I.A.S.C., and Captain A.H.W. Rowlandson S. Waziristan Scouts. who have helped me with suggestions and idiomatic translations.

QAZI RAHIMULLAH,

I have read through the New Pushtu Instructor compiled by Qazi Rahimullah and find it extremely interesting and instructive. A real Pushtu Munshi, Qazi Rahimullah has brought the experience of years of teaching to bear on the subject he has so skilfully handled and I have not the slightest hesitation in stating that this "Instructor "has supplied the need which the existing Manuals on the market fail to supply. Comparisons are odious, but as it is, the Manuals referred to above were prepared, not with a view of bringing up Pushtu Grammar to a level with grammars written in other languages, but were simply attempts at organising a few facts of Pushtu Grammar to present them to students with scanty knowledge of the language. To a real student of the language, therefore, the need for properly organised facts of Grammar was imperative and Qazi Rahimullah has done well to undertake the work. About 150 Syntax Rules have been framed, which I am sure will be appreciated by those who have something to do with Pushtu and its Grammar.

It is very easy to understand, explain and even criticize rules but it is very difficult to

frame rules where no rules are in existence.
Besides these the author has left out nothing
that a Pushtu Manual should contain and I
hope and trust that students of Pushtu
Grammar will find in it all that they require
for the proper understanding of the idiom and
the spirit of the people who use the language.
The author has collected such proverbs as are
commonly used by the Pathan as he sits in
his Hujra (Club) and effort has been made to
supply their equivalent where possible or at
least their nearest translation where an
equivalent proverb in English could not be
found. Idioms and proverbs relating to the
various parts of the body have been similarly
incorporated and effort has been made to
take the students into the very midst of the
Pathans sitting in their Hujras and transa-
cting their daily business. I am confident
that the "Modern Pushtu Instructor" will be
welcomed by all lovers of the Pathan and his
language and it is to the attention of such
that I would commend this book.

Every language has certain irregularities
and peculiarities and Pushtu is not immune
About 130 tricky sentences have been
collected and translated in Section 13

and a student of Pushtu will find great help in mastering the language if he studies them. In Volume II are to be found a number of Examination Question papers of the various Military and Civil Examinations to give students a little practice and this I am sure will be welcomed by many students who burn midnight oil to get through their examinations. There is also one special feature of Volume II which must be mentioned, and it is that the author has collected and classified the vocabulary of the various Pathan tribes like the Afridis, the Mohmands and others and I am sure this could not be found anywhere in any book written on Pushtu Grammar.

In short the "Modern Pushtu Instructor" is a valuable contribution to Pushtu literature and I hope the Author's efforts will produce the result we all desire such a book to produce.

Maulana Abdul Qadir (Yousafzai)
M.A., LLB., B. T. (Honours in
Arabic) Headmaster Islamia
Collegiate School, Peshawar,
and Member Text Book
Committee Department of
Education N.- W. F. P.,
Peshawar.

The greatest difficulty I found in learning Pushtu was that no two grammar books used the same rules and that the manuals of those days were very limited in scope. Each was compiled for one special group of learners, Civil, Militia or Army.

None of these by itself was sufficient for the modern Military Examinations, nor, if combined, would they cover the syllabus.

A new book was needed to put the study of Pushtu on a footing with the study of the other languages.

With his "Modern Pushtu Instructor" Munshi Qazi Rahimullah has produced what was required.

The new system of verb diagrams and the grammar sections are clear ; the papers and vocabularies useful.

But, for myself, I am particularly taken with the Syntax Rules (section 10 of Part I) the tricky sentences (section 13 of Part II) and the idioms and Proverbs in Volume II When a student has mastered these he should be able correctly to use Pushtu idiom, in other words, to be able to talk sense instead of nonsense or worse. For instance, what is meant by :—

هغه پۀ سپين آس باند سوردى

compared with— هغه پۀ سپين آس كنس سوردى

or again, which do you mean to say ?

هغه پۀ مور باند تلى دى

or :— هغه مور ته تلى دى

A mistake here may easily be disastrous for the speaker !

I wish Qazi Sahib all good luck with his new book.

(Sd.) F. J. DILLON,
Major R. I. A. S. C.

I have read through Qazi Rahimullah's Pushtu Instructor and feel certain that it will be a success as it fills a much felt want. The book should be of great assistance to students of the language, as the author has taken great pains to be clear and concise in the explanation of the various Syntax Rules etc. The idioms and proverbs in Vol. II of the book should prove most useful as also should the various vocabularies especially the Afridi and Court vocabularies. I wish the author every success which he well deserves for taking the trouble to write a really up to date book on the language.

(Sd.) A. ROWLANDSON,
Captain.
South Waziristan Scouts.

———

PART I.

Pushtu Alphabet.

1. The Pushtu Alphabet consists of forty letters :—

Form	Power.	Name.
ا	A	*Alif*
ب	B	*Bé*
پ	P	*Pé*
ت	T (Soft)	*Thé*
ټ	T (Hard)	*Té*
ث	S	*Sé*
ج	J	*Jim*
ح	H (Arabic)	*Hé*
خ	Kh	*Khé*
څ	Ch	*Ché*
ځ	S or Z	*Sim* or *Zim*
د	D (Soft)	*Dāl*
ډ	D (Hard)	*Dāl*
ذ	Z	*Zāl*
ر	R (Soft)	*Ré*
ړ	R (Hard)	*Ré*
ز	Z	*Zé*
ژ	Jh	*Jhé*
ږ	G	*Gé*

Form	Power.	Name.
س	S	*Sin*
ش	Sh	*Shin*
ښ	Kh	*Khin*
ص	S	*Swād*
ض	Z	*Zwād*
ط	T	*Twé*
ظ	Z	*Zwé*
ع	A or I	*Ain*
غ	Gh	*Ghain*
ف	F	*Fé*
ق	Q	*Qāf*
ک	K	*Kāf*
ګ	G	*Gāf*
ل	L	*Lām*
م	M	*Mim*
ن	N	*Nūn*
و	O, W, U	*Wāo*
ه	H (Round)	*Hé*
ۀ	H (Butterfly)	*Hé*
ء	Á	*Hamza*

{ Used generally in
conjunction with
ي = Y. broadening
the sound.
ئ = ai
for example = جنئ
= *Jinai*
= Girl.

ي =   E, I, or Y.

2. The following seven letter-forms are purely Pushtu viz:—

ټ	T (Hard)	*Té*
ځ	S or Z	*Sim* or *Zim*
ډ	D (Hard)	*Dal*
ړ	R (Hard)	*Ré*
ږ	G	*Gay*
ښ	Kh	*Khin*
ګ	G	*Gaf*

The following eight letter-forms are Arabic viz:—

ث	S	*Sè*
ح	H̤	*Hé*
ص	S	*Swād*
ض	Z	*Zwād*
ط	T	*Twé*
ظ	Z	*Zwé*
ع	A	*Ain*
ق	Q	*Qaf*

The following three letter-forms are common to Pushtu. Hindustani and Persian, but not found in Arabic viz:—

پ	P	*Pé*
چ	Ch	*Ché*
ژ	Jh	*Jhé*

The remaining letter forms are common to Pushtu, Arabic, Persian, and Hindustani.

3. Pushtu Script is written from right to left.

4. When writing a word, all except the following letters are joined together from the right hand side and not from the left :—

١	A	*Alif*
د	D	*Dāl*
ड़	D	*Dāl*
ذ	Z	*Zāl*
ر	R	*Ré*
ड़	R	*Ré*
ز	Z	*Zé*
ژ	Jh	*Jhé*
ژ٠	G	*Gé*
و	O, W	*Wao*
ه	H (Round)	*Hé*

See the shape of above letters in the middle of a word :—

ـا	A		ـو	O, W
ـد	D		ـه	H
ـر	R			

NOTE :—When writing a word in which any of the above letters occurs, a space is left between this letter and the next. See the position of the letter in the middle of the following words :—

خيال	*Khyāl*
عدالت	*Adālat*
صدر	*Sadar*
سرَى	*Saray*
خراپ	*Kharāp*
خوار	*Khwār*

5. The following are initial, medial and final forms of the letters :—

NAME	FINAL	MEDIAL	INITIAL
Alif	...ا	...ا...	ا
Bé	...ب	...ب...	ب...
Pé	...پ	...پ...	پ...
Thé	...ت	...ت...	ت...
Té	...ٹ	...ٹ...	ٹ...
Sé	...ث	...ث...	ث...
Jim	ج...	...ج...	ج...
Hé	ح...	...ح...	ح...
Khé	خ...	...خ...	خ...
Ché	چ...	...چ...	چ...
Sim or *Zim*	ژ...	...ژ...	ژ...
Dāl	د...	د...	د

NAME	FINAL	MEDIAL	INITIAL
Dal	د...	د...	د
Zal	ذ...	ذ...	ذ
Ré	ر...	ر...	ر
Ré	ړ...	ړ...	ړ
Zé	ز...	ز...	ز
Jhé	ژ...	ژ...	ژ
Gé	ږ...	ږ...	ږ
Sin	س...	...س...	...س
Shin	ش...	...ش...	...ش
Khin	ښ...	...ښ...	...ښ
Swād	ص...	...ص...	...ص
Zwād	ض...	...ض...	...ض
Twé	ط...	...ط...	...ط
Zwé	ظ...	...ظ...	...ظ
Ain	ع...	...ع...	...ع
Ghain	غ...	...غ...	...غ
Fé	ف...	...ف..	...ف
Qaf	ق...	...ق.	...ق
Kaf	ک...	...ک...	...ک
Gaf	ګ...	..ګ...	..ګ
Lām	ل...	...ل...	ل
Mim	م...	...م...	...م
Nūn	ن...	...ن...	...ن
Wāo	و...	...و...	و...
Hé	ه...	.. ه ..	...ه
Yé	ى...	...ى ..	..ى

6. Vowels :—

SHORT.	LONG.

$\overline{Zabar}$ = a, u   ا - ح - ع - ه - ء .

$\underline{Zer}$ = é,   ی = é ی = ee, i, ئ = ai

$\acute{P\acute{e}sh}$ = o   و = ō, w. ؤ = ū, oo

EXAMPLES.

بِت But	جَل Jal
بِت Bét	جِل Jél
بُت Bot	جُل Jol
كَل Kal	دَر Dar
كِل Kél	دِر Dér
كُل Kol	دُر Dor

يَ ay	i. e. سَرَی Saray	A man
ی é (like 'a' in English)	i. e. ونی Wané	Trees
يِ ee, i	i. e. مالی Māli	Gardener
ئ ai	i. e. جنئی Jinai	Girl
ۃ ā (H. soft)	i. e. ونۃ Wana	Tree
ۃ uh (H. hard)	i. e. نیکۃ Nikuh	Grand father.

NOTE—The short vowels are not written explicitly, but they are understood and consequently pronounced.

(a) words ending in "ah" are pronounced as "a" = ۃ = h (Soft) i. e. تبۃ = *Taba* = Fever.

(b) o, or u (short) at the beginning or a word = اُ = o or u i. e. اُستاذ = *Ostāz* = Teacher.

(c) 'E' (short) or 'I' at the beginning of a word ۱ = é, i i. e., اِقرار = *Iqrār* = Agreement, promise.

7, In addition to the above vowels, there are certain signs used with consonants, to modify their sound ; they are :—

(i) - *mad*, only used on the top of ۱ = *alif* to lengthen the sound, thus = آمین = *āmin* = so be it.

(ii) ـ *tashdid* ; an Arabic sign causing the consonant over which it is placed to sound double ; thus = اتّفاق = *Ittefāq* = a chance, union.

(iii) ٴ *two zabars* on the top of alif sounds "an" as فوراً *fauran*   At once.

تخمیناً *takhminan* Nearly.

Section 2.

(READING AND WRITING EXERCISES).

(I)

کور ـ مور ـ خور ـ جوړ ـ کار ـ مار ـ لار ـ سَر ـ وَر ـ پَر ـ نَر ـ الم

رِګ ـ نَر ـ لور ـ سور ـ سُور ـ پُل ـ چپ ـ سَل ـ مینځ ـ رِبَړ

وینس ـ رَنګ ـ بَر ـ حَق ـ پیر ـ چَل ـ جال ـ مال ـ کال ـ میل

کز ـ تنګ ـ لبر ـ واک ـ خر ـ سیند ـ بازار ـ قبول ـ مَد ـ اوبس

آس ـ اسپه ـ کپ ـ اوز ـ چرګ ـ خوار ـ سردار ـ إقرار ـ آختر

أستاذ ـ اوبه

Kōr. Mōr. Khōr. Jōr. Kār. Mār. Lār. Sar.
War. Par. Nar. Lām. Rag. Ghar. Lōr.
Sōr. Sūr. Pul. Chup. Sal. Maikh. Raig.
Wĭkh. Rang. Bar. Haq. Pir. Chal. Jāl.
Māl. Kāl. Mĭl. Gaz. Tang. Lag. Wāk
Khar. Sĭnd. Bāzār. Tōl. Mad. Ŭkh. Áss
Áspa. Kat. Aor. Charg. Khwār. Sardār.
Iqrār. Akhtar. Ostāz. Obuh.

(II)

دفتَر ـ چَرته ـ دوست ـ خراپ ـ دَلته ـ پلار ـ ورور ـ غریب ـ کوهاټ
لاهور ـ جلال آباد ـ کابل ـ نوکر ـ کتاب ـ ماښام ـ وروکی
پیښور ـ چترل ـ مردان ـ روند ـ چرګه ـ زور ـ مَیز ـ کُرسۍ
ناوخته ـ ټوکرۍ ـ جواب ـ جنګ ـ واښه ـ کلی ـ سپی ـ سری
مالیان ـ هلته ـ راشه ـ کینه ـ فارسی ـ پښتو ـ پښتون ـ هندوستانی
انګریزی ـ بادشاه

Daftar. Charta. Dōst. Kharāp. Dalta. Plār.
Vrōr. Gharib. Kohāt. Lāhōr. Jalālabād.
Kābal. Nōkar. Kitāb. Mākhām. Warūkay
Pékhawar. Chatrāl. Mardān. Rūnd. Charga.
Zōr. Maiz. Kursai. Nāwākhta. Tōkrai.
Jawāb. Jang. Wākhuh. Kalay. Spay.
Saray. Māliān. Halta. Rāsha. Kaina.
Fārsi. Pukhtō. Pukhtūn. Hindustāni. Angrézī.
Bādshāh.

(III)

زۀ دَ صاحب نوکريم ۔ دا هلك ځما ورور دیَ ۔ ځما کور پۀ کوهاټ کښ دیَ ۔ دا لار چرته تلی دَه ۔ ځما سپیَ ناجوړ دیَ ۔ دننه راشه ۔ ستا پلار دلته راغلیَ نۀ دی پرته دَ هغۀ څۀ کیږی ۔ اوس ناوخته دیَ بیا راشه ۔ داڅوک دیَ ۔ دَ هغۀ کور چرته دیَ ۔ دَ هغی مور چرته وَه سړی باهر وَه ۔ ځما سلام ورکړه ورته ووایه چه دلته راشی ۔ زۀ به ډاکټر وبام ۔ مردان خراب ځای نۀ دیَ ۔ دا لار ښهر ته تلی دَه ۔ ډیره ښه ده

Zuh da Sāhib naukar yam. Dā halak zamā
vrōr day. Zmā kōr puh Kohāt ké day. Dā lār
charta talé dah. Zamā spay nājōr day.
Danana rāsha. Stā plār dalta rāghalay nuh
day. Tuh da haghuh suh kége. Ôss nāwakhta
day. Biā rāsha. Dā sōk day. Da haghuh kōr
charta day. Da haghé mōr charta wah. Saray
bāhar woh. Zamā salām warkra. Warta wo
wāya chi dalta rāshi. Zuh ba dāktar wo balam.
Mardān kharāp zāi nuh day. Dā lār khahar
ta talé dah. Déra kha dah.

(IV)

دوه تن سړی ولاړ روؤ ۔ يو بادشاه ځما مُلک ته راغی ۔ دَ بادشاه څوی
ناجوړ شو ۔ دوه کال پس هغه مړ شو ۔ دَ کور پۀ خواکښ يو جماعت
دیَ ۔ دَ کلی خلق ډیر ښۀ دی ۔ هغوی ټول پۀ کوزِ نوکښ اوسیدِ وی

خپل سپاهیان اوس آرام کوي ۔ څما طلب چرته دی ۔ کمان افسرصاحب
بنه سری دی ۔ خپل افسران بنه دی ۔ دمغو پلتن اوس پۀ کراچي
کښ ده ۔ زراورشه بیا دلته مۀ راخه ۔ زر زر کار کوه۔ زۀ دفتر تۀ ځم ۔ پۀ
څلور بجی به بیرته راځم ۔

*Dawa tana sari walār woo. Yao bādshāh zamā
mulk ta rāghay. Da bādshāh zōi, nājōr sho
Dwa kāla pas hagha mar sho. Da kōr puh khwā
ké yao jumait day. Da kali khalq dair khuh di
Haghūi tōl puh kōrūno ké oségi. Tōl spāhyān
oss arām kawi. Zamā talab ūharta day. Kamān
afsar sāhib khuh saray day. Tōl afsarān khuh
di. Da hagho paltan oss puh Karāchai ké dah.
Zar lārsha biā dalta muh rāza. Zar zar kār
kawa. Zuh daftar ta zam. Puh salōr bajé ba
biartā rāzam.*

Section 3.

There is no article in Pushtu, corresponding
to the "a" or "an" in English, the article being
inherent in the noun itself.

یو = *Yau* = one, which is an indefinite numeral,
is some times used as an article, as :—

یو بادشاه = *Yau bādshāh* = A king.

PERSONAL PRONOUNS.

زهٔ	*Zuh*	I	
تهٔ	*Tuh*	Thou	} Singular.
هغه	*Hagha*	He, she, it or that	

موؤنږ	*Mūng*	We	
تاسو	*Tāso*	You	} Plural.
هغوي	*Haghūi*	They (Masculine and Feminine)	

POSSESSIVE PRONOUNS.

زما	*Zamā*	My or mine	
ستا	*Stā*	Thy or thine	
دَ هغهٔ	*Da haghuh*	His	} Singular.
دَ هغی	*Da haghé*	Her	

ځموؤنږ	*Zamūng*	Our or ours	
ستاسو	*Stāso*	Your or yours	
دَ هغوي	*Da haghūi*	Their or theirs (m. or f.)	} Plural.

THE VERB "TO BE."

Present Tense.

زهٔ یم	*Zuh yam*	I am	
تهٔ یی	*Tuh yé*	Thou art	
هغه دی	*Hagha day*	He is	} Singular.
هغه ده	*Hagha ḥah*	She is	

مُوَنْږ يوْ	Mūng yū	We are	
تاسوئُږی	Tāso yai	You are	Plural
هغوی دی	Haghūi di	They are (M. and F.)	

FUTURE TENSE.

زۀ به یم	Zuh ba yam	I will be or I shall be	
تۀ به یی	Tuh ba yé	Thou wilt be	Singular
هغه به یِی	Hagha ba yi	He, she, it	
or		will be	
هغه به وی	Hagha ba wi		
مُوَنْږ به یوْ	Mūng ba yū	We will be	
تاسو به یئ	Tāso ba yai	You will be	
هغوی به یِی	Haghūi ba yi		Plural.
or		They will be	
هغوی به وی	Haghūi ba wi	(M. and F.)	

PAST TENSE.

زۀ وم	Zuh wam	I was	
تۀ وی	Tuh wé	Thou wast	
هغه وۀ	Hagha woh	He was	Singular
هغه وه	Hagha wah	She was	
مُوَنْږ وُ	Mūng woo	We were	
تاسو وئ	Tāso wai	You were	
هغوی وُ	Haghūi woo	They were	Plural.
هغوی یی	Haghūi wé	They were (Feminine)	

Section 4.

PREPOSITIONS AND POST-POSITIONS

A preposition is composed of two parts and the noun or pronoun qualified is placed in the middle, while a postposition is always placed after the noun or pronoun.

NOTE :—The inflected form of زۀ = *Zuh* is ما = *mā*; and تۀ = *tuh* is تا = *tā*, of هغۀ = *hagha* is هغۀ = *hqghuh* and in the case of feminine singular هغۀ = *hagha* becomes هغې = *haghé*; while in 1st 2nd and 3rd person plural the pronouns remain uninflected, as :—

لۀ نه = *Luh-na* from

لۀ ما نه	*Luh mā na*	from me	
لۀ تا نه	*Luh tā na*	from thee	⎫
لۀ هغۀ نه	*Luh haghuh na*	from him	Singular
لۀ هغې نه	*Luh haghé na*	from her	⎭

لۀ موږ نه	*Luh mūng na*	from us	⎫
لۀ تاسو نه	*Luh tāso na*	from you	
لۀ هغوی نه	*Luh haghūi na*	from them	Plural
لۀ هغوی نه	*Luh haghūi na*	from them (Feminine)	⎭

NOTE:—Either of the two parts can be used to express the same meaning as above, but the first part can only be used with nouns and pronouns ending in consonants, in which case

Zabar = *a*, should be put over the last consonant letter of the noun and pronoun, instead of نه = *na*, as :—

نه پیښور لۀ	*Luh pekhawar na*	
پیښور نه	*Pekhawar na*	}From Peshawar.
لۀ پیښور	*Luh pekhawara*	

ته = *ta* له = *la* لرِ = *lara* or وته = *wata* = to as :—

ماته	*mā ta*	to me	
تاته	*tā ta*	to thee	
هغۀ ته	*haghuh ta*	to him	}Singular.
هغې ته	*haghé ta*	to her	
مونږ ته	*mūng ta*	to us	
تاسو ته	*tāso ta*	to you	
هغوی ته	*haghūi ta*	to them	}Plural.
هغوی ته	*haghūi ta*	to them (Feminine)	

NOTE :—Decline the personal pronouns with the following post or prepositions as above :—

پۀ کښ	*puh-ké*	In
پۀ ماکښ	*puh mā ké*	In me etc.

NOTE :—The last part of above can also be used to express the same meaning as:—

پۀ پیښور کښ	or *puh pekhawar ké*	
یا	or	}In Peshawar.
پیښور کښ	*pekhawar ké*	
پۀ باندی	*puh-bāndé*	On.
پۀ ما باندی	*puh mā bāndé*	On me etc.

NOTE :—Either of the two parts of above can be used to express the same meaning as :—

پۀ ميز باندې	Puh méz bāndé	⎫
پۀ ميز	Puh méz	On the table.
ميز باندې	Méz bāndé	⎭
لاندې	Lāndé	Beneath, below, under.
ماالاندې	Mā lāndé	Beneath, below or under me etc.

NOTE :—Certain post-positions can also be used with the noun or pronoun in the Genitive Case *e. g.* :—

دـدلاندې يا	da-da lāndé	⎱ Beneath, below or
دـکلاندې	or da-lāndé	⎰ under.
څما دلاندې	zamā da lāndé	Under me.
څما لاندې	Zamā lāndé	Under me.
څما ميز دلاندې	Zamā méz da lāndé	Under my table.
څما ميز لاندې	Zamā méz lāndé	Under my table.
سره	Sara	With.
ماسره	Mā sara	With me.
	or	
دسره	da sara	With.
څما سره	Zamā sara	With me etc.
دپاره	Dapāra	⎫ For
دـدپاره	Da dapāra	⎭
ما دپاره	Mā dapāra	⎫ For me etc.
څما دپاره	Zama da pāra	⎭

پشان	Pashān	} Like
دَپشان	Da pashān	
ما پشان	Mā pashān	} Like me
څما پشان	Zamā pashān	
کره	Kara	} In the house of
دَ-کره	Da kara	
ما کره	Mā kara	} In my house etc
څما کره	Zamā kara	
پوری	Pōré	Near or by
ما پوری	Mā poré	Near or by me etc.
ته نیزدی	Ta nizdé	Near
ما ته نیزدی	Mā ta nizdé	
سخه	Sakha	} Near; it is also used for the possessive case in the verb to have.
دَ-سخه	Da sakha	

EXAMPLE I

ما سخه - یا	Mā sakha or	} Near me etc:
څما سخه	Zamā sakha	

EXAMPLE II

ما سخه کتاب دی یا	Mā sakha kitāb day or	} lit, near me book is = I have a book.
څما سخه کتاب دی	Zamā sakha kitāb day	
تا سخه کتاب دی	Tā sakha kitāb day or	} lit near thee book is = thou hast a book.
ستا سخه کتاب دی	Stā sakha kitāb day	

هغهٔ سخه کتاب دیَ	*Haghuh sakha kitāb day*	lit near him book is =
یا	or	he has a book.
دَ هغهٔ سخه کتاب دیَ	*Da haghuh sakha kitab day*	

NOTE:—سخه *sakha*, can only be used when the object is light and moveable as well as to denote owner-ship otherwise the possessive case should be used as :—

ما سخه یو قلم دیَ	*Mā sakha yau qalam day*	I have a pen
ماک سخه یوه اسپد دَه	*Malak sakha yawa aspa dah*	The malik owns a mare
ستا څو کوروند دي	*Stā so korūna dee*	How many houses have you ?
ستا څو ورونړه دي	*Sta so vrūnra dee*	How many brothers have you ?

دَ پاس	*Da pāsa*	above.
دَ...دَ پاس	*da...da pāsa*	
ما دَ پاس	*Mā dapāsa*	above me etc.
ځما دَ پاس	*Zamā dapāsa*	
دَ...په مینځ کښ	*da...pa mianz ké*	in the middle of or through, among.
دَ باغ په مینځ کښ	*da bāgh pa mianz ké*	Through the garden.
لهٔ...نه ورانده	*luh na varāndé*	before (in place)
دَ...دَ ورانده	*da...da varāndé*	

لۀ مانه وراند	luh mā na vrāndé	
	or	before me (etc).
ځما دَوراند	Zamā da vrāndé	
لۀ ..نه ورمبی	luh-na vrūmbay or	before (in time.)
يا اﺆ۔نه اول	awal	
لۀ ما نه ورمبی	luh mā na vrūmbay	before me
لۀ ما نه اول	luh mā na awal	
لۀ ..نه ورستو	luh-na vrosto	b e h i n d (in
ن ..دَ ورستو	da...da vrosto	place)
لۀ ما نه ورستو	Luh mā na vrosto	
يا	or	behind me.
ځما دَ ورستو	Zmā da vrosto	
لۀ ..نه پس	Luh-na pas	after (in time).
لۀ ما نه پس	Luh mā na pas	after me etc.

NOTE:—پس = Pas, does not inflect any noun of time.

پسی = Pasé = after (in the case of a person or business).

ما پسی	Mā pasé	after me.
څۀ پسی	suh pasé	after what business).
لۀ ..نه دی خوا	Luh-na dé khwā	this side of.
لۀ دفتر نه دی خوا	Luh daftar na dé khwā	this side of the office.
لۀ ..نه هغه خوا	Luh-na hagha khwā	beyond.
لۀ دفتر نه هغه خوا	Luh daftar na hagha khwa	Beyond the office.
لۀ ..نه گير چاپيره	Luh-nā gér chāpéra	around.
لۀ ښهر نه گير چاپيره	Luh khahar na gér chāpéra	Around the City.

دَ... پهٔ باب کښی	Da...puh bāb ké	About, concerning.
زما پهٔ باب کښی	Zmā puh bāb ké	About me etc.
دَ... پهٔ سبب یا	Da...puh sabab or	Owing to, on account of or
دَ... پهٔ وجه	Da puh waja	by reason of
دَ باران پهٔ سبب یا	Da bārān puh sabab or	Owing to the rain
دَ باران پهٔ وجه	Da bārān puh waja	
دَ... پهٔ موجب	Da...puh mūjeb	According to
دَ حکم پهٔ موجب	Da hukam puh mūjeb	According to order
بی لهٔ .. نه	bé luh...na	Without, except, besides.
بی لهٔ ما نه	bé luh mā na	Without me etc.
دَ... پهٔ شا	Da...puh shā	At the back of
دَ کور پهٔ شا	Da kor puh shā	At the back of the house.
دَ	Da	Of
دَ میجر صاحب آس	Da maijar sāhib ass	The Major's horse.

The particles را = Rā, در = Dar, ور = War are
used with post positions and with the 2nd part of
prepositions as well as with some verbs denoting
the singular and plural both numbers and they
have the force of personal pronouns :—

را Rā   For 1st   person singular and
                         plural.

در Dar   For 2nd   ,,   ,,   ,,

ور	*War*	For 3rd person singular and plural.

as :—

را نه	*Rā na*	From me or from us.
درنه	*Dar na*	From thee or from you.
ورنه	*War na*	From him or from them, her, or it.
را باند	*Rā bāndé*	On me or on us.
در باند	*Dar bāndé*	On thee or on you.
ور باند	*War bāndé*	On him or on them, her or it.
را ته	*Rā ta*	To me or to us.
در ته	*Dar ta*	To thee or to you.
ور ته	*War ta*	To him or to them.
را سره	*Rā sara*	With me or with us.
در سره	*Dar sara*	With thee or with you.
ور سره	*War sara*	With him or with them, her or it.
و تل	*Watal*	To go out.
را و تل	*Rā watal*	To come out towards me or us.
در و تل	*Dar watal*	To come out towards thee or you.
ور و تل	*War watal*	To come out towards him or them, her or it.

Section 5.

THE NOUN.

A noun is a word denoting a person, place or thing, and has two Genders—Masculine and

Feminine and two numbers—Singular and Plural :—

ENDINGS OF MASCULINE NOUNS.

I. Nouns ending in ى = *ay*. are masculine as :—

سړي	*Saray*	A man.
كلى	*Kalay*	Village.
پوړ	*Paray*	Rope.
سپى	*Sŗay*	Dog.
مړى	*Maray*	Dead body.
كانړى	*Kānray*	Stone.

II. Nouns ending in consonants are masculine as :—

چرګ	*Charg*	Cock.
هلك	*Halak*	Boy.
ميز	*Méz*	Table.
كور	*Kōr*	House.
دفتر	*Daftar*	Office.
ملك	*Malak*	Head man.

EXCEPTIONS:—

لار	*Lār*	Road.
پاتن	*Paltan*	Regiment.
ورځ	*Vraz*	Day.
وريځ	*Woriaz*	Cloud.

میاشت	*Miąsht*	Month, half moon.
بِرستن	*Brąstan*	Quilt.
دُرمن	*Sąrman*	Skin, leather.
خنہل	*Sangal*	Elbow.
دُرشل	*Durshal*	Frame of a door.
بِرمنز	*Gumanz*	Comb.
ستن	*Stan*	Needle. Pillar, Telegraph Post.
لمن	*Lman*	Skirt.
میچن	*Mechan*	Hand Mill.

III. Nouns ending in ی = *ī*, denoting profession are masculine as :—

مالی	*Mālī*	Gardener.
دوبی	*Dōbī*	Washerman.
نائی	*Nāyī*	Barber.
قاٰضی	*Qāzī*	Judge.
موچی	*Mochi*	Shoe Maker.

IV. Nouns ending in ﮦ = *uh*. (Hard) are masculine as :—

وادﮦ	*Wāduh*	Marriage.
نیکﮦ	*Nikuh*	Grand father.
کارغﮦ	*Kārghuh*	Crow.
مارغﮦ	*Marghuh*	Bird.

EXCEPTIONS :—

چارﮦ	*Chāruh*	Knife (Fem).
تیارﮦ	*Tyąruh*	Darkness (Fem).

ENDINGS OF FEMININE NOUNS.

I.   Nouns ending in ه = *h* (soft) are feminine as :—

ونه	*Wana*	Tree.
تبه	*Taba*	Fever.
ښځه	*Khaza*	Woman or wife.
چغه	*Chagha*	Pursuit party.
مږه	*Maga*	Rat.
خټه	*Khata*	Mud.

II.   Nouns ending in ۍ = *ai* are feminine as:—

جنۍ	*Janai*	Girl.
چتۍ	*Chitai*	Letter.
ټوکرۍ	*Tokrai*	Basket.
ګلۍ	*Galai*	Hail-storm, Hail-stone.
نالۍ	*Nālai*	Quilt.
سيلۍ	*Silai*	Sand or dust-storm.
څپلۍ	*Saplai*	Sandals.

III.   Nouns ending in ي = *i* denoting qualities are feminine as :—

دوستي	*Dosti*	Friendship.
بدي	*Badi*	Enmity, feud.
دُشمني	*Dushmani*	Enmity.
غريبي	*Gharibi*	Poverty.

نيكي   *Nekī*   Goodness.

نا مردي   *Nāmardī* Cowardice.

IV.   Nouns = ending in ‍ا = ā (*alif*) are feminine as :—

بلا   *Balā*   Calamity.

قلا   *Qalā*   Fort.

سزا   *Sazā*   Punishment.

نيا   *Niā*   Grand-mother.

ژرا   *Jharā*   Crying, weeping.

خندا   *Khandā* Laughter.

EXCEPTIONS —

ملا   *Mulā* A priest   ملا يان   *Mulayan* Priests.

گدا   *Gadā* A beggar   گدايان   *Gadayan* Beggars.

كك   *Kakā* An uncle (Polite term of calling an old man   كك گان   *Kākāgān* Uncles.

سنڍا   *Sandā*   Male buffalo.

سنڍ گان   *Sandgān* Male Buffaloes.

V.   Nouns ending in و = o, are feminine as :—

پيشو   *Pisho*   Cat.

بيزو   *Bizo*   Monkey.

ورشو   *Warsho* Grazing ground.

لانبو   *Lānbo*   A swim.

FORMATION OF FEMININE FROM MASCULINE.

I. Nouns ending in سَي = *ay*, form their feminine by changing this letter in سِي = *ai* as :—

سپَي *Spay*	Dog.	سپِي *Spai*	Bitch
چيلَي *Chelay*	He goat.	چيلِي *Chelai*	She goat.
نوسَي *Nwasay*	Grand son	نوسِي *Nwasai*	Grand daughter.
اوسَي *Osay*	Antelope.	اوسِي *Osai*	Female antelope

II. Nouns ending in consonants form their feminine by adding ه = *h* (soft) as : —

چرګ *Charg*	Cock	چرګه *Charga*	Hen
خر *Khar*	He ass	خره *Khara*	She ass
ګډ *Gad*	Male sheep	ګډه *Gada*	F. sheep
غل *Ghal*	Thief	غله *Ghla*	F. thief
آس *Ass*	Horse	آسپه *Aspa*	Mare.

(Persian = آسپ = *Asp* = horse)

III. Nouns ending in سِي = *i* form their feminine by changing this letter into نره = *nra* (or *narah*) as :—

دوبي	*Dobi*	Washerman.
دوبنره	*Dobanra*	Washer woman.
نائيي	*Nāi*	Barber.
نائينره	*Nāyanra*	Barber's wife.

مالی *Māli*   Gardener.

مالنره *Mālanra* Gardener's wife, f. gardener.

بذهی *Bangi* Sweeper.

بَذهنِره *Banganra* Sweeper's wife.

NUMBER OF MASCULINE NOUNS.

I. Nouns ending in ـَي = *ay* form their oblique singular and nominative plural by changing this letter into ـِي = *i* as:—

سړَی *Saray* A man.   سړِي *Sari* Men.

سپَی *Spay* A dog.   سپِي *Spi* Dogs.

له سړِي نه *Luh Sari na* from a man (ob. s.)

II. Nouns ending in consonants denoting animate objects and those ending in ـِي = *i* remain un-changed in the oblique singular and form their nominative plural by adding ـان = *ān*, and those denoting time, measure, and weight, form their plural by adding——*zabar* over the final letter as :—

هلک *Halak* Boy.   هلکان *Halakān* Boys.

ملک *Malak* Head Man ملکان *Malakān* Head men.

د ملک *da malak* of the head man (remains un-changed).

Singular.   Plural.

کال *Kāl* Year.   کالَ *Kāla* Years.

ګز *Gaz* Yard.   ګزَ *Gaza* Yards.

Singular.   Plural.

مَن   Man   Maund.   مَن   Mana   Maunds
سیر   Sér   Seer.   سیَر   Séra   Seers.
میل   Mĭl   Mile.   میلَ   Mĭla   Miles.
قدَم   Qadam Pace.   قدَم   Qadama Paces.
جیرب   Jirub   ½ acre.   جیرب   Jiruba   Jiribs.
ملټ   Mélat   Minute.   ملټ   Mélata   Minutes

III. Nouns ending in consonants denoting
in-animate objects remain unchanged in the
oblique singular and form their nominative
plurals by adding ونه = ūna as:—

کور   Kōr   House.   کورونه   Korūna   Houses
کتاب   Kitāb   Book.   کتابونه   Kitābūna Books.
میز   Méz   Table.   میزونه   Mézūna   Tables
په کور کښ   Pa kōr ké   In the house (ob.s.)

IV. Nouns ending in و = ū. They remain
unchanged in the oblique singular and form
their nominative plural by adding ګان = gān as:—

بابو   Bābū   Clerk.   بابوګان   Bābūgān Clerks.
میاو   Mélū   Bear.   میاوګان   Mélūgān Bears.
پارو   Pārū   Snake   پاروګان   Pārūgān Snake
              charmer.   charmers
تارو   Tārū   Francolin.   تاروګان   Tārūgān Franc-
                                         olins.

دبابﺍ   Da bābū   of the clerk. (ob. s.)

V. Nouns having و = *ū* in the last syllable, change the و = *ū* into ا = *ā* = (alif) and ه = *H* (hard) after it to form their nominative plural and they remain unchanged in the oblique singular:—

پښتون	*Pukhtūn*	Pathan.	پښتانه	*Pukhtā-nuh*	Pathans
شپون	*Shpūn*	Shepherd,	شپانه	*Shpānuh*	Shepherds.
سور	*Sōr*	Horse man, rider.	سواره	*Swāruh*	Riders.

دَ پښتون *Da pukhtūn* of the Pathan. (ob. s.)

VI. Some nouns form their nominative plural irregularly as :—

ورور	*Vrōr*	Brother	ورونړه	*Vrūnrah*	Brothers
ځوي	*Zōi*	Son	ځامن	*Zāman*	Sons.
تره	*Truh*	Uncle	ترونه	*Trūna*	Uncles (Paternal)
ماما	*Mā mā*	Uncle	ماماگان	*Māmā gān*	Uncles. (Maternal)
اس	*Ass*	Horse	اسونه	*Assūna*	Horses.
غل	*Ghal*	Thief	غله	*Ghluh*	Thieves.
میلمه	*Mélma*	Guest	میلمانه	*Mélmānuh*	Guests.
زړه	*Zruh*	Heart	زړونه	*Zrūna*	Hearts.

VII. Some nouns, are only used in the plural as :—

شراپ	*Sharāp*	Wine.
غنم	*Ghanam*	Wheat.
جوار	*Jowār*	Maize.

پئِي	*Pai*	Milk.
ما ستة	*Māstuh*	Curds.
کُچ	*Kuch*	Butter.
تیل	*Tail*	Oil.
اپیم	*Apim*	Opium.
ما غزهٔ	*Māghzuh*	Brain.
زهر	*Zahar*	Poison.
با نړهٔ	*Bānruh*	Eye-lashes
اوړهٔ	*Oruh*	Flour.
سکارهٔ	*Skāruh*	Charcoal.
ریښم	*Rékham*	Silk.

NUMBER OF FEMININE NOUNS.

1. Nouns ending in ٔ = *h* (soft) form their oblique singular and nominative plural by changing this letter into ی = *é* as :—

| ونه | *Wana* | Tree | ونی | *Wané* | Trees. |
| تبه | *Taba* | Fever | تبی | *Tabé* | Fevers. |

دَوَنی *Da wané* of the tree. (ob. s.)

NOTE :—In the locative case feminine singular they are not inflected.

پهٔ ونه کیښ *Puh wana ké*   In the tree.

پهٔ ونه باندِ *Puh wana bāndé* On the tree.

EXCEPTION.

Feminine nouns ending in ی = *i*.

دو ستی *Dōsti*   Friendship.

په دوستيِ کیښ *Puh dōstai ké*   In friendship.

II. Nouns ending in ي = *ī* form their oblique singular and nominative plural by changing this letter into ئي = *ai*, as :

دوستی *Dōsti* Friendship دوستئي *Dōstai* Friendships

دشمنی *Dush* Enmity دشمنئي *Dush* Enmities.
mani manai

پۀ دوستئي کښ *Puh dostai ké* In friendship (Ob. S.)

III. Nouns ending in consonants form their oblique singular and nominative plural by adding ي = *é*, or *zer* under the final letter.

يوه ورځ *Yawa vraz* One دوورځ *Dwa* Two days.
day *vrazé*

پالټن *Paltan* Regiment پالټنـ *Paltané* Regiments.

د ورځ *Da vrazé* of the day (idiomatic "in the day time") Ob. S.

IV. Nouns ending in ئي = *ai*, remain unchanged in the oblique singular and nominative plural as :—

جنئي *Jinai* Girl or girls جنکئي *Jinakai* Girls.
(In Khalil and Mohmand.)

درئي *Darai* Carpet or Carpets.

څپلئي *Saplai* Sandal or Sandals.

د جنئي *Da jinai* of the girl. (Ob. S.)

V. Nouns ending in ١ = *ā* (alif) remain unchanged in the oblique singular and nominative

plural in Yusafzai, but in Khalil and Mohmand
add کانے = *gāné* as :—

قلا　*Qalā*　　Fort or Forts.

(Khalil and Mohmand قلا کانے = *Qalā gāné* =
Forts.)

نيا　*Niā*　　Grand mother or Grand mothers.

(In Khalil and Mohmand نيا کانے = *Niā gāné* =
Grand mothers)

په قلا کښں　*Puh qalā ké*　In the fort.

VI.　Some nouns form their plural irregularly as :—

لور *Lūr*　Daughter　لونړه *Lūnra*　Daughters

مور *Mōr*　Mother　ميندى *Méndé*　Mothers

خور *Khōr*　Sister　خويندى *Khwéndé* Sisters.

ترور *Trōr*　Aunt　تروريانې *Trōryāné* Aunts

VII.　Some nouns are only used in the
plural as :—

اوربشي　*Orbashé*　　Barley

شوملى　*Shōmlé*　　Butter milk.

وريژې　*Vrijhé*　　Rice (in shop)

شولى　*Shōlé*　　Rice (in field)

توکانړى　*Tukānré*　　Spittle.

اوبه　*Obuh*　　Water.

OBLIQUE PLURAL.

All masculine and feminine plural nouns

form their oblique plural by adding ﺟ = "o" to
the last consonant letter of the word as :—

لۀ سړونه	*Luh sarō na*	From men.
پۀ ښځو بانده	*Puh khazō bāndé*	On the women
مالیانو ته	*Māliāno ta*	To the gardeners
پۀ کورونو کښ	*Puh korūno ké*	In the houses.

CASE OF NOUN.

There are eight cases of noun in Pushtu :—

1. Nominative. Subject always, but object in the past tenses of a transitive verb.

2. Accusative Object in the present and future.

3. Agentive Subject in past tenses of a transitive verb.

4. Genitive Possessive ($د = da =$ of)

5. Dative In direct object ($ته = ta$, $له = la$ or $لره = lara =$ to)

6. Ablative Distance from a place ($لۀ-نه = luh-na =$ from)

7. Locative Remaining in a place :
   (پۀ-کښ *pa-ké* in)
   (پۀ-باند *puh-bāndé* on)

8. Vocative Used in calling.

INFLECTION OF MASCULINE NOUNS.

I. Nouns ending in ي = *ay* are thus inflected :—

Singular.	Plural.

1. Nominative :

سَرَى *Saray* A man سَرِي *Sari* men

2. Accusative :

سَرَى *Saray* The man سَرِي *Sari* The men

3. Agentive :

سَرِي *Sari* By a man سَرُو *Saro* by men

4. Genitive :

د سَرِي *Da sari* Of a man د سَرُو *da saro* of the men

5. Dative :

سَرِي ته *Sari ta* To a man سَرُو ته *Sarō ta* To men

6. Ablative :

له سَرِي نه *Luh sari na* From a man له سَرُو نه *Luh saro na* From men

7. Locative :

په سَرِي کښِ *Puh sari ké* In a man په سَرُو کښِ *Puh saro ké* In men

8. Vocative :

اى سَرِيَّ *Ay sariya* Oh man! اي سَرُو *Ay saro* Oh men !

NOTE :—The nominative and accusative are the same in both Singular and plural, therefore if one knows nominative, then one will know the accusative, and if one knows the agentive one will also know all the rest.

II. Nouns ending in consonants denoting animate objects are thus inflected :—

	Singular.	Plural.
Nominative	هلک *Halak* Boy	هلکن *Halakān* Boys
Agentive	هلک *Halak* by boy	هلکانو *Halakāno* by boys.

III. Nouns ending in consonants denoting in animate objects are thus inflected :—

	Singular.	Plural.
Nominative	کور *Kōr* House	کورونه *Korūna* Houses
Agentive	کور *Kōr* by house	کورونو *Korūno* by houses.

INFLECTION OF FEMININE NOUNS.

I. Nouns ending in ه = *h*, are inflected thus:--

	Singular.	Plural.
Nom	ونه *Wana* Tree	ونی *Wané* Trees.
Agent	ونی *Wané* by tree	ونو *Wanō* by trees

II. Nouns ending in ي = *i*, are inflected thus:-

	Singular.	Plural.
Nom	دوستي *Dōstī* Friendship	دوستي *Dostai* Friendships.
Agent	دوستي *Dostai* by Friendship	دوستو *Dōsto* by Friendships.

III.   Nouns ending in consonants are inflected thus :—

	Singular.	Plural.
Nom	ورځ *Vraz* Day	ورځ يا ورځے *Vrazé* Days.
Agent	ورځے *Vrazé* by day	ورځو *Vrazō* by days.

IV.   Nouns ending in ﻰ = *ai,* are declined thus :—

	Singular.	Plural.
Nom	جنۍ *Jinai* girl	جنۍ *Jinai* or جنکۍ *Jinakài* girls.
Agent	جنۍ *Jinai* by girl	جينو *Jino* or جنکو *Jinakō* by girls.

V.   Nouns ending in ا = a (*alif*) are declined thus :—

	Singular.	Plural.
Nom	قلا *Qalā* Fort	قلا *Qalā* or قلاګانى *qalāgàné* forts.
Agent	قلا *Qalā* by fort	قلاؤ *Qalāo* or قلاګانو *Qalāgānō* by forts.

Section 6.

THE ADJECTIVE.

The adjective follows the rules of the noun for Gender, number and case. It is generally placed before its noun.

EXAMPLE :—

I.   نرى سرى *Naray saray* A thin Man.

نري سري *Nari sari*   thin men.

دَ نری سړی   *Da nari sari* of a thin man (m. ob. s)

دَ نرو سړو   *Da narō sarō* of thin men (mas. ob. plu).

نرۍ ښځه   *narai khaza* thin woman.

نرۍ ښځی   *narai khazé* thin women.

دَ نرۍ ښځی   *da narai khazé* of a thin woman (f. ob. s.)

دَ نرو ښځو   *da narō khazō* of thin women (f. ob. plu.)

II. But note :—Expressing sympathy.

سړی نری دی   *saray naray day* the man is thin.

ښځه نرۍ ده   *khaza narai dah* the woman is thin.

سړی نا جوړ دی   *saray nā jora day* the man is (unfortunately) ill.

2. The following adjectives ending in ی = *ay*

Change ي = *ay* into ی = *i.* in the nominative plural and form their feminine singular and plural by changing ی = *ay* into ي = *é* as:—

m. s.		f. s. & f. p.		
نوی	*naway*	نوي	*nawé*	new.
تږی	*tagay*	تږي	*tagé*	thirsty.
غلی	*ghalay*	غلي	*ghalé*	silent.
خوشی	*khūshay*	خوشي	*khushé*	useless
اوږی	*ogay*	اوږي	*ogé*	hungry.

وروکَی	warūkay	وروکَي	warūké	small.
ورکوتَی	warkōtay	ورکوتَي	warkōté	small.
کمزورَی	kamzōray		kamzōré	weak.

3. Adjectives ending in consonants do not change in the nominative plural and follow the rules of nouns for feminine singular and plural as:—

خراپ سرَي	kharāp saray	A bad man.
خراپ سرِي	kharāp sari	Bad men.
خراپه ښځه	kharāpa khaza	A bad woman.
خرابي ښځی	kharāpé khazé	Bad women.

4. The following adjectives remain unchanged except in the oblique plural :—

خائيسته	Khāiesta	beautiful or handsome.
ناکار	nā kāra	bad, ugly.
خپه	khapa	unhappy.
دروغ	darogh	lie.
رښتیا	rikhtiā	true.
ځینی	ziné or bāzé	some.
پوره	pūra	complete.
بی حیا	bé hayā	shameless.
بی وفا	bé wafā	faithless.
ویریا	wéryā	free, gratis.
مفت	muft	free, gratis.
تکړه	takra	strong.

5. The following adjectives are irregular as :—

M. S.	M. P.	F. S.	F. P.	
مړ Mar	مرو mruh	مړه mra	مړى mré	dead
لوُند lūnd	لاونده lāunduh	لونده launda	لوندى laundé	wet.
کوږ kōg	کاږه kāguh	کږه kaga	کږى kagé	crooked.
دروُند drūnd	درانه drānuh	درنه drana	درنى drané	heavy.
موړ mōr	ماړه māruh	مړه mara	مړى maré	rich, replete.
پروت prōt	پراته prātuh	پرته prata	پرتى prate	prostrate.
زوړ zōr	زاړه zāruh	زړه zara	زړى zaré	old.
توُد tōd	تاوده tāuduh	توده tauda	تودى taudé	hot.
تريو triw	تاروه tārwuh	ترو ه trawa	تروى tarwé	sour
خوږ khōg	خواږه khwā-guh	خوږه khwaga	خوږى khwagé	sweet.
تريخ trikh	تارخه tārkhuh	ترخه tārkha	ترخى tarkhé	bitter
وروست vrōst	وراسته vrāstuh	ورسته vrasta	ورستى vrasté	rotten.
شين shin	شنه shnuh	شنه shna	شنى shné	green.

روُنْد *rūnd*   رانده *rānduh*   رنده *randa*   رندی *randé*
blind.

كوُنْر *kūnr*   كانْرُه *kānruh*   كنره *kanra*   كنری *kanré*
deaf.

پوُښ *pōkh*   پاښه *pākhuh*   پښه *pakha*   پښی *pakhé*
cooked, ripe.

6. COMPARISON OF ADJECTIVE.

There is no special form for the Comparative Degree in Pushtu. Comparison is expressed by using the Positive Degree with the Ablative case as :—

أَس لۀ اوښ نه ګرندی دی = *Ass luh ūkh na garanday day* the horse is swifter than the Camel.

SUPERLATIVE.

There is no special form for the superlative degree in Pushtu. It is expressed by using the positive degree with the following phrases as :—

لۀ ټولو نه *luh tōlō na*   ⎫   Used by Khalils.
لۀ وارو نه *luh wārō na*   ⎬ than all   ,,   ,, Yusafzais
لۀ جمله ونه *luh jumlaō na* ⎭   ,,   ,, Afghans.

as :—

دا هلک لۀ ټولو نه هوښیار دی   *dā halak luh tōlo na hukhyār day*

This boy is the cleverest

Section 7.

THE NUMERAL CARDINAL NUMBERS.

1	—	۱	یو *Yau.*
2	—	۲	دوہ *dwa.*
3	—	۳	دری *dré.*
4	—	۴	څلور *salōr.*
5	—	۵	پنځه *pinzuh.*
6	—	۶	شپږ *shpag.*
7	—	۷	اوۀ *owuh.*
8	—	۸	اتۀ *atuh.*
9	—	۹	نهۀ *nahuh.*
10	—	۱۰	لس *las.*
11	—	۱۱	یولس *yaolas.*
12	—	۱۲	دولس *dōlas.*
13	—	۱۳	دیارلس *diārlas.*
14	—	۱۴	څوارلس *swārlas.*
15	—	۱۵	پنځۀ لس *pinzalas.*
16	—	۱۶	شپاړس *shpāras.*
17	—	۱۷	اولس *owalas.*
18	—	۱۸	اتَلس *atalas.*
19	—	۱۹	نُولس *nūlas.*
20	—	۲۰	شل *shal.*
21	—	۲۱	یو ویشت *yau wisht.*
22	—	۲۲	دوہ ویشت *dwa wisht.*
23	—	۲۳	در ویشت *dar wisht.*
24	—	۲۴	څلریشت *salréisht.*
25	—	۲۵	پنځۀ ویشت *pinza wisht.*

26	—	۲۶	شپږ ویشت	shpag wisht.
27	—	۲۷	اوۀ ویشت	owuh wisht.
28	—	۲۸	اتۀ ویشت	atuh wisht.
29	—	۲۹	نهۀ ویشت	nahuh wisht.
30	—	۳۰	دیرش	dérsh.
31	—	۳۱	یو دیرش	yau dérsh.
32	–	۳۲	دوه دیرش	dwa dérsh.
33	—	۳۳	درې دیرش	dré dérsh.
34	—	۳۴	څلور دیرش	salōr dersh.
35	—	۳۵	پنځۀ دیرش	pinzuh dérsh.
36	—	۳۶	شپږ دیرش	shpag dérsh.
37	—	۳۷	اوۀ دیرش	owuh dérsh.
38	—	۳۸	اتۀ دیرش	atuh dérsh.
39	—	۳۹	نهۀ دیرش	nahuh dérsh.
40	—	۴۰	څلویښت	salwékht.
50	—	۵۰	پنځوس	panzōs.
60	—	۶۰	شپیتۀ	shpétuh
70	—	۷۰	اویا	auyā.
80	—	۸۰	اتیا	atyā.
90	—	۹۰	نوي	navi.
100	—	۱۰۰	سلَ	sal.
200	—	۲۰۰	دوه سوَ	dwa swa.
1000	—	۱۰۰۰	زر	zar.
2000	—	۲۰۰۰	دوه زرَ	dwa zara.
100000	۱۰۰۰۰۰		لک	Lak.

پۀ سلګونو	*Puh salgūnō*	Hundreds of
پۀ زرګونو	*Puh zargūnō*	Thousands of.
پۀ لکونو	*Puh lakūnō*	"Laks" of.

Numerals (both cardinal and ordinal) are used in Pushtu as adjectival nouns. When governed by any preposition and post position they are put into the Oblique Plural as :—

په څلورو سرو باندې *Puh saloro saro bānde* On four men.

يو = *Yau* becomes يوه = *Yawa* in the case of Feminine as :—

يوه ښځه *Yawa Khaza* One woman.

The Ordinal numbers are formed (with the exception of اول = *Awal* = 1st and دويم = *Dwem* = 2nd) by adding م = *m* to the Cardinals. They form the Feminine by the addition of ه = *h* (soft).

CARDINAL.

Masculine.	Feminine.
درى سړي *Dre sari* three men	درى ښځي *Dre khaze* three women

ORDINAL.

Masculine.	Feminine.
دريم سړى *Drem saray* 3rd man.	دريمه ښځه *Drema khaza* 3rd woman
څلورم *saloram* 4th	
پنځم *pinzam* 5th	
شپږم *shpagam* 6th	

In Pushtu only the simpler fractions can be expressed :—

EXAMPLES.

1/4	پاؤ	*Pāw*
1/2	نیم	*Nim*
3/4	دری پاؤ	*Dré Pāwa*
1¼	پاؤ پنځه	*Pinzuh Pāwa*
1½	یو نیم	*Yau Nim*
1¾	پاؤ کم دوه	*Pāw kam dwa*
2¼	پاؤ باندی دوه	*Pāw bāndé dwa*
2½	دوه نیم	*dwa nim*

Some times the villagers count by *Shal*=a score the plural of which is *Shalé* as

دوه شلی *dwa shalé*   two scores 40.

دری شلي *dré shalé*   three scores 60

پنځه دا پاس دری شلي *Pinzuh dapāsa* 5 over 3 scores *dréshalé*   65.

پنځه کم دری شلي *Pinzuh kam* 5 less of *dréshalé* 3 scores 55.

واړه *Wāra* all. put after a cardinal number indicates universality.

دواړه *dwāra*   both.

دری واړه *dré wāra*   all three.

څلور واړه *salōr wāra*   all four.

Multiplication by degree is expressed by using the particle په = *Puh* between the cardinal یو = *yau* and any other cardinal as :—

یو په دوه *yau puh dwa*   twice as much.

یو په دری *yau puh dré*   thrice as much.

یو په څلور *yau puh salōr*   four times as much.

Some times the word چه = *chand* is used after any cardinal number to express the same meaning as above.

دو چند   *do chand*   twice as much.

دری چند   *dré chand*   thrice as much.

څلور چند   *salōr chand*   four times as much.

Section 8.

PRONOUNS.

1st Person.

Singular.			Plural.		
Nom :	زه *zuh*	I.	مونږ *mūng*	we.
Acc :	ما *mā*	me.	مونږ *mūng*	us.
Agent :	ما *mā*	by me.	مونږ *mūng*	by us.
Gent:	زما *zamā*	my.	زمونږ *zamūng*	our.
Dat :	ما ته *mā ta*	to me.	مونږ ته *mūng ta*	to us.

Abl: له ما نه *luh mā* from   له مونږ نه *luh mūng* from
       na   me.   *na*   us.

Loc : —

پ ما کښے *puh mā* in me   پ مونږکښے *puh mūng* in us.
      ké   *ké*

Voc :—

اے زه *ay zuh* oh me!   اے مونږ *ay mūng* oh us!

2nd Person.

Singular.			Plural.		
Nom :	ته *tuh*	thou.	تا سو *tā so*	you.
Acc :	تا *tā*	thee.	تا سو *tā so*	you.
Agent:	تا *tā*	by thee	تا سو *tā so*	by you

Singular.   Plural.

Gent: ستا *stā*   thy.   سناسو *stā so*   your.

Dat : تاته *tā ta*   to thee. تا سو ته *tā so ta* to you.

Abl: له تا نه *luh tā* from   له تا سونه *luh tā-* from
                      na   thee.   *so na*   you.

Loc :—

پۀ تا کښ *puh tā* in thee. پۀ تاسو کښ *puh* in you.
           ké   *tāso ké*

Voc :—

اي تۀ *ay tuh* oh thou   اى تا سو *ay tāso* oh you

3rd Person.

Singular.   Plural.

Nom : هغه *hagha*   he   هغوي *haghūi* they.

Acc : هغه *hagha*   him.   هغوي *hughūi* them.

Agent: هغۀ *haghuh* by him هغوي *haghūi* by
                                          them.

Gent: د هغۀ *da*   his.   د هغوي *da*   their.
         haghuh   *haghūi*

Dat :—

هغۀ ته *haghuh* to him هغوي ته *haghūi* to
      ta   *ta*   them.

Abl :—

له هغۀ نه *luh*   from   له هغوي نه *luh*   from
      haghuh him.   *hughūi* them.
      na   *na*

Loc :—

پۀ هغۀ کښ *puh*   in   پۀ هغوي کښ *puh*   in
      haghuh him.   *haghūi* them.
      ké   *ké*

Voc :—

اى هغۀ *ay*   oh him ! اى هغوي *ay*   oh
      haghuh   *haghūi* them.

NOTE:—A. Some times دَى = *day* is used
for هغه = *hagha*, when the object is close at hand
and it is inflected thus :—

	Singular.		Plural.	
Nom:	دَى *day*	he	دُوى *dui*	they
Agent:	دُ *duh*	by him	دُوى *dui*	by them.

B. The following particles are used as pronouns in three cases, accusative, agentive and
genitive.

Singular.   Plural.

مِ *mé* me, by me or my مُو *mō* us, by us or our.

دِ *dé* thee, by thee or مُو *mō* you, by you or
thy   yours

یِى *yé* him, by him or یِى *yé* them, by them
his   or their

EXAMPLE :

Accus : هغه مِ وهِى *hagha mé wahi* He beats me

Agent : هغه مِ ووهلو *hagha mé wo wahalo*
I beat him

Geni : کتاب مِ *kitab mé*   My book

Ordinarily in Pushtu sentences the subject
is placed first, the object second and the Verb
last, but where the above particles are used, in
the case of a transitive verb Past-Tense, the
object is put first and the subject second.

هغه مِ و لیدلو *hagha mé wo lidalo* I saw him.

C. The following particles are used as prepositions and have the force of personal pronouns :—

پرِ *pré* on him, on them, on her, or on it.

ترِ *tré* from him, from them, from her or from it.

There was only one chair in the room and he himself was sitting on it.

" پهٔ کمره کښ خالی یوه کُرسۍ وه " *puh kamra ké khāli yawa*
اِو هغه پخپله پرِناست وهٔ *kursai wah aw hagha*
pakhpala pré nāst woh ".

DEMONSTRATIVE PRONOUNS.

There are only three Demonstrative Pronouns in Pushtu which are inflected thus :—

Nom دا *dā* this or these دغه *dagha* this or these.
          هغه *hagha*   that or those.

Agent دی *dé* by this د غی *daghé* by this
                or these   or these.

          هغی *haghé*   by that or by those.

دا خما نوکر دی *dā zamā*   this is my servant.
                    naukar day

لهٔ دی هلک نه *luh dé halak na* from this boy.

دغه څوک دی *dagha sōk day* who is this.

د دغی هلک *da daghé*   this boy's father is

پلار مِ نوکر دی *halak plār mé* my servant.
                    naukar day

هغه خما كلّیَ دیَ *haghá zamā*   that is my village.
kalay day

دَ هغیَ كلّیَ ندهغه خوا *da haghé kali* beyond that
na hagha khwā   village.

THE INTERROGATIVE PRONOUNS.

څوک	*sok*	who.
څه	*suh*	what.
كوم	*kum*	which
كوم يو	*kum yeu*	which one.
څو يا څومره	*sō or somra*	how many or how much.
څوک	*sōk*	is inflected thus :—

Nom   څوک *sōk* who   } used in singular and
Agent   چا *chā* by whom   } plural both numbers.

m. s.	m. p.	f. s.	f. p.	ob. p.
كوم سړی	كوم سړي	كومه ښځه	كومی ښځی	دَكومو خلقو
kum saray	*kum sari*	*kuma khaza*	*kumé khazé*	*da kumo hhalqo*
which man.	which men	which woman	which women	of which people.

THE RELATIVE PRONOUNS.

There is only one relative pronoun in Pushtu
چه = *Chi*, which is also used as a conjunction
for joining two sentences. It also makes any
interrogative word relative as :—

1. هغه سړی راوبله چه   *hagha saray*   Call that man
   پرون دلته وه   *rā wōbala chi*   who was here
   parūn   dalta   yesterday.
   woh

2. هغه و چه نوم م   *haguh   wō*   he said that my
   احمد دی   *wé chi nūm*   name is Ahmad
   mé Ahmad   (direct speech)
   day   he said his
   name was
   Ahmad.

3. خوک چه   *sōk chi*   he who.

   هر خوک چه را شي   *har sōk chi*   whoever may
   rāshee   come.

   کوم چه د خوښ وي   *kum chi dé*   whichever you
   khwakh wé   like.

   کوم یو چه د خوښ وي   *kum yau chi*   which ever one
   dé khwakh wé   you like.

   څۀ چه کوی   *suh chi kawé*   whatever you
   do.

THE CORRELATIVE PRONOUNS.

Interrogative			Correlative		
که	*kuh*	if	نو	*no*	then.
چه	*chi*	} when.	نو	*no*	then.
کله چه	*kala chi*		نو	*no*	then.
څومره چه	*sōmra chi*	as much as	دومره	*dōmra*	that much.
څنګه چه	*sanga chi*	what ever	هسې	*hasé*	thus.

EXAMPLE.

كه ستا خوښد	*kuh stā khwakha*	
وی نو لاړشه	*wī nō lārsha*	go if you like.
چه یا کله چه	*chi or kala chi mā*	he also spoke
ما وو نو هغۀ	*wo wé no haghuh*	when I spoke.
هم وو	*hum wo wé*	
خو مره چه	*sōmra chi ghwāré*	take as much as
غواړی دومره	*dōmra wākhla*	you want Liter-
واخله		ally : as much as
		you want take so
		much.
خذه چه د	*sanga chi dé khwa-*	do as you like.
خوښه وی	*hha wi hasé kawa*	Literally : what-
هسی کوه		ever you wish,
		thus do.

INDEFINITE PRONOUNS.

In Pushtu the simple indefinite pronouns
are :—

څوک	*sōk*	some one.
څه	*suh*	some, something or anything.
څینی	*ziné*	some.
هیڅ	*hiss*	no, or nothing. anyone, any-thing which is followed by a negative e. g.
هیڅوک نشته	*hiss sōk*	
	nishta	there is no body.
هیڅ نشته	*hiss nishta*	there is nothing.

څوک *sōk* beeomes چ *chā* in the oblique case e. g.

هيڅ چا ته مۀ وايه   *hiss chā ṭta*   Don't tell any one
يا   *muh wāya*

هيچا ته مۀ وايه   *hichā ḍū muh*   „   „   „   „
wāya

خينې = *ziné* takes the regular inflection and
څۀ = *suh* and هيڅ = *hiss* are indeclinable.

EXAMPLE.

څوک په دی کور کښی شته   *sōk puh dé*   is there any-
kor ké shta   one in this
house?

څوک خو شته   *sōk kho shta*   there is
someone
(*Kho* = really.)

څۀ شیَ راکړه   *suh shay rākra*   give me
something.

خينې هوښياردي خينې   *ziné hukhyār*   some are
di ziné kam   clever, some
کم عقل   *akal*   foolish.

خينو خلقو ته   *zinō khalqō ta*   to some
people.

Numerous compound indefinite pronouns are
formed from the above thus :—

هر = *har* every, combining with څوک = *sōk*,
څۀ = *suh* and يو = *yau* makes:— هرڅوک = *har sōk*
every one هر څۀ = *har suh* every thing

هر يو = *har yau* every one and similarly بل = *bal*
another and نور = *nōr* more or others   make:—
بل څوک = *bal sōk* anyone else.

نور څوک = *nōr sōk* any others بل څه = *bal suh* anything else نور څه = *nōr suh* something more. نور هيڅ = *nōr hiss* nothing else بل يو = *bal yau* another.

VERBAL NOUNS.

In Pushtu the verbal nouns can be formed in two ways Viz:—

1. By changing the final ´ل = L of the infinitive into نه = *na* which is always feminine singular as :—

تړل *taral* to bind. تړنه *tarana* binding

هيرول *hérawal* to forget هيرونه *herawana* forgetting.

خودل *khodal* to show. خودنه *khōdana* showing

2. The infinitive itself can be used as a verbal noun as :—

تړل *taral* to bind or binding.

هيرول *hérawal* to forget or forgetting.

NOTE :—This form of the verbal noun is always masculine plural. So when it is governed by a preposition or post position the oblique plural should be used as :—

په تړلو کښ *puh taralo ké* in binding.

په هيرولو باند *puh hérawalo bāndé* on forgetting

The Noun of agency is formed by changing the final ل = *l*, of the infinitive into ونکی = *ūnkay* which is declinable as :—

ليكل *likal* to write ليكونكى *likūnkay* writer.

دَ ليكونكي نوم *da likūnki* the name of the writer
nūm

In the case of an intransitive verb it also
expresses the meaning of "to be about to" as:—

راتلل *rātlal* to come هغه را تلونكى دى *hagha rā-*
tlūnkay day
He is about
to come.

NOTE :—To express "to be about to" use the
preposition *pa-ké* with verbal noun as :—

هغه پۀ تلو كښ دي *hagha puh*   he is about to go.
tlo ké day

ABSTRACT OR DERIVED NOUNS.

(Substantive and Adjective.)

Secondary nouns are derived from primary
by the following suffixes : — ١ = *ā,* ى = *i*

ستيا = *stiā* توب = *tōb* والى = *wālay* ګلي = *galī.*

تون = *tūn* تيا = *tiā* :—

غل *ghal*   a thief becomes غلا *ghlā* theft.

خوښ *khwakh* pleased   ,,   خوښى *khwakhi*
pleasure.

سپاهي *spāhi* soldier   ,,   سپاهي توب *spāhi tōb*
توب soldiering.

شين *shin* green   ,,   شيذوالي *shin wālay*
green-ness

پيژندل *péjhandal* knowing becomes پيژندنگلي *péjhandgali*
کلی acquaintance.

بيل *bial* separate ,, بيلتون *bīltān* separation.

ناجور *nājōr* ill ناجورتيا *nājōrtiā* illness.

ميلمه *mélma* guest ميلماستيا *mélmastia* hospitality

Section 9.

THE VERB.

Ás regards their formation, the Pushtu verbs are devided into seven different classes: —

1. Regular transitive.
2. Regular intransitive.
3. Irregular transitive.
4. Irregular intransitive.
5. Compound transitive.
6. Compound intransitive.
7. Verbs which are irregular in the formation of the present Tense and Tenses derived from it.

Class I.

REGULAR TRANSITIVE.

All verbs in Pushtu end in ل = *l* :—

وهل *Wahal* to beat, strike.

تړل	*taral*	to bind, tie.
ليکل	*likal*	to write.
بلل	*balal*	to call.
خوړل	*khwaral*	to eat.
سکل	*skal*	to drink.
منل	*manal*	to obey, agree, accept.
سا تل	*sātal*	to keep, guard, cherish
استول يا ليږل	*astawal* or	
	légal	to send.
کرل	*karal*	to sow.
ګنډل	*gandal*	to sew.
خرېل	*khrayal*	to shave.
ګنړل	*ganral*	to consider.
چيچل	*chichal*	to bite.
ښيل	*khayal*	to show or direct.

THE PRESENT TENSE.

Change the final ل = L of the infinitive into:—

1st P.	م *m*			ؤ *oo*	
2nd P.	ې *é*	} Singular.		ئ *ai*	} Plu.
3rd P.	ي *ee*			ي *ee*	

as

زۀ وهم	*zuh waham*	I beat	
تۀ وهې	*tūh wahé*	thou beatest	} Sing.
هغه وهي	*hagha wahee*	he beats.	

مۇ ز, به و هۇ   *Mūng wahoo* We beat
تا سو و هئ   *tāso wahai*   you beat   }Plu.
هغړی وهی   *haghūi wahee* they beat

THE FUTURE TENSE.

Prefix به = *Ba*, to the Present tense as : —

ز ۀ به و هم   *zuh ba waham* I will beat
تۀ به و هی   *tuh ba wahé*   thou wilt beat   }Sing.
هغه به و هی   *hagha ba*   he will beat
      wahee

مۇ ز,ب به و هۇ   *Mūng ba*   we will beat
      wahoo
تا سو به وهئ   *tāso ba wahai* you will beat   }Plu.
هغوی به وهی   *haghui ba*   they will
      wahee   beat.

THE AORIST (PRESENT SUBJUNCTIVE.)

Prefix : —و = *wo*, to the present tense as : —

زۀ و وهم   *zuh wo waham* I may beat
تۀ و وهی   *tuh wo wahé* thou mayst beat   }Sing.
هغه و وهی   *hagha wo*   he may
      wahee   beat

مۇ ز,ب و و هۇ   *Mūng wo wahoo* we may beat
تا سو و وهئ   *tāso wo wahai*   you may beat.   }Plu.
هغوی ووهی   *haghūi wo*   they may beat.
      wahee

THE IMPERATIVE.

Is formed by changing the final $م = m$ of the aorist into $ه = a$ (H. soft) to form singular and into $ی = ai$ to form plural as :—

وَ وَهَ   *wo waha*   beat (thou)

وَ وَهَی   *wo wahai*   beat (you)

THE PROHIBITIVE.

Is formed by changing the first $و = wo$ of the imperative into $مه = muh$ as : —

مه وَهَ   *muh waha*   don't beat (thou)

مه وَهَی   *muh wahai*   don't beat (you)

THE IMPERFECT TENSE.

Add to the infinitive the following suffixes :—

1st P.	$م$ *m*	$و$ *oo*	
2nd P.	$ی$ *é*	Singular.	$ی$ *ai*	Plural.
3rd P.	$و$ *ō*	infinitive	
3r P. F.	$ه$ *h*	$ی$ *é*	

NOTE :—(A) The verb agrees with the subject in the present and object in all past tenses.

(B) Object in the past tenses is always put into the nominative form as :—

هغه زه وهلم   *haghuh zuh wahulam*   he was beating me

هغه تَه وهلی   *haghuh tuh wahalé*   he was beating thee

هغه هغه وهلو   *haghuh hagha wahalō*   he was beating him

هغه هغه وهله   *haghuh hagha wahalō*   he was beating her

Sing.

وهلؤ .ر, موزُ هغۂ *haghuh mūng* he was beating ⎫
      wahaloo us |

وهلئ تاسو هغۂ *haghuh tāso* he was beating |
      wahalai you   ⎬ Plu.

وهل ہغوی هغۂ *haghuh haghūi* he was beating |
      wahal them |

وهلي هغوی هغۂ *haghuh haghūi* he was beating |
      wahalé them (fem.) ⎭

وهلو هغه ما *mā hagha wahalō* I was beating
           him.

هله وهله .ر,موزُ *mūng hagha wahala* We were beat-
           ing her.

PAST HABITUAL.

Prefix به = *ba* to the imperfect tense as :—
      Singular.

وهلم به زه هغۂ *haghuh zuh* he used to beat me or
      ba wahalam he would beat me.

وهلي به نَه هغۂ *haghuh tuh* do. thee
      ba wahalé

وهلو بد هغه هغۂ *haghuh hagha* do. him
      ba wahalō

هله بۂ هغه هغۂ *haghuh hagha* do. her
      ba wahala
      Plural.

وهلؤ به .ر,موزُ هغۂ *haghuh mūng* he used to beat us or
      ba wahaloo he would beat us

وهلئ بد تاسو هغۂ *haghuh tāso* do. you
      ba wahalai

وهل بد هغوی هغۂ *haghuh haghui* do. them
      ba wahal

هغهٔ هغوي بِه وهلي *haghuh haghui* he used to beet them
  ba wahalé or   he   would   beat
                 them (fem.)

ما هغوي بِه وهل *mā haghui*   I used to beat them.
  ba wahal

PAST DEFINITE.

Prefix و = *wo*, to the imperfect tense as :—

هغهٔ زهٔ و وهلم *haghuh zuh* *wō wahalam*	he beat me	
هغهٔ تهٔ و وهلي *haghuh tuh* *wō wahalé*	do. thee	
هغهٔ هغهٔ و وهلو *haghuh hagha* *wō wahalo*	do. him	Sing.
هغهٔ هغهٔ و وهله *haghuh hagha* *wō wahalah*	do. her	
هغهٔ مونږ و وهلو *haghuh mūng* *wō wahaloo*	he beat us.	
هغهٔ تاسو و وهلي *haghuh tāso* *wō wahalai*	do you.	
هغهٔ هغوي و وهل *haghuh haghū* *wō wahal*	do them.	Plu.
هغهٔ هغوي و وهلي *haghuh haghui* *wō wahalé*	do them. (feminine).	

جنۍ هلک و وهلو *jinai halak wō* the girl beat the
  wahalo   boy.

هلک جنۍ و وهله *halak jinai wō* the boy beat the
  wahāla   girl.

THE PAST PARTICIPLE.

Is formed by adding ی = *ay*, to the infinitive
as :—

وهلی *wahalay* beaten.

This is used as an adjective and is inflected
as nouns ending in ‎ی‎ = *ay* as :—

‎و هلی سری‎	*wahalay saray*	beaten man.
‎و هلی سری‎	*wahali sart*	beaten men:
‎د و هلو سرو‎	*da wahalo saro*	of the beaten men (Ob. Plu.)
‎و هلی جنئ ته‎	*wahalé jinai ta*	to the beaten girl (F. Ob. S.)
‎و هلو ښڅو ته‎	*wahalo khazo ta*	to the beaten women (F. Ob. P.)

PERFECT TENSE.

Conjugate the present tense of the verb to
be after the past participle as :—

‎هغۀ زۀ و هلی یم‎	*haghuh zuh wahalay yam*	he has beaten me	
‎هغۀ تۀ و هلی یې‎	*haghuh tuh wahalay yé*	he has beaten thee	
‎هغۀ هغه وهلی دی‎	*haghuh hagha wahalay day*	he has beaten him.	Sing
‎هغۀ هغه و هلی دہ‎	*haghuh hagha wahalé dah*	he has beaten her.	
‎هغۀ مۇږ وهلی یۇ‎	*haghuh mūng wahali yū*	he has beaten us.	
‎هغۀ تاسو وهلی یئ‎	*haghuh tāso wahali yai*	he has beaten you.	
‎هغۀ هغوی وهلی دی‎	*haghuh haghui wahali dee*	he has beaten them.	Plu.
‎هغۀ هغوی وهلی دی‎	*haghuh haghui wahalé dee*	he has beaten them (Feminine.)	

خَنْثَى سِرِى وهلَى *khazé saray*   the woman has
دى *wahalay day*   beaten the man.

سِرِى خَشَه وهلى دَه *sari shaza*   the man has beaten
wahalé dah   the woman.

هلكا نو هندو وهلى *halakāno*   the boys have
hindū   beaten a Hindu.
دى *wahalay day*

PLUPERFECT TENSE.

Conjugate the past tense of the verb to be
after the past participle as :—

هغهٔ زهٔ و هلَى وم *hāghuh zuh*   he had beaten
wahalay wam me. ⎫

هغهٔ تهٔ و هلَى وى *hāghuh tuh*   he had beaten
wahalay wé thee. ⎬ Sing

هغهٔ هغهٔ وهلَى وهٔ *haghuh hagha* he had beaten
wahalay woh him. ⎪

هغهٔ هغهٔ وهلى وَه *haghuh hagha* he had beaten
whalé wah her. ⎭

هغهٔ مونږ وهلى وُو *haghuh mūng* he had beaten ⎫
wahali woo us.

هغهٔ تاسو وهلِي وَى *haghuh tāso* he had beaten
wahali wai you. ⎬ Plu.

هغهٔ هغوِي وهلِي وُو *haghuh*   he had beaten
haghui them.
wahali woo ⎪

هغهٔ هغوِي وهلى *haghuh*   he had beaten
haghui them
دى *wahalé wé* (feminine). ⎭

هلك بنسته وهلی وه‌ *halak khaza wahalé wah* — The boy had beaten the woman.

بنستی هلك وهلی وه‌ *khazé halak wahalay woh* — The woman had beaten a boy

PRESENT POTENTIAL.

Add ‌ی = *ay* to the infinitive and conjugate the word شم = *sham* after it according to the present personal terminations as :—

زۀ وهلی شم *zuh wahalay sham* I can beat.

تۀ وهلی شی *tuh wahalay shé* Thou canst beat.

هغه وهلی شی *hagha wahalay shee* He or she can beat.

Sing.

موْژر وهلی شوْ *mung wahalay shoo* We can beat.

تاسو وهلی شئ *tāso wāhalay shai* You can beat.

هغوی وهلی شی *haghui wahalay shee* They can beat M. & F.

Plu.

هغه ما وهلی شی *hagha mā wahalay shee* or
هغه م وهلی شی *hagha mé wahalay shee* He can beat me.

زۀ هغه وهلی شم *zuh hagha wahalay sham* or
زۀ یی وهلی شم *zuh yé wahalay sham* I can beat him.

THE PAST POTENTIAL.

Add ‌ى = *ay* to the infinitive and conjugate the word شوم = *shwam* afrer it according to the past personal terminations :—

هغهٔ زهٔ وهلَى شوم	*haghuh zuh wahalay shwam*	He could beat me or he was able to beat me.
هغهٔ تهٔ وهلى شوى	*haghuh tuh wahalay shwé*	He could beat thee.
هغهٔ هغه وهلَى شو يا شهٔ	*haghuh hagha wahalay sho* or *shuh*	He could beat him.
هغهٔ هغه وهلى شوه يا شوله	*haghuh hagha wahalay shwa* or *shwala*	He could beat her.
هغهٔ موُږ وهلى شوُ يا شُ	*haghuh müng wahaly shwoo* or *shoo*	He could beat us.
هغهٔ تاسو وهلى شوئي	*haghuh tāso wahalay shwai*	He could beat you.
هغهٔ هغوى وهلى شوُ يا شوَل	*haghuh haghūi wahalay shwoo* or *shwal*	He could beat them,
هغهٔ هغوى وهلى شوى يا شوَلى	*haghuh haghui wahalay shwé* or *shwalé*	He could beat them (Feminine.)

} Sing

} Plu.

ځما نوكر هغه وهلى شو	*zamā naukar hagha wahalay sho*	My servant could beat him
هلك جنى وهلى شوه	*halak jinai wahalay shwa*	The boy could beat the girl.

REGULAR INTRANSITIVE VERBS CLASS II.

رسیدل *rasédal* to arrive څښیدل *sasédal* = to leak.

اوسیدل *osédal*   to live.

بهیدل *bahédal*   to flow.

زغلیدل *zghalédal*   to run.

تښتیدل *takhtédal*   to flee.

زلیدل *zalédal*   to shine.

خوزیدل *khwazédal* to move.

رپیدل *rafédal*   to tremble.

کږیدل *karédal*   to pine.

غوریدل *ghwarédal* to spread.

غوریدل *ghurédal*   to thunder.

From the above examples it is quite clear that all regular intransitive verbs end in یدل = *édal*.

PRESENT TENSE.

Change the final د = *d* of the infinitive into ږ = *g* and apply the rules of regular transitive verb as :—

زۀ رسیږم *zuh raségam*	I arrive.	
تۀ رسیږي *tuh raségé*	thou arrivest.	⎫
هغه رسیږي *hagha raségee*	he arrives.	⎬ Sing.
,, ,, ,,	she ,,	⎭
مونږ رسیږو *mūng raségoo*	we arrive.	
تاسو رسیږي *tāso raségai*	you arrive.	⎫
هغوی رسیږي *haghūi raségee*	they arrive.	⎬ Plur.
,, ,, ,, ,, ,, (f.)		⎭

NOTE :—See syntax rule No. 3 for explanation of the formation of transitive from intransitive verbs of class II.

COMPOUND VERBS CLASS V & VI.

The Compound verbs are formed by adding adjectives and nouns to كول = *Kawal* and كيدل = *Kédal.*

Transitive.		In Transitive.	
وركول *war kawal*	to give	وركيدل *war kédal*	to be given,
مړ كول *mar kawal*	to kill or put out.	مړ كيدل *mar kédal*	to die or to be put out.
جوړكول *jōr kawal*	to make, build.	جوړ كيدل *jōr kédal*	to be made, to be built.
پوه كول *pōh kawal*	to inform instruct.	پوه كيدل *pōh kédal*	to understand, to be instructed
لوكول *law kawal*	to harvest.	لوكيدل *law kédal*	to be harvested
اوبۀكول *obuh kawal*	to irrigate.	اوبۀ كيدل *obuh kédal*	to be irregated
خراپكول *kharāp kawal*	to spoil.	خراپ كيدل *kharāp kédal*	to be spoilt.
لرى كول *laré kawal*	to open	لرى كيدل *laré kédal*	to be opened.
پورى كول *pōré kawal*	to shut.	پورى كيدل *pōré kédal*	to be shut.
تپوس كول *tapōs kawal*	to ask.	تپوس كيدل *tapōs kédal*	to be asked.
پُښتنه كول *pukhtana kawal*	to ask	پُښتنه كيدل *pukh-tana kédal*	to be asked.

برباد کول barbād to kawal destroy.   برباد کیدل barbād to be kédal destroyed

کندر کول kandar to kawal burgle.   کندر کیدل kandar to be kédal burgled

ژوبل کول jhōbal to wound kawal   ژوبل کیدل jhōbal to be kédal wounded

خوږر کول khūg to hurt. kawal   خوږر کیدل khūg to be kédal hurt.

بل کول bal to light. kawal   بل کیدل bal to be lit. kédal

پري کول pré to cut. kawal   پری کیدل pré to be kédal cut.

مات کول māt to break. kawal   مات‌کیدل māt to be kédal broken.

NOTE:—See syntax Rule No. 5. for full explanation of the formation of derivative verbs from Class V & VI.

CLASS VII.

Verbs which are irregular in the formation of Present and tenses derived from it.

Infinitive		Present.	
غوښتل ghukhtal	to want.	غوارم ghwāram	I want.
راغوښتل rāghukh- tal	to send for.	راغوارم rāghwā- ram	I send for
پریوتل préwatal	to fall.	پریوځم préwō- zam	I fall.
پوریوتل pōréwatal	to cross.	پوریوځم pōréwo- zam	I cross.

پریشودل	prékhō-dal	to leave, let off.	پریردم	prégdam I leave.
پیژندل	péjhan-dal	to recognize.	پیژنم	péjha-nam I recognize.
موندل	mūndal	to get, obtain, receive, find.	مومم	mūmam I get, obtain, receive, find.
ویشتل	wishtal	to shoot.	ولم	wōlam I shoot.
وژل	wajhal	to kill.	وژنم	wajhnam I kill.
لوستل	lwastal	to read.	لولم	lwalam I read.
لیدل	lidal	to see.	وینم	wīnam I see.
کتل	katal	to look.	گورم	gōram I look.
اوریدل	aurédal	to hear.	اورم	auram I hear.
اخستل	akhistal	to take.	اخلم	akhlam I take.
اغوستل	aghustal	to wear, to put on, to dress.	اغوندم	aghun-dam I put on. etc.
ختل	khatal	to climb.	خیژم	khéjham I climb.
الوتل	alwatal	to fly.	الوځم	alūzam I fly.
کنودل	kanōdal	to dig.	کنم	kanam I dig.
اوریدل	aurédal	to hear.	اورم	auram I hear.
ویل	wayal	to say, speak, tell.	وایم	wāyam I say, speak, tell.
وتل	watal	to go out.	وځم	wozam I go out.
راوتل	rāwatal	to come out.	راوځم	rawozam I come out.
ویستل	wistal	to take out.	وباسم	wobā-sam I take out.
ننوتل	nanawa-tal	to go in.	ننوځم	nanawo-zam I go in.

ننويستل	*nanawis-* *tal*	to take in.	ننباسم *nanabā-* *sam* I take in.
خندل	*khandal*	to laugh.	خاندم *khāndam* I laugh.
ژړل	*jharal*	to cry, weep.	ژاړم *jhāram* I cry, I weep.
نښتل	*nakhatal*	to be ca- ught.	نښلم *nakha-* *lam* I am caught.
چاودل	*chāwdal*	to split, burst.	چرم *chwam* I am burst.
لنبل	*lānbal*	to bathe.	لانبم *lānbam* I bathe.
نيول	*niwal*	to catch, seize, arrest, hold.	نيسم *nīsam* I catch etc :—
زنګل	*zangal*	to swing.	زانګم *zāngam* I swing.
پاخيدل	*pāsédal*	to get up.	پاخم *pāsam* or I get up. *pāségam*
راښکل	*rākhkal*	to pull.	راکاږم *rākāgam* I pull.
نغښتل	*nghakh-* *tal*	to wrap- up.	نغاړم *nghāram* I wrap- up.
پرانتل	*prānatal*	to untie.	پرانځم *prāna-* *zam* I untie.

Section 10.

THE SYNTAX RULES.

1. Verbs commencing with ‎را = *rā*   د = *dar*
و‎ر = *war*   پا = *pā*   ‎پري = *ŧré*   پوري = *pōré*   ‎کي = *ké*
نه = *nan*   بي = *bé*   تي = *té* do not take "و = *wo*" in their
past, aorist and imperative:—

راوتل *rāwtal*   to come out towards
                          (me or us)

دروتل *dạr wtal*   to come out towards
(thee or you)

ورونل *war watal*   to come out towards
(him or them, her, it)

پاخیول *pāsédal*   to get up.

تیرباسل *térbāsal*   to mislead.

پریونل *prewatal*   to fall.

پوریونل *porewatal*   to cross.

کیښودل *kékhōdal*   to put, place.

ننونل *nanawatal*   to go in, enter

بیلل *bélal*   to lose.

راښکل *rākhkal*   to pull.

EXAMPLE.

I got up زۀ پاخیدم = *zuh pāsédam* (Not *wo pāsé-dam*) past).

May I get up پاخم = *pāsam* (aorist)

Get up پاخه = *pāsa* (The imperative)

EXCEPTIONS.

Which take *wo* after the را = *rā*   در = *dar* and
ور = *war* :—

راغوښتل *rāghukhtal*   to send for.

رابلل *rābalal*   to call for, recall.

رازغلیدل *rāzghalédal*   to run towards me or us.

راتښتیدل *rā takhtédal*   to flee towards me or us.

راویستل *rā wistal*   to bring out, towards me
or us.

راوتل rā watal   to come out towards me or us.

راګرزیدل rā garzédal   to return.

رانغختل rā nghakhtal   to wrap up.

راګرزول rā garzawal   to bring back, to make to return.

راشړل rā sharal   to drive back towards me or us.

EXAMPLES.

ما هغه را و غوښتلو = *Mā hagha rā wo ghukhtalo* = I sent for him (past).

زۀ یی را و غواړم = *Zuh yé rā wo ghwāram* = May I send for him? (aorist)

را و یی غواړه = *Rā wo yé ghwāra* = Send for him! (imperative).

NOTE :—-Verbs which take را = *rā*, in the 1st person, take در = *dar*, and ور = *war* in the 2nd and 3rd person singular and plural as well as :—

هغه را و زغلیدلو   *hagha rā wo zghalédalo*   he ran towards me or us.

هغه در و ز غلیدلو   *hagha dar wo zghalédalo*   he ran towards thee or you.

هغه ور وۀ ز غلیدلو   *hagha war wo zghalédalo*   he ran towards him or them, her, it.

2 The subject of the following verbs although they are intransitive, is put in the Agentive case and the verb always goes into the 3rd person masculine plural in past tenses :—

دنهل	*dangal*	to jump.
غهل	*ghapal*	to bark.
خندل	*khandal*	to laugh.
ژرل	*jharal*	to weep.
زنهل	*zangal*	to swing.
توُ كل	*tūkal*	to spit.
توخس	*tōkhal*	to cough.
لنبل	*lanbal*	to bathe.
جار باسل	*jārbāsal*	to vomit.

Examples as :—

ما و دنهل	*mā wō dangal*	I jumped.
سري و دنهل	*sari wō dangal*	The man jumped.
جنيى و دنهل	*jinai wō dangal*	The girl jumped.
سرو دنهلي دي	*saro dangali di*	The men have jumped.
خهى دنهلي دى	*khazé dangali di*	The woman has jumped.
ما دنهلي وُو	*mā dangali woo*	I had jumped.

In the absence of an object the following verbs also follow the above rules

ليكل	*likal*	to write.
لوستل	*lwastal*	to read.
و يل	*wayal*	to say, speak. tell.
كتل	*katal*	to look.
ليدل	*lidal*	to see.

غوښتل *ghukhtal*   to wish, want.

اوريدل *aurédal*   to hear.

As :—

ما وا وريدل	*Mā wā wrédal*	I heard.
تا وا وريدل	*Tā wā wrédal*	Thou heard
هلک وا وريدل	*Halak wā wrédal*	The boy heard.
جنۍ وا وريدل	*Jinai wā wrédal*	The girl heard.
سړو وا وريدل	*Saro wā wrédal*	The men heard
ښځو وا وريدل	*Khazo wā wrédal*	The women heard.
ما اوريدلي دي	*Mā aurédali di*	I have heard.
ما اوريدلی وؤ	*Mā aurédali woo*	I had heard.
جنۍ اوريدلی وؤ	*Jinai aurédali woo*	The girl had heard.
هلک اوريدلی وؤ	*Halak aurédali woo*	The boy had heard.
ما و ليکل چه...	*Mā wo likal chi...*	I wrote that...
ما په اخبار کښ ولوستل	*Mā puh akhbār ké wo lwastal*	I read in the paper.
ما په اخبارکښ لوستلي دي	*Mā puh akhbār ké lwastali di*	I have read in the paper.

3. To form transitive from class II, Regular intransitive verbs, change يدل = *édal* of the infinitives into ول = *awal* as :—

رسيدل *rasédal* to arrive   رسول *rasawal* to make to arrive

اوسيدل *osédal* to live   اوسول *osawal* to make to live

پاخیدل *pāsédal* to get up پاخول *pāsawal* to make to
get up.

NOTE :—In conversation some times the
present tense of Class II is formed irregularly.

رسیدل *rasédal*	to arrive	رسم *rasam*	I arrive
اوسیدل *osédal*	to live	اوسم *ōsam*	I live
زغلیدل *zghalédal*	to run	زغلم *zghalam*	I run
تښتیدل *takhtédal*	to flee	تښتم *takhtam*	I flee
خوزیدل *khwazédal*	to move	خوزم *khwazam*	I move
رپیدل *rapédal*	to tremble	رپم *rapam*	I tremble
څښیدل *sasédal*	to leak	څښم *sāsam*	I leak.

4. Compound verbs formed from adjectives
never take و = *wo*, in their past, aorist and imperative and those formed from nouns always
do as :—

ما میز صاف کړلو *mā méz sāf kralo* I cleaned the table.

ستا بوټونه صاف کړم *sta būtūna sāf* May I clean your
kram ? boots ?

لوکوتی یی صاف کړه *lūkūti yé sāf kra* Please clean them.

ما کار و کړلو *mā kār wo kralo* I worked.

زه کار وکړم *zuh kār wo kram* May I work ?

خپل کار و کړه *khpal kār wo kra* Do your work.

5. Compound verbs formed from some
adjectives are Derivative Verbs which are
formed by leaving out the first letter ک = *k* of
کول = *kawal* and کیدل = *kédal* and add $\overline{zabar}$ over

the last letter of the adjective only in case of transitive verb, as :—

from صاف کول *sāf kawal* صافول *sāfawal* to clean.

from صاف کیدل *sāf kédal* صافیدل *sāfédal* to be cleaned.

from پوه کول *pōh kawal* پوهول *pōhawal* to inform

from پوه کیدل *pōh kédal* پوهیدل *pōhédal* to understand.

EXAMPLES.

زهٔ صافوم	*zuh sāfawam*	I clean.
زهٔ به صافوم	*zuh be sāfawam*	I will clean.
مهٔ صافوه	*muh sāfawa*	don't clean.
ما صافولو	*mā safawalo*	I was cleaning.
زهٔ صافولیَ شم	*zuh sāfawalay sham*	I can clean.

NOTE :—In the Past, Aorist, Imperative and Past Participle of Derivative Verbs however کول = *kawal*, and کیدل = *kédal*, are conjugated in full.

EXAMPLES.

ما میز صاف کړلو	*mā méz sāf kralo*	I cleaned the table.
صاف کړم ؟	*sāf kram* ?	my I clean ?
هو صاف کړه	*ho sāf kra*	yes, clean.
میز تیار شو	*méz tayār sho*	the table was (became) ready.
تیار شم ؟	*tayār sham* ?	may I became ? ready ?

هو تیار شه *ho tayār sha*   yes, be ready.

Not : ما میز و صافولو *mā méz wo sāfawalo.*

وصافوم = *wo sāfawam* or وصافوه = *wo sāfwa*

The list of adjectives from which the derivative Verbs are formed.

Adjective.   Verbs.

خراپ *kharāp*	خراپول *kharapawal*	to spoil.
جوړ *jor*	جوړول *jorawal*	to make, build.
پوه *poh*	پوهول *pohawal*	to inform or instruct.
موړ *mōr*	موړول یا *mōrawal* or	
	مړول *marawal*	to feed.
لوند *lūnd*	لوندول *lūndawal*	to make wet.
کوږ *kōg*	کوږول با *kōgawal* or	to make
	کږول *kagawal*	crooked.
دروند *drūnd*	دروندول *drundawal*	
	یا درنول *or dranawal*	to make heavy.
تود *tōd*	تودول *tōudawal*	to make hot.
پوخ *pōkh*	پښول یا *pakhawal* or	
	پوخول *pokhawal*	to cook.
تریو *triw*	تریوول *triwawal*	to make sour.
خوږ *khōg*	خوږول یا *khōgawal* or	
	خوږول *khwagawal*	to make sweet.
تریخ *trikh*	تریخول یا *trikhawal* or	
	ترخول *tarkhawal*	to make bitter.

Adjective.   Verbs.

خُوږ *khūg*	خُوږَوَل *khūgawal*		to hurt.
وروست *vrōst*	یا وروسْتَول *vrostawal* or		
	ورسْتَول *vrastawal*		to make rotton.
شین *shin*	شینَول *shinawal*		to make green
رُوند *rūnd*	یا رُوندَول *rūndawal* or		
	رانْدَول *randawal*		to make blind.
سپین *spin*	سپینَول *spinawal*		to make white.
زیر *ziar*	زیرَول *ziarawal*		to make yellow.
بند *band*	بنْدَول *bandawal*		to close.
لوی *loi*	لویَول *loyawal*		nurse up or make bigger.

PRESENT CONTINUOUS.

6. When the action is continuous use simple present in the first sentence and simple future in the second, the 1st: sentence commences with که = *kuh* if, and the 2nd: with نو = *no* then.

EXAMPLE.

که هغه راځی نو زهٔ به ځم = *kuh hagha rāzee, no zuh ba zam*

If he keeps on coming, I shall keep on going.

PAST CONTINUOUS.

7. Use imperfect in the first sentence and Habitual in the 2nd as:—

كه هغه راتلو نوزۀ به تلم *kuh hagha-rātlo, nō zuh ba tlam*
If he had kept on coming I would have kept on
going.

PRESENT CONDITIONAL.

8 Use aorist in the first sentence and aorist
preceded by به = *ba* in the 2nd as: —

كه هغه راشي نوزۀ به لارشم *kuh hagha rāshee, no zuh ba
lārsham* If he comes I will go.

NOTE:—Some times in the present conditional idiomatically, the Past tense is used
instead of the aorist, in the first clause when the
condition is assumed to be realised, as :—

كه تا دا كار وكړلو نو انعام به درکړم *kuh tā dā kār wokralo, no
inām ba darkram*
If you do this work I will reward you.

PAST CONDITIONAL.

9. Use the word وی = *way* unchangeably
after the uninflected Past Participle in the first
sentence and pluperfect preceded by به = *ba*, in
the 2nd: as: —

كه هغه راغلی وی نوزۀ به تلی وم *kuh hagha rāghalay
way, nō zub ba talāy wam*
If he had come, I would have gone.

PAST POTENTIAL CONDITIONAL.

10. Use the word شوی = *shway*, unchangeably after the original uninflected Past participle

in the first half and Pluperfect tense preceded
by به = *ba*, in the 2nd as :—·

كه زۀ راتلى شوى	*kuh zuh rātlay*	If I could have
نوزه به را غلى وم	*shway, no zuh*	come, I would
	ba rāghalay	have
	wam	
كۀ م و هلى شوى	*kuh mé*	If I could have
نو به م وهلى وه	*wahalay,*	beaten him, I would
	shway, no ba	have done so.
	mé wahalay	
	woh	

PASSIVE VOICE.

11.   In Pushtu the Passive Voice is only
used in those cases wnen the subject of the
verb is not mentioned at all.

Formation :—

Conjugate the required tense of كېدل = *kédal,*
after the uninflected Past Participle of an other
Verb as :—

دوډۍ خوړلى كېږي	*dodai khwaralay kégi*	The bread is being eaten.
دوډۍ به خوړلى كېږي	*dodai ba khwaralay kégi*	The bread will be eaten.
دوډۍ خوړلى شوى ده	*dodai khwaralay shawé dah*	The bread has been eaten.

NOTE :—To form Passive Past and Aorist add سی = *ay* to the Past Tense 3rd. Person masculine Plural with کیدل = *kédal* conjugated after it *e. g.*

هغه و وهلی شو	*hagha wo wahalay sho*	He was beaten.
که هغه و وهلی شی	*kuh hagha wo wāhalay shī*	If he is beaten.
کتاب یوړلی شو	*kitāb yauralay sho*	The book was taken away.
که کتاب یو ړلی شی	*kuh kitāb yauralay shī*	If the book is taken away.
آس بوتللی یا	*āss bōtlalay* or	The horse was taken away.
بوتلی شو	*bōtlay sho*	
که آس بو تللی	*kuh āss bōtlalay*	If the horse is taken away.
یا بوتلی شی	or *botlay shi*	
کار و کړی شو	*kār wo kray sho* or	The work was done.
(یا وکړای شو)	*kār wo kralay shō*	
که کار و کړی شی	*kuh kār wo kray shi*	If the work is done.
یا وکړی شی	or *wo kralay shi*	
میزصاف کړی شو	*méz sāf kray sho*	The table was cleaned.
یا کړی شو	or *kralay sho*	
که میز صاف کړی	*kuh méz sāf kray*	If the table is cleaned.
یا کړی شی	or *kralay shi*	

NOTE :—کړی = *kray*, is a short form of کړلی *kralay*.

12. The Infinitive of Purpose is always inflected and it is followed by the Post Position
ﺩ ﺩَ ﭘﺎﺭﻩ = *da dapāra* as :—

زﻩ دَ رِپوٹ کولو دَ ﭘﺎﺭﻩ	*zuh da rapōt kawalo*	I have come
ﺭﺍ ﻏﻠﮯ ﻳﻢ	*dapāra rāghalay*	to make a
	yam	report.

13. In the Negative Past and Aorist, the
نﮦ—*nuh*, is placed after the following Particles:—
ﺭﺍ *rā* در *dar* ور *war* ﭘﺎ *pā* ﭘﺮے *pré* ﭘﻮﺭے *pōré*.
و *wo* وﺍ *wā* ﻻ *lā* ﻛﮯ *ké* ﺑﮯ *bé* نﻦ *nan*
ﭘﺮﺍ *prā*, as :—

ﻫﻐﮧ ﺭﺍ ﻏﻠﻮ	*hagha rāghlo*	He came.
ﻫﻐﮧ ﺭﺍ نﮧ ﻏﻠﻮ	*hagha rā nuhghlo*	He did not come.
زﮦ ﻻﺭﻢ	*zuh lāram*	I went.
زﮦ ﻻ نﮧ ﺭﻢ	*zuh lā nuh ram*	I did not go.
تﮧ ﭘﺎ ﺧﻴﺪﻟﯽ	*tuh pāsédalé*	You got up.
تﮧ ﭘﺎ نﮧ ﺧﻴﺪﻟﯽ	*tuh pā nuhsédalé*	You did not get up.
ﻣﺎ و وﻳﻞ	*mā wo wayal*	I said, spoke or told
ﻣﺎ و نﮧ وﻳﻞ	*mā wo nuh wayal*	I did not say etc.
ﻣﻮﻧﮋ وﺍﺧﺴﺘﻠﻮ	*mūng wā khistalo*	We took it.
ﻣﻮﻧﮋ وﺍ نﮧ ﺧﺴﺘﻠﻮ	*mūng wā nuh khistalo*	We did not take it.
تﺎ ﺳﻮ ﻛﻴﻨﻮ دﺍﻟﻮ	*tāso kékhōdalo*	You placed it.
تﺎ ﺳﻮ ﻛﻴﻨﮧ نﻮدﻟﻮ	*tāso ké nuh khōdalo*	You did not place it.

هغوی ننو تل	*haghui nanawatal*	They entered.
هغوی نننۀ وتل	*haghui nana nuh watal*	They did not enter.
چا پرا نتلو	*chā prānatlo*	Who opened it ?
چا پرا نۀ نتلو	*chā prānuh natlo*	Who did not open it ?

14. In the case of all verbs commencing with ا = *ā*, (alif) the sound of و = *wo*, becomes وا *wā*, in their Past, Aorist and Imperative as :—

ما يو كتاب واخستلو   *mā yau kitāb* I took a book.
                                                      wākhistalo

15. When an infinitive is used after an imperative, the last part of the sentence should be put into the aorist preceded by چه = *chi* as :—

ورته و وايه چه   *warta wō wāya*
لارشي   *chi lārshee*   Tell him to go.

16. Use the word ځان = *zān*, self or خپل ځان *khpal zān* oneself when the person of the subject is concerned as :—

يو كتاب م دَ ځان   *yau kitāb mé da*
سره وا خستلو   *zān sara wākhistalo*   I took a book with me.

څۀ او بۀ دَ ځان   *suh obuh da zān* Take some water
سره واخله   *sara wākhla*   with you.

17. The words تن = *tana* or كس = *kasa* = individuals, are used before persons as :—

شل تنَ سړی	shal tana sari	Twenty men
راغلل	rāghlal	came
څلور تنَ ښځی	salōr tana khazé	Four women.
پنځهٔ کس ښځی	pinzuh kasa khazé	Five women.
څو کسَ	sō kasa	How many persons ?

18. When a possessive pronoun refers to the nominative of the sentence it should always be translated by خپل = khpal. own :—

زهٔ خپل کور ته ځم	zuh khpal kōr ta zam	I go to my house.
ټول خپلو خپلو	tōl khpalo	Each man went.
کورونو ته لاړل	khpalo korūnō ta lāral	to his own house, or they all went to their own houses.
زهٔ خپله کمره کښی	zuh khpala kamra ké wam	I was in my room

19. The particle د = dé. is used before the aorist tense at the end of a sentence only in the 3rd person singular and plural to express command and permission, but to show negation, permission and continuation use Present Tense as :—

هغهٔ د لاړ شی	hagha dé lārshee	He should go.

د هغهٔ خور دِ هم لاړه شي	*da haghuh khōr dé hum lāra shee*	His sister should also go.
هغهٔ دِ نهٔ راشي	*hagha dé nuh rāzee*	He should not come.
هغهٔ دِ راشي يا راشي دِ	*hagha dé rāzee* or *rāzee dé*	He may come or he is allowed to come or let "him come.
هغهٔ دِ مدام راشي راشي	*hagha dé mudām rāzee*	He should always come.

NOTE (A)—لار = *lār* is used as an adjective declinable .

NOTE (B)—د = *dé* with لکه = *laka* after it is used after the subject of the verb in all persons to express the following idioms *e. g.*

تهٔ دلکه خوب کوې او زهٔ دِ لکه ستا بوټونه صافوم	*tuh dé laka khōb kawé aw zuh dé lakā stā būtūna sāfawam*	Is it reasonable that you should go to sleep and I should clean your boots.

20. Use the word پکار = *pakār di* it is necess-ary, after the uninflected infinitive at the end of a sentence and the subject of the verb should be put into the dative case to express should, must or ought as :—

ماله تلل پکاردي	*mā la tlal pakār di* lit	To me going necessary is I must go.

تا له تلل پکاردي *tā la tlal pakār di* You should go.

(نهر) مونږ.دلوپه‌خوار *mūng la puh khār* We must live in

كښ اوسيدل پکاردي *ké osédal pakār di* The city.

21. Use the word پکار دي چه = *pakār di chi* at the beginning of a sentence followed by the aorist tense to express the same meaning as above as :—

پکاردى چه زۀ پريډ	*pakār di chi zuh* I must go on
ته لارشم	*paraid ta lārsham* parade.
پکار دى چه تا سو	*pakār di chi tāso* You must go
وختى لارشي	*wakhtī lārshai* earlier.

22. To express should have or ought to have, use پکار ژو چه = *pakār woo chi* at the beginning of a sentence followed by وى = *way* after the uninflected past participle at the end of a sentence as :—

پکار ژو چه زۀ تلى	*pakār woo chi zuh* I ought to have
وى	*talay way* gone.
پکار ژو چه هغه	*pakār woo chi* He should have
راغلى وى	*hagha rāghalay* come.
	way

23. وى = *wi* the aorist tense of the verb "to be", is only used in the 3rd person singular and plural to express doubt, continuation, present conditional in the verb "to be" and general statement as :—

گُنَد هغه هلته وي	gundė haga haltā wi	Perhaps he is there.
هغه مدام پٔه ښهر کښې وي	haga mudām puh khahar kė wi	He is always in the city.
که هغه پٔه مردان کښې وي	kuh hagha puh mardān kė wi	If he is in Mardan.
نو زۀ به ورسره خبرې دکړم	no zuh ba warsara khabarė wo karm	I will speak to him.
پۀ دې وطن کښې هر رنګ ښکار وي	pa dė watan kė har rang khkār wi	There are all kinds of shooting in this country.

24. Aorist preceded by به = *ba* is called strong future, which stands for certainty and fixed time as :—

| هغه به صبا راشي | hagha ba sabā rāshee | He will (certainly) come tomorrow. |
| هغه به پۀ کور کښې وي | hagha ba puh kōr kė wi | He will (certainly) be in the house. |

25. The Imperative formed from the Present Tense denotes continuation, or habit as :—

| هره ورځ ښما کور ته راځه | hara wraz zamā kōr ta rāza | Come to my house every day. |
| هره ورځ مدرسې ته ځه | hara wraz madrasė ta za | Go to the school every day. |

26. The Plural of Onomatopœic Nouns is formed by adding ,هار—*ahār*, which takes the verb to be into 3rd person masculine singular, as :—

دز *daz*	sound of a shot.	دزهار *dazahār*	sound of shots.
کرپ *krap*	foot fall	کرپهار *krapahār*	sound of footfalls.
شرنگ *shrang*	chink of money.	شرنگهار *shranga-hār*	chink of rupees.
پنس *pus*	sound of whisper	پنسهار *pasahār*	whisper-ing.
هینر *henr*	neigh of a horse.	هینرهار *hénrahār*	neighing of horses.

27. Use the word لګیا = *lagyā* = busy, as an adjective with the subject of the Verb, when the action is continuous as :—

زۀ لګیا یم پښتو زده کوم	*zuh lagyā yam pukhtu zda kawam*	I am busy learn-ing Pushtu.
هغه لګیا دی چټۍ لیکی	*hagha lagyā day chitai likee*	He is busy writ-ing letters.
موږ لګیا یؤ غنم کړؤ	*mūng lagyā yū ghanam karoo*	We are busy sowing wheat.

28. The following words take the Genitive Case followed by the Verb to be (بدی = *badi* is the only one which takes the aorist of "to become ".)

خوښ *khwakh*	pleasant.
پکار *pakār*	required.
بدي *badi*	unpleasant.
پیرزو *pérzo*	wish.

EXAMPLES.

دا کتاب خما خوښ *dā kitāb zamā*
دی *khwakh day* — I like this book.

خما درې روپۍ پکار *zamā dré rupai* — I requirè three
دی *pakār dee* — rupees.

د هغۀ ورور خما بدي *da haghuh vror*
شی *zamā badi shee* — I hate his brother.

دا انعام خما پۀ تا *dā ināam zamā* — I wish you to
پیروز دی *puh tā pérzo day* have this reward.

29. The word معلوم = *māl ūm* = known, takes dative case followed by the Verb to be as :—

دا ما ته معلوم دی *dā mā ta mālūm* I know this.
day

30. The phrases given below are followed by the aorist tense :—

راځه چه *rāza chi* — Let us.

پریږده چه *prégda chi* — Let him, them, her, it.

EXAMPLES.

راځه چه دغه کلی *rāza chi dagha* — Let us go to that
ته لارشو *kali ta lārshoo* — village.

پریږده چه لارشی *prégda chi lārshee* Let him go.

31. The verbs "to sell" and "sell for" always take the preposition په باند = *puh bāndé* on as :—

ما خپل آس په هغۀ *mā khpal ass*
باند پۀ لس روپۍ *puh haghuh*
خرڅ کړلو *bāndé puh las*   I sold my horse
    rūpai khars   to him for 10
    kralo   rupees.

32. The verb "to understand" takes پۀ = *puh* as :—

زۀ پۀ پښتو پوهېږم *zuh puh pukhtu*   I understand
    pōhégam   Pushtu.

33. پس = *pas* = after (in time) does not inflect any nouns of time as :—

درى مياشتى پس *dré miāshté pas*   After three
                     months.

څلور کالَ پس *salōr kāla pas*   After four years.

34. پسى = *pasé* after (position or business) inflects its nouns or pronouns e. g.

ما پسى دفتر ته راشه *mā pasé daftar*   Come after me to
     ta rāsha   the office.

زۀ نوکرۍ پسى *zuh naukarai*
راغلى يم *pasé rāghalay*   I have come
      yam   after a job.

35. The following Verbs take Ablative Case (لۀ - نه = *luh - na*) from.

تپوس کول يا پښتنه *tapōs kawal* or
کول   *pukhtana kawal* To ask.

ویریدل veyarédal	to fear.
پوریوتل pōréwatal	to cross.
هیرکیدل hér kédal	to be forgotten.

EXAMPLES.

لۀ هغۀ نه تپوس وکړه luh haghuh na tapōs wokra	Ask him.
لۀ ـ سیند نه پوریوتلم luh sind na pōré-watalam	I crossed the river.
را نه کتاب هیر شو rā na kitāb hér shō	I forgot the book.

36. When the action is unintentional an Intransitive Verb with the Ablative case should be used as :—

گلاس را نه مات شو galās rā na māt shō	I broke the glass (by accident).

37. To do something by means of any thing, the indirect object is always governed by پۀ - باند = puh - bāndé on as :—

زۀ پۀ قلم باند لیکم zuh puh qalam bāndé likam	I write with a pen.
زۀ یی پۀ لرگی و وهلم zuh yé puh largi wo wahalam	He beat me with a stick.

38. For the Pluperfect Tense after "when" the past tense should be used and for Perfect, the Aorist as :—

کله چه ما خپل کار وکرلو یا وکړ kala chi mā khpal kār wō kralo or wo kar	When I had done my work

و كله چه زۀ ډوډۍ *kala chi zuh dodai* When I have
خورم *wo khuram* eaten my food.

39. "Until" at the beginning of an English
sentence is always translated by ترڅو پورې چه
= *tar sō pōré chi.* and followed by the Negative
Aorist tense as : —

تر څو پورې چه څما *tar sō pore chi* Until you come
دفتر له رانۀ شي *zamā daftar la* to my office.
rā nuh shé

40. "Since" (in the sense of time) at the
beginning of an English sentence, is translated
by كله راسى چه = *kala rāsé chi,* as : —

كله راسى چه هغه *kala rāsé chi*
څما نوكردى *hagha zamā* Since he has been
naukar day in my service.

41. To express "See if" the negative tense
with خو *kho,* before it, should be used as : —

ګوره چه څما كتاب پۀ *gora chi zamā* See if my book
ميز باندې خو نشته *kitāb puh méz* is on the table.
bāndé kho
nishta

42. To express Present Optative, change
the last م = *m,* of the past tense 1st. person
singular into ى = *ay,* for all persons.

To express Past Optative, use the word
way, unchanged after the uninflected past participle and to form Past Potential Optative,

use the word شوی = *shway.* unchanged after the original uninflected past participle. All these Optative expressions commence with :—

ار مان دئ چه   *armān day chi*   I wish that
(Lit : I regret.)

EXAMPLE.

ار مان دئ چه زۀ   *armān day chi*   I wish I could
لارئ   *zuh lāray*   go.

ار مان دئ چه زۀ   *armān day*   I wish I had
تلئ وئَ   *chi zuh talay*   gone.
way

ار مان دئ چه زۀ   *armān day chi*   I wish I could
تلئ شوئَ   *zuh tlay shway*   have gone.

43. To express compulsion, کم نا کم = *kām nā kām* or خوا مخواه = *khwā makhwāh* = some-how or other, should be used as :—

زۀ خوا مخواه لارم   *zuh khwā*   I had to go.
makhwāh lāram

ما کم نا کم نوم   *mā kām nā kām*
کټ کړه   *nūm kat kro*   I had to resign.

زۀ به خوا مخواه   *zuh ba khwā*
خم   *makhwāh zam*   I will have to go.

44. Adverbial phrases of time and place are sometimes put before the subject of the verb as :—

پۀ شپږ بجی زۀ   *puh shpag bajé*   I will go to the
به د فتر ته لارشم   *zuh ba daftar*   office at 6.
ta lārsham

45. شته = *shta* Is there or are there ? It is also used for a question and an answer to a question in the verb to have, but in case of using any interrogative, Adjective and Adverb in the sentence, شته = *shta* can not be used as :—

تا سخه كتاب شته *tā sakha kitāb shta*	Have you a book ?
هو ما سخه كتاب شته *ho mā sakha kitāb shta*	Yes, I have a book.
خو ما سخه قلم نشته *kho mā sakha qalam nishta*	But I have not a pen.
تا سخه څومره كتابونه دي *tā sakha sōmra kitabūna di*	How many books have you ?
تا سخه كوم كتاب دي *tā sakha kum kitāb day*	What book have you?
تا سخه ډير دولت دي؟ *tā sakha dér daulat day ?*	Have you much wealth ?

46. The post position سخه = *sakha* = In the possession of, can be used when the object possessed, is light and moveable and can be carried about.

In the case of parts of the body, relations and heavy property the possessive case should be used as:—

ما سخه يو قلم دى *mā sakha yau qalam day*	I have a pen.
ملك سخه يوه اسپه ده *malak sakha yawa aspa dah*	The headman owns a mare.

زه سترګه یوه خما *zama yawa*
starga dah I have one eye.

شته ورور ستا *stā vrōr shta ?* Have you a
brother ?

شته کور ستا *stā kōr shta* Have you a house ?

47. The use of two similar numerals together denotes "each" as :—

انی دوه دوه ته یو یو *yau yau ta dwa* Give them two
ورکړه *dwa ané warkra* annas each.

48. The Past Conditional of the verb to be
is formed by using the word وی = *way* (indecline-
able) at the end of a sentence as :—

وی هلته زه کۀ *kuh zuh halta*
way If I had been there.

وی هلته تۀ کۀ *kuh tuh halta* If you had been
way there.

وی هلته خان کۀ *kuh khān halta* If the khan had
way been there.

49. In the Negative Tenses formed from
the Past Participle, the Past Participle in
conversation is sometimes put last as :—

راغلی دی نۀ هغه *hagha nuh day*
rāghalay He has not come.

راغلی وۀ نۀ خان *khān nuh woh* The Khan had
rāghalay not come.

راتلی شم نۀ زه *zuh nuh sham* I cannot come.
rātlay

خَتَه يِهْ لارَ نَهْ شوه *khaza puh lāra* The woman could
تلَى *nuh shwa tlay* not go on the road.

50. In Yusafzai Pushtu the last ب = *lo*, of
the 3rd. person Masculine singular of the past
tense is left out as : —

كينا ستلو *kénāstalo* or كيناست *kénāst* He sat.

خملا ستلو *samlāstalo* or خملاست *samlāst* He lay
down.

51. The following nouns take the verb in
the 3rd. person masculine singular :—

مال *māl*   Cattle.

يرغمل *yarghamal*   Hostage or Hostages.

فوځ *fauz*   Troops, Army.

ملاتْرِ *mlā tar*   Followers, Fighting men.

دښمن *dukhman*   Enemy (in War.)

52. The following words take the verb in
the 3rd ; person Masculine Plural :—

دروغ *darōgh*   Lie.

رښتيا *rikhtiā*   Truth.

كنزل *kanzal*   Abuse,

څه *suh*   What, anything.

هيڅ *hiss*   Nothing (takes negative tense.)

53. To forget = هير كَوَل = *hér kawal*, is only
used transitively if the act of forgetting is
delibrate ; ordinarily = هير كيدل = *hér kédal*. with
the ablative case is used e. g.

ما ماك هيروه = *mā muh hérawa* = Don't forget-me

پهٔ دفتر کښې کتاب *puh daftar ké*
رانه هیر شو *kitāb rā na*   I forgot the book
            hér sho   in the office.

Lit : — In the office the book from me was forgotten.

54. (A) Terms of politeness used in address-
ing the following are :—

Old man	کاکا یا کاکا جي *kākā ji* or *kākā*	Uncle.
Blind man	حافظَ *hāfiza*	The man who knows the Quran by heart.
Stranger	ذوانَ *zowāna*	Young man.
Known person	هلکَ *halaka*	Boy.
Father	بابا *bābā*	Father.
Mother	ادي *adé*	Mother.
Brother	لالا *lālā*	Brother.
Sister (older)	بی بی *bébé*	Sister.
Uncle	چاچا *chāchā*	Uncle.
Grand-mother	نانا *nā nā*	Grand-mother.
Maternal uncle	ماما *māmā*	Maternal uncle.
Wife or husband	وَي *way*	Oh !
Urdu knowing person	مرزا صاحب *mirzā sāhib*	Urdu writer.
English knowing person	بابو صاحب *bābū sāhib*	Clerk.
A sweeper	جمعدار *jamādār*	Jemadar.
Mali	چودري *chōwdhri*	Manager.

(B) The following are the terms of calling and driving away different kinds of animals etc :—

	Calling.	Driving away.
Dog	تو تو تو	کوری شه یا چغی شه
	to to to	*kurésha* or *chakhaysha*
Cat	پیش پیش پیش	پشی شه
	peesh peesh peesh	*pashéysha.*
Cow or	شو شو شو	هاوشه
Bullock	*sho sho sho*	*hawsha*
Buffalo	تی تی تی	هی شه
	té té té	*hai sha*
Hawk	بیا بیا بیا	سو سو سو
	biā biā biā	*sū sū sū*
		or
		هان هان هان
		hān hān hān
Goat	بچی بچی بچی	کچی شه
	baché baché baché	*kaché sha*
Sheep	درزی درزی درزی	درزی شه
	darray darray darray	*darray sha*
Horse or	کوز کوز کوز	تپو شه
Donkey	*koor koor koor*	*tpo sha*
Hen or	پاپ پاپ پاپ	کوی شه
Cock	*pāp pāp pāp*	*karé sha*
Camel	پش پش پش	او شا
	pash pash pash	*oosha*
Crow	آ آ آ	دو شه
	ā ā ā	*dōsha*

(C) Driving a person out ‎شه ‎ورک = *vraksha* = Confound you, go and lose yourself.

(D) When speaking of any defective person use the word ‎معذور = *mazūr* = the one who has objection.

هغه ‎یه ‎ورځ ‎سترګه *hagha puh yawa*
‎معذور ‎دی   *starga mazūr*   He has only one
          day   Eye.

هغه ‎یه ‎لاس ‎معذور ‎دی *hagha puh lās*   He has only one
          mazūr day   hand.

هغه ‎یه ‎خپه ‎معذور ‎دی *hagha puh khpa* He has only one
          mazūr day   foot or leg.

55. When two similar post positions are used together, their meaning is intensified as :—

ورستو ‎ورستو ‎راخه *vrosto vrosto*
          rāza   Come far behind.

لاند ‎لاند *lāndé lāndé*   Right underneath, the lower most ones.

پورته ‎پورته *pōrta pōrta*   Upper most ones.

مخ ‎کښی ‎مخ ‎کښی ‎ځه *makhké makhké*
          zah   Go right ahead.

56. The following words have an additional meaning derived from the characteristic of the language and the people as :—

پښتو *pukhtu*   Pashto or modesty.

پښتون *pukhtūn* Pathan or modest, self respecting, firm.

EXAMPLES.

پهٔ هغهٔ کښې هیڅ   *puh haghuh ké*   He has no mode-
پښتو نشته   *hiss pukhtō*   sty (shame) in
nishta   him.

کرنیل صاحب یو   *karnél sāhib yau*   The colonel is a
پښتون سړی دی   *pukhtūn saray*   modest yet firm
day   person.

57. The following words are used as regular adjectives with the verb to be :—

ناست   *nāst*   Sitting.

و لاړ   *walār*   Standing.

ملا ست   *mlāst*   Lying.

اودهٔ   *ūduh*   Sleeping.

EXAMPLE

هغه پهٔ کرسۍ   *hagha puh kursai*   Lit: he is seated
نا ست دی   *nāst day*   on the chair = he
  is sitting on the
  chair.

جنۍ پهٔ کرسۍ   *jinaī puh kursai*   The girl is sit-
ناسته ده   *nāsta dah*   ting (seated) on
  the chair.

58. خندل=*khandal*, to laugh takes پورې=*pōré*
as :—

هغهٔ ما پورې   *haghuh mā*
و خندل   *pōré wo khandal*   He laughed at me

ما هغهٔ پورې   *mā haghuh*
و خندل   *pōré wo khandal*   I laughed at him.

59. The future perfect and past dubious are formed by conjugating the future tense of the verb to be after the past participle of another verb as :—

هغه به راغلیَ وی *hagka ba*   He must, will, or
           rāghalay wee   may have come.

NOTE :— به = *ba* the sign of the future can be put anywhere after the subject of the verb, so long as it is before the verb as :—

زهٔ به پهٔ پنڅهٔ بجی *zuh ba puh pinzuh*
دَ کرنیل صاحب سره *bajé da karnail*   I will go for shoot-
         sāhib sara khk-   ing with the colo-
ښکار دَ پاره ځم *ār da pāra zam*   nel at 5 o'clook.

60. To express "to be about to" either change the final ل = *l* of the infinitive into ونکیَ = *ūnkay* or use the preposition پهٔ-کښ = *puh-ké* with the verbal nouns as :—

هغه راتلونکیَ دیَ *hagha rātlūnk-*   He is about to
         ay day   come.

هغه پهٔ راتلوکښ دی *hagha puh rātlo*   He is about to
         ké day   come.

61. To express "to be about to be" conjugate the verb راتلل = *rātlal* = to come or کیدل = *kédal* = become after the verbal nouns governed by پهٔ-بندی = *puh-bānde* as :—

کوهی پهٔ ډکیدلو راغیَ *kuhy puh dakédalo*   the well
         rāghay   is about
کوهی ,, پهٔ ډکیدلو شو ,, ,, *sho*   to become
کوهی ,, پهٔ ډکیدلو دی ,, ,, *day*   full

62. To express "either......or," use يا = *yā* at the beginning of both sentences and to express "neither nor," use نه = *nuh* at the beginning of both sentences as :—

يا دا واخله يا *yā dā wākhla*
هغه واخله *yā hagha* take either this *wākhla* or that.

زه نه دا اخلم نه هغه *zuh nuh dā*
اخلم *akhlam nuh* I will take neith-
hagha akhlam er this nor that.

63. ياد کول = *yād kawal* to remind and ويل = *wayal* to say, speak or tell, take the dative case ته = *ta* = to.

ما ته ياد کړه *mā ta yād kra* Remind me.
ورته و وايه *war ta wo wāya* Tell him.

64. In some districts the imperfect tense 3rd. person masculine singular and plural of the Class II, III, IV and VII verbs, is formed by changing the final ل = *l*, of the infinitive into ه = *uh*, as :—

هغه ر سيده *hagha raséduh* He was arriving.
هغوی ر سيده *haghui raséduh* They were arriving.
ما هغه راوستۀ *mā hagha rāwastuh* I was bringing him.
ما هغوی راوستۀ *mā haghui rāwastuh* I was bringing them.
هغه مر کيده *hagha mar kéduh* Hé was dying.

هغوی مړهٔ کیدهٔ	*haghui mruh kéduh*	they were dying.
ما کتاب لو ستهٔ	*mā kitāb lwastuh*	I was reading a book.
ما کتا بونه لوستهٔ	*mā kitābūna lwastuh*	I was reading books.

In Class I. Verbs the above rule applies only to 3rd. person masculine singular as :—

ما هغه و وههٔ	*mā hagha wo wahuh*	I beat him, struck him.
ما هغوی ووهل	*mā hughui wo wahal*	I beat them, struck them.

Some times the imperfect tense 3rd person masculine singular is formed irregularly :—

هغه تهٔ	*hagha tuh*	He was going.
هغه راتهٔ	*hagha rātuh*	He was coming.

65. Sometimes in forming the potential mood the final ل = *l*, of the past participle is dropped.

زهٔ رسیدی شم	*zuh raséday sham*	I can arrive.
زهٔ او سیدی شم	*zuh oséday sham*	I can live.
زهٔ رسیدی نهٔ شم	*zuh raséday nuh sham*	I cannot arrive.
زهٔ کینا ستی شوم	*zuh kénāstay shwam*	I could sit.
زهٔ راوری شم	*zuh rāwray sham*	I can bring.
ما راوری شو	*mā rawray sho*	I could bring.

66. The past tense of the following verbs is sometimes formed thus :—

راتلل = *rātlal* = to come,

Singular.	Plural.
راغم *rāgham* (I) came	راغُو *rāghū* (we) came.
راغې *rāghé* (thou) came	راغئ *raghai* (you) came.
راغی *rāghay* (he) came or *ragho*	راغهٔ *rāghuh* (they) came.
راغه *rāgha* (She) came (F)	راغې *rāghé* (they) came. (F. P.)

کول = *kawal* = to do.

(زهٔ یی مۀ) (*zuh yé mar*) kram	(He killed) me.
(تهٔ یی مۀ) (*tuh yé mar*) kré	(he killed) thee.
(هغهٔ یی مۀ) (*hagha yé mar*) kro	(He killed) him.
(هغهٔ یی مۀه) (*hagha yé mra*) kra	(He killed) her (F. S.)
(مونږونږي مۀه) (*mūng yé mruh*) kroo	(He killed) us.
(تٔ سو ئی مۀه) *tāsō yé mruh*) krai کړئ	(He killed) you.
(هغوی یی مۀه) (*haghui yé mruh* kruh کړهٔ	(He killed) them.
(هغوی یی مړی) (*haghui yé mré*) kré کړی	(He killed) them (F. P.)

کیدل‎ = *kédal* = to become.

شولم‎ *shwalam* (I) became.   شولو‎ *shwaloo* (we) become.

شولی‎ *shwalé* (thou) become.   شولۍ‎ *shwalai* (you) became.

شولوباشۀ‎ *shwalo* (he) or *shuh* become.   شوۀ‎ *shwuh* (they) became.

شوله‎ *shwalah* (she) became.   شوي‎ *shwé* (they) became. (F. P.)

وبل‎ *wayal*   to say, speak, tell.

ما وو‎ *mā wo wé* I said, spoke, or told.

ما و‎ *mā wé* I was saying.   (Imperf. tense.)

67. To express "unless or until" use the negative aorist tense of the required verb as :—

که تۀ پخپله رانۀ شی‎ *kuh tuh pakh-pala rā nuh shé*   Unles you come yourself.

ترخو پوری چه زۀ را‎ *tar so pōré chi zuh rā nuh sham* نۀشم‎   Until I come my-self.

68. داره‎ = *dāra* raid or raiding party and جرم‎ = *jurm* fine (on the village or tribe) both take the verb to fall = پریوتل‎ = *préwatal.*

زما پۀ کلی باند‎ *zamā puh kali bāndé dāra préwatala* داره پریوتله‎   My village was raided.

زما پۀ کلی باند‎ *zamā puh kali bāndé jurm préwatalo* جرم پریوتلو‎   My village was fined.

69. افسوس = *afsōs*, sorrow. must always be used with كول = *kawal* = to do, as :—

زۀ افسوس كوم = *zuh afsōs kawam*,　I am sorry.

70. Nouns ending in consonants governed by ablative case sometimes take ــَ *zabar* over the last consonant letter of the noun instead of نه = *na*, the second Part of the Post position as :—

لۀ كور نه *luh kōr na* or　لۀ كورَ *luh kōra*
　　　　　　　　　　　　　　From the house.

لۀ مسكوټ نه *luh miskōt na* or لۀ مسكوټَ *luh miskota*
　　　　　　　　　　　　　　From the Mess.

71. بل = *bal*, next or other (stands for number) Its Plural is نور = *nōr*, = more or others (Stands for both number and quantity) as :—

بل سړى راغى　*bal saray rāghay*　Another man came.

نورى اوبۀ نشته　*noré obuh nishta*　There is no more water.

72. څو = *so*, how many (stands for number.) څومره = *somrā*, how many or how much (Stands both for number and quantity) e. g.

څو هلكان دى　*so halakān di*　How many boys are there.

پۀ گلاس كښ　*puh gélas ké*　How much water

څومره اوبۀ دى.　*sōmra obuh di*　is there in the glass.

73. When an adjective is used to qualify two or more nouns of different Genders the verb agrees with last one as :—

يو سړی او دوه	*yau saray aw*	One man and two
ښځی ناستی وی	*dwa khazé*	women were
	nāsté wé	sitting.

74. When two or three or more than three nouns of different genders are used in the sentence, the verb agrees with the last one and if two nouns of different genders in the singular number are used, the verb goes into the 3rd person masculine plural. In the case of the verb "to be" however agreement is with the last noun as :—

هلته دوه سړی او	*halta dwa sari*	There were two
دری هلکان او	*aw dré halakān*	men and three
	aw dré khazé	boys and three
دری ښځی وی	*wé*	women three.
پۀ کور کښ څلور	*puh kōr ké salōr*	There were four
ښځی او دوه	*khazé aw dwa*	women and two
سړی وُو	*sari woo*	men there in the house.
یو هلک او یوه	*yau halak aw*	One boy and one
جنۍ ولاړۀ وُو	*yawa jinai walār woo*	girl were standing
هلته یو هلک او	*halta yau halak*	There are one
یوه جنۍ دَه	*aw yawa jinai dah*	boy and one girl there.
زما پۀ خیال کښ	*zamā puh kheyāl*	I thing there were
یوه جنۍ او یو	*ké yawa jinai aw*	one girl and one
هلک وۀ	*yau halāk woh*	boy there.

75. خپل = *khpal* Own—comes under the rules of regular adjectives ending in consonants and is used as a reflexive pronoun as :—

زۀ خپل کورته ځم *zuh khpal hōr ta zam*	I go to my house.
ځما خپل کورونه دی *zamā khpal kōrūna di*	They are my own houses.
ځما خپله لُور ده *zamā khpala lūr dah*	She is my own daughter.
ځما خپلی لُونړه دی *zamā khpalé lūnra di*	They are my own daughters.
دَ خپلی اسپی زین راوړه *da khpalé aspé zin rāwra*	Bring the saddle of your mare.
خپلو اسپونه واښۀ واچوه *khpalo aspo ta wākhuh wāchawa*	Give grass to your mares.
مۆنږ خپلو کورونو ته ځُو *mūng khpalo kōrūno ta zoo*	We are going to our houses.

NOTE :—When the particle پۀ = *pa* is prefixed to خپل = *kapal*, the ۀ = *h* of the particle پۀ = *pa* is placed after the same word :—

پخپله = *pakhpala* = Myself, yourself, himself, herself, itself, etc.

زۀ پخپله ځم *zūh pakhpala zam*	I go or will go myself.
هغه به پخپله راشی *hagha ba pakhpala rāshi*	He will come himself.

76. The Causative verbs are formed by using the preposition پِه‑باند = *puh-bānde* with a transitive verb as :—

ما پِه مُنْشی باند *mā puh munshi*
چِنْی ولیکله *bāndé chitai*   I made the munshi
                wo likalah   write a letter.

77. The interrogative is often used to indicate strong negative as :—

ما سخه روپِی چرتەدِي *mā sakha*   I have no money
                  rupai charta di? at all.

78. The past participle of any verb can be used as an adjective as :—

تښتیدلیَ آس *takhtédalay āss* Run away horse.

وهلیَ شوی سړیَ *wahalay*
                    shaway saray The beaten man.

79. Prefix د = *da* = of, (the genitive) to a noun to use it as an adjective as :—

د میوی دوکان *da mewé dūkān*   The fruit shop.

دَ کور خاوند *da kōr khāwand* The owner of the
                                house.

80. لؤ‌وتی = *lūkūti* or لر = *lag* = little, is used at the beginning of a sentence to express "Please" as :—

لؤ کوتی زر راشه *lūkūti zar rāsha* Please come
                                    quickly.

لؤ کوٹی اوبۂ راوړہ	*lūkūti obuh rāwra*	Please bring some water.
لری اوبۂ راکړہ	*lagé obuh rākra*	Please give me some water.

81. غوندی = *ghundé* Like, added to adjectives signifies "Somewhat" :—

وړوکی غوندي	*warūkay ghundé*	somewhat small or smallish.
سپين غوندي	*spin ghundé*	somewhat white or whitish.

82. The plural is used for the 2nd and 3rd person singular for politeness, but if the name of the person is mentioned then the Verb remains singular as :—

تا سو کله راغلي يِي	*tāso kala rāghali yai*	instead of.
تۀ کله راغلی يِي	*tuh kala rāghalay yé*	When have you come ?
هغۀی کله راغلي دی	*haghūi kala rāghali dī*	Instead of.
هغۀ کله راغلی دی	*hagha kala rāghalay day*	(lit) when has he come, when did he come ?
افضل خان کله تلی دی	*afzal khān kala talay day*	when did Afzal Khan go ?

83. پۀ مخه راتلل = *puh makha rātlal* to meet. When using this in a sentence, the subject of the English verb is always left out as :

راغلو هغه پۀ مينه *hagha puh makha*
rāghlo   I met him.

درغلو هغه پۀ مينه *hagha puh makha*
daraghlo   Thou met him.

ورغلو هغه پۀ مينه *hagha puh makha*
waraghlo   He met him.

84. To express strong negation in question form repeat, the tense in affirmative after the negative tense with خو = *kho* before it as :—

زۀ ستا نوکر، خو نۀيم *zuh stā naukar*
چه نوکريم *kho nuh yam*   I am not your
chi naukar yam servant am I ?

85. The expression "Will you" the sign of a question or force after an imperative in English is always translated by که نه = *ka na* = if not, or not as :—

دا واخله که نه *dā wākhla ka na* take this will you ? but when used with هو = *ho*, it means "Of course" as :—

هو که نه *ho ka na* of course, certainly.

86. For blessing and cursing use د = *dé* before the imperative for 2nd person singular as :—

خدای دلات کړه *khudāi dé lāt* May God make
kra   you a lord.

خدای د خوار کړه *khudāi dé* May God make
khwār kra   you poor.

NOTE : —For the rest of the persons use the following particles.

‍م = *mé*		‍مو = *mo*	
‍د = *dé*	Singular.	‍مو = *mo*	Plural.
‍ی = *yé*		‍ئي = *yé*	

before the aorist tense 3rd, person with ‍د = *dé* before it as :—

خدای م د خان کړی	*khudāi mé dé khān kri*	May God make me a Khan.
خدای مو د خوار کړی	*khudāi mō dé khwār kri*	May God make you poor.
خدای د یی خوار کړی	*khudāi dé yé khwār kri*	May God make him (them) poor.

NOTE :—The above particles are idiomatically used after :—

را = *rā*	در = *dar*	ور = *war*	پ = *pā*	پری = *pré*
پوری = *pōré*	‍کی = *ké*	‍و = *wo*	وا = *wā*	نن = *nan*
‍بی = *bé*, e. g.				

را یی نه کړ	*rā yé nuh kar*	He did not give it to me.
پا یی نه خولو	*pa yé nūh sawalo*	He did not make him get up.
و م نه ویل	*wo mé nuh wayal*	I did not say.

كېم نۀ ښودلو   *ké mé nuh khōdalo*   I did not place it.

راېې نۀ ورو   *rā yé nuh vro*   He did not bring it.

87. An inanimate object can never be used in the Agentive case. The verb is changed into intransitive governed by the Ablative case as : —

ستا چټۍ مې ولوستله او وز نه پوه شوم چه تۀ نوره نوکری نه کوې

stā chitai mé wo lwastalah aw war na poh shwam chi tuh nōra naukari nuh kawé

I read your letter which made me think that you were not going to serve any more.

لۀ دى سيند نه ښمنوزر ټوله زمکه اوبۀ کېږي

luh dé sind na zamūng tōla zmaka obuh kégi

This river irrigates all our land.

ښمونږ پټو له پۀ وله کښې اوبۀ راخلی یا له ولې نه اوبۀ راخلی

zamūng patō la puh wala ké obuh rāzee or *luh walé na obuh rāzee* The irrigation channel brings water to our fields.

88. The first letter of a noun is changed into م = *m* and then it is repeated for emphasis and etc. but when the noun begins with م = *m* it should be repeated without any alteration as :—

تا سخه کتاب متاب شته   *tā sakha kitab mitāb shta*   Have you any book etc ?

پۀ کمره کښې خه میز   *puh kamra ké suh méz méz*   Is there any میز شته   *shta*   table etc. in the room ?

NOTE :—The following are the exceptions :—

غږ غوږ	*ghag ghūg*	Human voice (in answer)
هان هون	*hān hūn*	,, ,, ,,
تس تُوس یا	*tas tūs* or	
دز دوس	*daz dūz*	Sniping.
غلا غلتیا	*ghlā ghultia*	Theft etc.
کاڼری بوټی	*kānri būti*	Stones etc.
کرو کور	*karū kōr*	Rendered homeless.
چنگ رباپ	*chang rabāp*	Squandered.
خل پل	*khal pal*	Leaves and twigs.
غال بول	*ghāl būl*	Harum scarum.
ټیل ما ټیل	*tail mātail*	Pushing each other.
درب دروب	*drab drūb*	Fisticuffs.
گار گور	*gār gūr*	Thunder and lightning.

89.   The use of خو = *kho* = but

دغه کتاب خو راکوه	*dāgha kitāb kho rākra*	Just hand me that book please.
زۀ خو دا کار نۀ کوم	*zuh khō dā kār nuh kawam*	I shall not do this really.
دا سړی خو ځما نوکر وو	*dā saray khō zamā naukar woh*	I believe this man was my servant.
هغه خو به پاس شی	*hagha khō ba pāss shi*	He will certainly pass.
آخر گوره خو چه د دی به څۀ نتیجه وی	*ākher gora kho chi da dé ba suh natija wee*	Any way do at least wait and see what the result of it will be.

تۀ نا جوړ خو	tuh nā jōr kho	I hope you are
نه یی	nuh yé	not ill. (you look as if you are.)
جوړ خوبی که نه	jōr kho yé ka na	I hope you are well. (you look as if you are not.)
کم عقل خو دی	kam aqal khō	Admitted that he
خوغل نۀ دیَ	day kho ghal nuh day	is a fool but he is not a thief.
دا خو رښتیا خبره	dā kho rikhtiā	This indeed is
دَه	khabara dah	true.
زۀ خو نۀ ځم	zuh khō nuh zam	I (as you know) am not going.

پښتو خو پښتو دَه چه زۀ پۀ انګریزي هم نۀ پو هیږم

pukhtō kho pukhtō dah chi zuh puh angrézai hum nuh pōhégam

or

پښتو خو پریږده چه زۀ پۀ انګریزي هم نۀ پو هیږم

pukhtō kho prégda chi zuh puh angrézai hum nuh pōhégam

Let alone (or to say nothing of) Pushtu I do not even understand English.

| ښه دا کار خو وشو | kha dā kār khō wo shō | Well that is done. |
| یو خو هغۀ غریب دیَ بل بد خوئی دیَ | yau khō hagha gharib day, bal bad khūi day | For one thing (or first) he is poor, and for another (or secondly) bad tempered, |

90. When a noun is repeated, it denotes entirety plurality and variety as :—

ما هغه کټ پۀ کټ والټولو	*mā hagha kat puh kat wo latawalo*	I searched for him in each and every bed.
رښتیا رښتیا وایه	*rikhtiā rīkhtiā wāya*	Speak the truth and nothing but the truth (i. e. the whole truth.)
مؤ نر پۀ سرک سرک راغلو	*mūng puh sarāk sarāk rāghlū*	We came by the road the whole way.
اوس هغه در پۀ در ګرځي	*us hagha dar puh dar garzee*	Now he wanders about begging from door to door

91. When a personal or pronominal adjective is repeated, it denotes plurality, variety and distribution.

تا څۀ څۀ ولیدل   *tā suh suh wo lidal*

What various things did you see ?

پۀ هغه وخت هلته څوک څوک موجود وو   *puh hagha wakht halta sōk sōk maujūd woo.*

What people were individually present there at that time ?

کوم کوم چه وګټی نو انعام به وموسی   *kum kum chi wo gati no inām ba wo mūmee*

Every one of those who wins will get a reward.

خینی خینی سړی هلته پاتي دي   *ziné ziné saray halta paté day*

There were only a few people left there.

بعضي بعضي په كښ ډير   *bazé bazé pa ké dér*
مُنصف وُه   *munsif woh*

Some of them (considered individually) were
very just.

هر سړی خپل خپل كور ته لاړ   *har saray khpal khpal*
    kōr ta lār

Everyone of them went to his own house.

ټول خپلو خپلو كورونو ته لاړل   *tōl khpalō khpalō*
    kōrūno ta lāral

All went to their respective houses.

ما هغه هغه يا داسى داسى   *mā hagha hagha* or *dāsé*
خيزونه وليدل چه ورته حيران   *dāsé sizūna wo lidal*
    chi war ta hairan pāté
پاتى شوم   *shwam*

I was astonished to see such things.

څه څه يا نا څه   *suh suh* or *suh nā suh*

Somewhat or to some extent.

هغه څه نا څه   *hagha suh nā*   He can speak
انګريزى ويلى   *suh angrezi*   English a little
شى   *wayalay shee*   (to some extent.)

اوس هغه څه   *os hagha suh*   He is somewhat
نا څه جوړ دى   *nā suh jōr day*   better now.

92. څوک = *sōk* = who, څه = *suh* = what, repeated in negative sentences have the additional
idiomatic meaning of all or whole. as :—

هلته څوک څوک   *halta sōk sōk*   Who was not present
نه وُه ؟   *nuh woh*   there ? (name them in-
    dividually) ? or every
    body was there.

ما خڅ خڅ رنه‌ *mā suh suh* I saw everything (lit :
ليدل ؟ *wo nuh lidal* what was it that I
did not see?)

93. When an adjective is repeated it
denotes plurality, entirety, and variety or
distribution.

پۀ هر طرف اوچت	*puh har taraf*	There were tall
اوچت کورونه وو	*ūchat ūchat korūna woo*	houses on every side.
لۀ سرک نه پورې	*luh sarak na*	Beyond the road
غاړه لوی لوی	*poré ghāra lōi*	there were many
پټی وو	*lōi pati woo*	large fields.
لۀ چاونۍ نه باهر	*luh chāwnrai na bāhar*	Outside the cant- onment there are
شنۀ شنۀ فصلونه		
دی	*shnuh shnuh faslūna di*	many green crops.

دَ هغوی لنډی لنډی ګیری وي *da haghūi landé landé giré wi*
They have (generally) short beards.

ورته تازه تازه پۍ ورکوه *war ta tāza tāza pai war kawa*
Give him (or them) very fresh milk or give him
milk while it is still fresh.

یخه یخه هوا الوزي *yakha yakha hawā alūzee*
A nice cool breeze is blowing (continued and
agreeable intensity).

ورته پنځۀ پنځۀ انی ورکوه *war ta pinzuh pinzuh ané war kra*
Give them five annas each.

صاحب سخه ښی ښی جامی دي   *sāhib sakha khé khé*
jāmé di

The sahib has many good clothes.

ورسخه خرڅ دَ پاره لس لس   *war sakha khars da pāra*
روپۍ دي   *las las rupai di*

Each of them has ten rupees to spend.

تا سو ټولو ته به پاؤ باند خلور   *tāso tōlo ta ba pāw*
خلور روپۍ ملاؤ شی   *bandé salōr salōr rūpai*
milāw shi

Everyone of you will get Rs. 4/4/-.

94. When an imperfect tense or a verbal
noun is repeated it denotes continuity.

تلم تلم کابل ته ورسیدم   *tlam tlam kābal ta wo*
rasédam

I went on till I reached Kabul.

هغه یُه لوستو لوستوکښې لیوني شو   *hagha puh lwasto*
lwasto ké léwanay sho

By continually reading he went mad.

پُه ناستی ناستی ستړی شوم   *puh nāsté nāsté staray*
shwam.

I became tired of continued idleness.

پُه ملاستی ملاستی یی روټۍ   *puh mlāsté mlāsté yé*
وخوړله   *rōtai wo khwarala*

He ate his food lying down all the time.

پُه لیدو لیدو مې زړه باغ باغ   *puh līdo lido mé zruh*
کیږي   *bāgh bāgh kégee*

By continuously looking I am delighted.

خهٔ خهٔ چه را نه یی غوښتل ما   *suh suh chi rā na yé*
به ورکول   *ghukhtal mā ba warkwal*

I gave him whatever he asked me for.

95. Note the force of repetition in the following :—

زر زر راځه	*zar zar rāza*	Come on quickly.
ورو ورو ځه	*vro vro za*	Go on slowly.
مخ کینں مخ کینں ځه	*makh ké makh ké za*	Go ahead or take the lead.
كله كله دلته راځی	*kala kala dalta rāzee*	He comes here occasionally.
تهٔ چرته چرته وگرزیدی	*tuh charta charta wo garzédé*	What various places have you been to ?

هوائی جهاز اوس لاندِ لاندِ راځی   *Hawāi jéhāz oss lāndé lāndé rāzee*

The aeroplane is now gradually coming down.

چرته چرته چه لورِ ژوورِ وی نو هغه برابره کړه   *charta charta chi lwara jhawara wee no hagha barābara kra*

Level the ground wherever it is rough.

اول اول هغهٔ ماسره ښهٔ سلوک کولو   *awal awal haghuh mā sara khuh salūk kawalo*

In the beginning (i. e. early days) he treated me very well.

ورستو ورستو را پسی راځه   *vrusto vrusto rā pasé rāza*

Follow me closely.

هغه كلیِ ته نیزدی نیزدی مال — *hagha kali ta nizdé*
خروه — *nizdé māl sarawa*

Keep on grazing your cattle near that village.

د سیند پهِ غاړه غاړه یوه كچه لارده — *da sind puh ghāra*
ghāra yawa kacha lār
dah

There is an unmetalled road along the bank of the river.

خپلی كمپنی سره سره روان اوسه — *khpalé kampanai sara*
sara rawān osa

Keep on with your company.

In this connection, note the following idioms :—

كلیِ پهِ كلیِ — *kalay puh kalay* Village to village or village by village

كال پهِ كال — *kāl puh kāl* Yearly.

جمعه پهِ جمعه — *jūma puh jūma* Weekly.

ورځ پهِ ورځ — *vraz puh vraz* Daily.

فصل پهِ فصل — *fasal puh fasal* Half yearly.

دیوال پهِ دیوال — *déwāl puh déwāl* Next door to.

څه نا څه — *suh nā suh* Something or other

څوک نه څوک — *sōk na sok* Someone or other.

چرته نا چرته — *charta nā charta* Somewhere or other.

كور پهِ كور — *kōr puh kōr* In each house.

لاس پهِ لاس — *lās puh lās* hand to hand or very quickly.

خپه پهِ خپه — *khpa puh khpa* Sitting doing nothing (idly).

جور پهٔ جور   *jōr puh jōr*   Like servant like master (or wife and husband both are of the same nature)

96.   To form a question in the absence of any interrogative word use كه نه = *kuh na* = or not, at the end of a sentence. Also, as in other languages a rising intonation at the end of a remark implies a question.

خان اوس پهٔ هسپتال کښے دے   *Khān oss puh haspatāl*
کهٔ نه ؟   *ké day kuh na*
Is the Khan in the hospital now ?

97.   كه نه = *kuh na* = or not, is some times put at the end of a sentence to make it interrogative and invites an answer accordingly as the rest of the sentence is couched e. g. if the rest of the sentence is put affirmatively the answer is expected to be in the affirmative, but if it is worded negatively, the answer is expected to be in the negative as :—

تهٔ خو به صبا ځی کهٔ نه   *tuh kho ba sabā zé*
kuh na
I believe you will go   tomorrow, wont you ?

بیا خو به داسی کارنهٔ کوی کهٔ نه   *biā kho ba dāsé kār*
nuh kawé ka na
Well, I hope you will not do so in future, will you ?

98. The names of places ending in ـِي = *i* are considered masculine plural, therefore when governed by any preposition they should be put into the oblique plural as :—

خوا دى پيونه لۀ *luh pabō na dé khwā* This side of Pabbi.

خم متنونه زۀ صبا *sabā zuh matano ta zam* I am going to Mattani tomorrow.

99. To show dislike or anger add ـے = *ay*, ـۍ = *gay*, to proper nouns and titles ending in consonants or vowels respectively.

احمد *ahmad*   احمدے *ahmaday*

ملا *mulā*   ملاۍ *mulāgay*

100. To animate or inanimate articles add ـۍ = *gay*, to express smallness or poor quality as :—

تتو *tattū* Pony   تتوۍ *tatūgay* Small pony.

تم تم *tam tam* Tonga   تم تمۍ *tam tamgay* Ordinary kind of tonga.

101. Generic Plural Animals etc. when seen in numbers from a distance are sometimes referred to as feminine plural and sometimes as masculine plural regardless of their actual sex.

e. g. Feminine Plural.

ميښى *Mékhé*   Buffaloes.

ګډى *gadé*   Sheep.

کونترى *kōntaré*   Pigeons.

Masculine Pural.

ميلؤ ګان	*mélūgān*	Bears.
اوښان	*ukhān*	Camels.
ډنګر	*dangar*	Cattle.
ها تیاں	*hāthiān*	Elephants.
قار غان	*qārghān*	Crows.
ټپُو خان	*tapūsān*	Kites.
طو طیان	*tōtyān*	Parrots.
امزري	*amzari*	Tigers.
بیزو ګان	*bizōgān*	Monkeys.

102. لرل = *laral* to have. is rarely used except in the present and imperative.

زۀ یو كتاب لرم	*zuh yau kitāb laram*	I have a book.
ټول رسد تیار لره	*tōl rasad tayār lara*	Have all supplies ready.

103. ماره = *māra*, give me, the imperative, has no infinitive, it only derived from Persian Dative case مارا *mā rā* = to me as :—

دا كتاب مارا	*dā kitāb māra* Give me that book.

104. مینه كیدل = *mina kédal* to have a desire for, takes Dative case and is followed by the genitive case :—

خما تلو تۀ مینه	*zamā tlo ta*	I have a desire
كیږی	*mina kégee*	to go.

105. The following nouns are masculine in the singular and feminine in the plural :—

مرز *maraz* Quail   مرزی *maraze* F. P.

كندر *kandar* ruined   كندری *kandaré* F. P.
house

كوتک *kōtak* big stick   كوتكی *kōtaké* F. P.

دز *daz* Gun shot   دزی *dazé* F. P.
(report)

106. Some nouns are feminine in the singular and masculine in the plural as :—

گناه *gunāh* Sin   گناهونه *gunāhūna* Sins M. P.

107. خدمت كول = *khidmat kawal* = To serve (without payment) takes genitive case as :—

مونږ د سركار خدمت كړی دی *mūng dā sarkār khidmat karay day*
We have served Government.

108. Use simple imperfect when the desire of a person i. e. subject of the verb is expressed as :—

كه هغه راتلو نو را دِ شی *kuh hagha rātla no rā dé shee*
Let him come if he wishes to come.

109. In the imperative of a transitive verb the direct object must be expressed as :—

را یی كړه *rā yé kra*   Give it to me.

وریی كړه *war yé kra*   Give it to him.

وهه ولّی   *wo yé waha*   Beat him.

كيم نوه   *ké mé nawa*   Make me sit.

110. When the intention of the subject in the conditional form is expressed, use the original uninflected past participle in the 1st sentence and the required tense in the 2nd; half as :—

كه هغه راتلّی نو به راغلّی وه   *kuh hagha rātlay nō ba rāghalay woh*

If he meant to come he would have come.

111. To express "nearly" or "about" use یو = *yau* = one. before the required numerals as :—

یو دوه سو   *yaw dwa sawa*   nearly two hundred.

112. List of common female animals and their male young.

غوا	*ghwā* Cow	سخی	*skhay*	calf.
مېښه	*mékha* Buffalo	كتی	*katay*	Buffalo calf.
اسپه	*aspa* mare	كوّ چانوّی	*kūchā nray*	Colt.
گډه	*gada* Sheep	اورّی	*oray*	Lamb.
چېلی	*chélai* She goat	بکرّی	*bakray*	Kid.
اوښ	*ūkha* Female camel	جوّنګی	*jōngay*	young camel.
سپی	*spai* Bitch	كوّترّی	*kūtré*	pup.

113. پہ قهر کیدل = puh qahar kédal to be enraged with. takes Dative case as :—

ما ته پہ قهر شو   mā ta puh   He got angry
              qahar sho   with me.

114. خپه کیدل = khapa kédal to be angry with, takes لہ نه = luh-na as :—

هغه رانه خپه شو   hagha rā na
یا هغه له ما نه   khapa sho or
خپه شو   hagha luh mā   He got angry
         na khapa sho   with me.

لہ ما نه مۀ خپه   luh mā na   Don't be angry
کیږه muh khapa kéga   with me.

115. بلا = balā = calamity, when used before plural nouns means innumerable and before singular number, denotes greatness, the biggest size and the best qualification of a person as :—

پہ جماعت کښ   puh jumāit ké   There are innu-
بلا خلق دی   balā khalq dee   merable people in
                          the mosque.

هغه بلا سړی دی   hagha balā   He is an exception-
              saray day   able person.

116. The Definite Habitual expressing a condition is formed by prefixing بہ = ba to the past definite as :—

چه سهر, ته بہ راغلو نو زۀ بہ یی   chi khahar ta ba rāghlo
ولیدم او بیا بہ لاړو   no zuh ba yé wo lidalam
              aw biā ba lāro

Whenever he came to the city, he would come to see me and then go back.

117. The Potential Habitual in the form of conditional in the 2nd half is formed by pre fixing به = *ba*, to the past potential.

کۀ سرکار ټول وطن ته دَ ټوپکو
ساتلو اجازت ورکړی وی ـ نو
خذۀه به م ، ټول پۀ قابو کښی
ساتلیٰ شول

kuh sarkār tōl watan ta da tōpakō sātalō ijāzat warkaray way, nō sanga ba mé tōl puh qābū ké sātalay shwal.

If the Government had allowed the whole country to keep rifles, how could I keep them all in hand.

118. هسی نۀ وی چه = *hasé nuh wi chi* = Lest. is followed by the Aorist tense as :—

هسی نۀ وی چه هغۀ راشی *hasé nuh wi chi hagha rāshee*

Lest he should come.

NOTE :—Also the use of چرته = *charta*, in this connection.

چرته هغۀ را نۀ شی *charta hagha rā nuh shee.*

I hope he will not come (i.e. I fear lest he should come.)

119. Politely speaking when referring to the son of gentleman call him صاحبزاده = *Sahibzāda*, or برخوردار = *Barkhurdār* and when referring to ones own son, call him غلام = *ghulām* = Slave. Similarly when talking about the house of a gentleman (other than your own) you will call it

دولت خانه = *daulat khāna* = (abode of wealth) and
when talking of your own house, you will call it.

غريب خانه = *gharib khāna* = Humble cottage,
as :—

ستا سو دَ برخوردار نوم څۀ دیَ   *stāso da burkhurdār*
nūm suh day
What is the name of your son ?

داستاسو غلام به جواب درووړی   *dāstaso ghulām ba*
jawāb dar wree
This son of mine lit your slave will bring you
the answer.

ستا سو دولت خانه چرته ده   *stāso daulat khāna*
charta dah
Where is your house ?

ځما غريب خانه پۀ ښهر کښ ده   *zamā gharib khāna puh*
khahar ké dah
My house is in the city.

120. When visiting a patient, or referring
to an unpleasant subject, say, first :—

نصيب دشمنان   *nasibé dushmanān*
May it (disease) fall to the lot of your enemies.

When praising something or somebody
belonging to another person say :—

ماشاء الله   *mā shā allāh*   As God wills.

چشم بد دُور   *chéshmé bad dūr*   Far be the evil eye.

نصيب دشمنان دا کله راسی ناجوړ
شوَیَ یی

nasibé dushmanān dā
kala rāsé nā jora
shaway yé

May your disease become the lot of your
enemies.   How long have you been ill ?

ماشاء اللّٰه ستا سو برخوردار پۀ
جماعت کښې اول لمبر دی

mā sha allah stāso
barkhurdār puh jamāat
ké awal lambar day

By God's will your son is first in the class.

چشم بد دُور ستا سو موټر دَ
چاونړۍ دَ موټرونو پلار دی

cheshmé bad dūr stāṣo
mōtar da chāunrai da
mōtarūno plār day

Far be the evil eye, your motor is the best in the
cantt; (lit: is the father of motors in the Cantt.)

121.   Strong Negation is sometimes expressed by using خاوري = *khāwré* = dust,   with the
subject of the verb as :—

هغه به په دی خاوری ده
شی څۀ

hagha ba pa dé khāwré
poh shee suh

How on earth can he understand this ?

122.   Interrogatives are often used to express
strong negation, surprise and impossibility as :—

زۀ په دی کښی څۀ کولی شم

zuh pa dé ké suh
kawalay sham

What can I do in this matter! (or it is impossible
for me to do anything in this matter).

زۀ څنګه هلته لارشم

zuh sangā halta lār
sham

How can I go there or I cannot go there or it is
impossible for me to go there.

تهٔ په دى څهٔ پوهيږي   *tuh pa dé suh pōhégé*

How do you know of this ? (you know nothing
of this).

هغه كله كابل ته تلى دىَ   *hagha kala kābal ta
talay day*

When has he been to Kabul ? (i e. he has
never been to Kabul).

123. Many Arabic and Persian adverbs
are commonly used :—

اتفاقاً	*ittefāqan*	by chance.
خصوصاً	*khusūsan*	especially.
تخميناً	*takhminan*	nearly.
قريباً	*qariban*	nearly.
فوراً	*fauran*	at once.
جبراً	*jabran*	by force.
مثلاً	*masalan*	for instance.
عموماً	*umūman*	generally.
ارادتاً	*irādatan*	intentionally.

etc :—

124. Some idiomatic uses of چرته—*charta*
where.

چرته زهٔ او چرته ته   *charta zuh aw charta tuh*
there is all the difference between you and me
(lit : where am I and where are you.) ?

چرته هغه بادشاهى او چرته دا   *charta hagha bādshāhi*
غريبى   *aw charta dā gharibi*
Once there was such a good time and now there
is this poverty.

زهٔ چرته او تهٔ چرته   *zuh charta aw tuh charta*

We were far apart from each other or you found me merely by luck.

چرته یی کیږ ده   *charta yé kégda*

Place it somewhere.

گوره کهٔ چرته څوک راشي   *gōra kuh charta sōk rāshee*

Wait and perchance someone may come.

ما چرته ایښی دی   *mā charta ikhay day*

I have placed it somewhere.

پهم کوه چه چرته نا جوړنه شی   *paham kawa chi charta nā jōra nuh shé*

Be careful lest you should fall ill.

چرته ورک شوی خو نه دی   *charta vrak shaway kho nuh day*

I hope he or it has not been lost by any chance.

125. Direct narration is always used in place of indirect narration as :—

هغهٔ و و چه څما نوُم جان دی   *haghuh wō wé chi zamā nāu Jān day*

He said his name was John.

هغهٔ و و چه زهٔ به لاړ شم   *haghuh wo wé chi zuh ba lār sham*

He said that he would go.

126. The required tense of کیدل = *kédal* with the ablative can be used to express Potential mood.

دا كارﻟﮧ تا نﮧ كﻴﮉﻯ *dā kār luh tā*
na kégee   You can do this.

دا كارﻟﮧ ما نﮧ نﮧ كﻴﮉﻯ *da kār luh mā*
na nuh kégee   I cannot do this.

نﮧ نﮧ ما ﻟﮧ كار داسﻰ *dāsé kār luh*   I could not do

كﻴﮉﻭ *mā na nuh kédo* such work.

ﻟﮧ ما نﮧ دانﮧ اوچتﻴﮉﻯ *luh mā na dā*   I cannot lift this
nuh ūchatégee up.

127. The negative potential mood with the
ablative case is also used to express impossibility and strong negation as :—

ﻟﮧ ما نﮧ نﮧ شﻰ كﻴﮉﻯ *luh mā na nuh shi*
kéday

I am not going to do it or it is impossible for me
to do it. (lit: from me it cannot become).

128. Pathans themselves are often puzzled
to know which is the subject and which is the
object in sentences with a transitive verb, where
the subject and object both are singular in
number and the subject remains uninflected in
form in the agentive case.

To distinguish the subject ابرﻯ كﻴﮉﻝ = *lagé*
kédal to act, is conjugated after it as :—

احمد خان ابرﻯ شو محمد خان *Ahmad Khan lagé sho,*
Muhamad Khan yé wo
ﻴﻰ ووهﻟﻭ *wahalo*

Ahmad Khan beat Muhamad Khan.

NOTE:—Normally the subject in the sentence is put first, but colloquially this is often disregarded.

129. The following nouns take ورکول = *war kawal* to give.

شکست ورکول	*shikast war kawal*	To defeat.
مدد ورکول	*madad war kawal*	To help.
قرض ورکول	*qarz war kawal*	To lend.
لاس ورکول	*lās war kawal*	To shake hands, help.
رنگ ورکول	*rang war kawal*	To colour, dye.
گذار ور کول	*guzār war kawal*	To give a blow.
رنج ور کول	*rabar war kawal*	To trouble.
سزا ور کول	*sazā war kawal*	To punish.

130. The following nouns take اخستل = *akhistal* = to take.

ساه اخستل	*sāh akhistal*	To breathe.
پناه اخستل	*panāh akhistal*	To take refuge.
لۀ ـنۀ پور اخستل	*luh-na por akhistal*	To borrow.
لۀ ـنۀ خولۀ اخستل	*luh-na khuluh akhistal*	To kiss.

131. The following nouns take لګول = *lagawal* = to add, to put, to apply etc, as :—

لاس لګول	*lās lagawal*	To fight, touch.
اور لګول	*aur lagawal*	To set fire to.
قلپ لګول	*qulp lagawal*	To lock.

ديل لرَوَل‎ *dīl lagawal* To delay.

زور لرَوَل‎ *zōr lagawal* To exert strength.

پته لرَوَل‎ *pata lagawal* To trace.

گلونه لرَوَل‎ *gulūna lagawal* To arrange flowers (in vases)

ميز لرَوَل‎ *méz lagawal* To arrange table.

روپي لرَوَل‎ *rupai lagawal* To spend money.

ديره لرَوَل‎ *déra lagawal* To pitch a tent, or encamp.

دوکان لرَوَل‎ *dūkān lagawal* To open shop.

132. The following nouns take لرَيدل‎ =
lagédal = to be applied.

پښـباند اور لرَيدل‎ *puh-bāndé aur lagédal* To catch fire.

پښـباند لوږه لرَيدل‎ *puh-bāndé luaga lagédal* To feel hungry.

پښـباند تنده لرَيدل‎ *puh-bāndé tanda lagédal* To feel thirsty.

پښـباند بد لرَيدل‎ *puh-bāndé bad lagédal* To take ill.

پښـباند باد لرَيدل‎ *puh-bāndé bād lagédal* To blow (wind.)

پښـباند خ لرَيدل‎ *puh-bāndé khuh lagédal* To like the sight of.

133. The following nouns take راتلل‎ = *rātlal*
to come.

(ته) غُصه راتلل‎ *(ta) ghusa rātlal* To feel angry.

پهٔ۔باندې) رحم راتلل	*(puh-bāndé) raham rātlal*	To feel compassion.
(ته) ژبه راتلل	*(ta) jhuba rātlal*	To know (the language).
(پهٔ) نظر راتلل	*(puh) nazar rātlal*	To come into sight.
(پهٔ) مينه راتلل	*(puh) makha rātlal*	To meet.
(پهٔ۔باندې تبه راتلل	*(puh bāndé) taba rātlal*	To catch fever.

134. The following nouns take خورل = *khwaral* to eat as :—

قسم خورل	*qasam khwaral*	To take an oath.
دوکه خورل	*dōka khwaral*	To be deceived.
شکست خورل	*shikast khwaral*	To be defeated
تيندک خورل	*tindak khwaral*	To stumble.

135. څه = *suh* What, is sometimes put at the end of a sentence to form a question as :—

ما خپل کار نهٔ دی کړی څهٔ؟	*mā khpal kār nuh day karay suh ?*	Have I not done my work ?

136. The following nouns are commonly met with as collective numerals :—

جوړ	*jōra*	Pair, couple.
درزن	*darzan*	Dozen.
کوړي	*kaurai*	Score.
سيکړه	*saikara*	Hundred (percent).

137. By adding دواړه = *wāra* all, to any numerals, with the exception of يو = *yau* one. totality is shown as :—

دواړه *dwāra*	Both.
دری واړه *dré wāra*	All three.
څلور واړه *salōr wāra*	All four.
پنځه واړه *pinzuh wāra*	All five.

Similarly پ = *puh* before and ګونه = *gūna,* after the numerals are used :—

پ سلګونو *puh sulgūmo*	Hundreds of.
پ زرګونو *puh zargūno*	Thousands of.
پ لکونو *puh lakūno*	Lakhs of.

*

138. The multiplicative numerals are formed by adding چند—*chand.* after any numeral or by prefixing يو پ—*yau puh* to it as :—

دو چند *dō chand*	twice more.
دری چند *dré chand*	thrice more.
څلور چند *salōr chand*	four times more.
پنځه چند *pinzuh chand*	five times more.

or

| يو پ دوه *yau puh dwa* | twice. |
| يو پ دری *yau puh dré* | thrice. |

---

* NOTE.—On account of *puh* or *puh bānde,* they are put into the oblique plural.

یو پۀ څلور   *yau puh salōr*   four times more.

یو پۀ پنځۀ   *yau puh pinzuh*   five times more.

139.   The adverbial numerals once, twice, thrice etc. are formed by adding څل—*zal* = time, in the singular. څل—*zala*, in the plural which is inflected to څلو—*zalō*, in the oblique plural as :—

یو څل   *yau zal*   once.

دوہ څلَ   *dwa zala*   twice.

دری څلَ   *dré zala*   thrice.

څلور څلَ   *salōr zala*   four times.

لۀ څلورو څلو   *luh salōro*

نه زیات   *zalō na ziāt*   More than four times.

140.   The fractional numerals are :—

نیم   *nim*   half.

پاو   *pāw*   quarter.

دری پاو   *dré pāwa*   three quarters.

پاو کم دوہ   *pāw kam dwa*   one and three quarters $1\frac{3}{4}$.

141.   دَ = *da* = is sometimes used instead of لۀ = *luh,* the first half of the ablative case as :—

دَ کور نه *da kōr na* or دَ کورۀ *da kora* from the house, instead of :—

لۀ کورنه *luh kōr na* or لۀ کورۀ *luh kōra* from the house.

142. ليكن = *léken*   خو = *kho*   مگر = *magar*

ولى = *walé* all mean "But" مگر = *magar* and
ولى = *walé* are used in the case of expressing
exceptions and بلكه = *balké* means on the other
hand or instead of as :—

ما ورنه تپوس وكړو چه كور دَ   *mā war na tapōs wo*
چرته دى لیكن یا خو جواب یى   *krō chi kōr dé charta*
رانه كړ   *day lekén* (or) *khō*
    jawāb yé rā nuh kar.

I asked him where his house was but he did not
answer.

ټول كليوال ښه دى مگر یو په   *tōl kali wāl khuh di*
كښ ښه نه دَى   *magar* (or *walé*) *yau*
    pa ké khuh nuh day

All the villagers are good except one who is not
good.

زَه نه صرف دَ هغهٔ ورور یم بلكه   *zuh nuh sirf da haghuh*
نوكر یى هم یم   *vrōr yam balké naukar*
    yé hum yam

I am not only his brother but (or on the other
hand) I am his servant as well.

143. The past tense is used to express past
conjunctive as :—

چه كابل ته ورسیدم نو ستا دوست   *chi Kābal ta wo*
مې ولیدلو یا ستا دوست رانه ملاؤشو   *rasédam no stā dōst mé*
    wo lidalo or *stā dōst rā*
    ta milāo sho

Having arrived in Kabul I met your friend.

144. The simple present is idiomatically used to express desire of a person, wish and present continous as :—

زۀ ځم   *zuh zam.*

I want to go.
I like to go.
I wish to go.
I am going.
I go.

145. ملاست = *mlāst* Lying is only used for animate objects acting of their own accord, while پروت = *prōt* prostrate or lying, is used for inanimate objects and an animate objects with any kind of disease or helplessness.

زۀ پۀ کټ باندې ملاست یم   *zuh puh kat bānde mlāst yam*

I am lying on the bed.

زۀ درې ورځی ناجوړ پروت وم   *zuh dré vrazé nājora prōt wam*

I was lying ill for three days.

کتاب پۀ میز باندې پروت دی   *kitāb puh méz bānde prōt day*

The book is lying on the table

146. حاضر = *hāzir* = Present or at the service of. while موجود = *maujūd* = present is used for superiors or in the case of inanimate objects denoting existing or available etc. as :—

ټول نوکران حاضر دی   *tōl naukarān hāzir di*

All the servants are present.

خان په موقعه موجود وه *khān puh mōqa maujūd woh*

The Khan was present at the spot.

دا حکایت په کتاب کښ موجود دی *dā hikāyat puh kitāb ké maujūd day*

This story is (present) in the book.

NOTE :— خدای حاضر دی = *khudāi hāzir day* = God is present.

147. It is not polite to address the following persons without using the word صاحب = *sāhib* =

مُنشی	*munshi*	Munshi, teacher, writer.
با بو	*bābu*	Clerk.
جمعدار	*jamādār*	Lieut. (Indian rank.)
صو بیدار	*subédār*	Captain (Indian rank.)
سردار	*sardār*	Indian officer in the Army.
حکیم	*hakim*	Physician.
دانگتر	*dāngtar*	Doctor.
مولوی	*maulvi*	Priest, learned.
قاضی	*qāzi*	Judge.

148. بعضی = *bazé* = Some, implies some out of a certain number and څینی —*ziné*—Some. implies some out of a certain number. Also it is a substitute for سخه = *sakha* = (Post position) as :—

بعضی خلق ښه دی *bazé khalq khuh di*

Some people are good.

پۀ بعضو کتابونو کښے راغلی دی *puh bazō kītabūno ké rāghali di*

It is written (lit : come) in some books.

څینی پۀ رساله کښے نوکری کوی *ziné puh résāla ké naukari kawī*

Some of them serve in the Cavalry.

تا څینی چاقو شته *tā ziné chāqū shta* Have you a pen knife.

149. مه = *ma* = is the sign of prohibition and is used at the end of a sentence to express fear or force as :—

ته نن ځه مه = *tuh nan za ma* = You must not go today (or else you will get into trouble).

150. In the present conditional, the past tense is sometimes used in the first clause to express definite action as :—

کۀ دا کار د وزرو نو مړ به د کړم *kuh dā kār dé wo kro, nō mar ba dé kram*

I will kill you if you do this.

151. ماوې = *mā wé* or ماووویل = *ma wo wayal* I said, spoke or told has a secondary idiomatic meaning "I meant" as :—

ما ویل زۀ بد پۀ رساله کښے نوکري کوم *mā wayal zuh ba puh resāla ké naukari kawam_*

I meant to serve in the Cavalry.

152. In the following examples it will be noticed that the use of different prepositions is highly idiomatic. Sometimes a change of preposition completely changes the meaning not only of the whole sentence but of the nouns and verbs used as :—

هغه پهٔ سپین آس باند سورديَ	*hagha puh spin āss bāndé sōr day*	He is riding on a white horse.
هغه پهٔ سپین اس کښن سوردیَ	*hagha puh spin āss ké sōr day*	He is riding in a trap with a white horse in the shafts.
هغه مورته تلیَ دیَ	*hagha mōr ta talay day*	He takes after his mother.
هغه مور باند تلیَ دیَ	*hagha mōr bāndé talay day*	Lit: He has gone back into his mother (term of abuse).
هغه موټر ته پريوتو	*hagha mōtar ta préwato*	He threw himself in front of a motor car.
هغه موټر باند پريوتو	*hagha mōtar bāndé préwato*	He bumped into a stationery motor car.
هغه کورته ننوتو	*hagha kōr ta nanawato*	He went into his house.
هغه پهٔ کور باند ننوتو	*hagha puh kōr bāndé nanawato*	He went into someone else's house.
هغه باغ ته ننوت	*hagha bāgh ta nanawat*	He went into a Garden.

هغه پۀ باغ ورننوت *hagha puh bāgh war nanawat* — He went into someone else's garden (because of fear) or he was chased into a garden.

هغه پۀ پیښور کښی دی *hagha puh pékhawar ké day* — He is in Peshawar.

هغه پۀ پیښور باندِ دی *hagha puh pékhawar bānde day* — He is in charge of Peshawar.

هغۀ ته اواز وکړه *haghuh ta awāz wo kra* — Call him.

هغۀ باندِ اواز وکړه *haghuh bānde awāz wo kra* — Challenge him.

153. Use the word ځان = *zān* = self, or خپلځان = *khapal zān* = oneself, with the Dative case before a compound transitive verb formed from an adjective to express "pretended to be", e.g :—

هغۀ ورته ځان مړ کړ *haghuh war ta zān mar kar* — He pretended to be dead.

هغۀ ورته خپل ځان اودۀ کړ *haghuh war ta khpal zān ūduh kar* — He pretended to be asleep.

ما ورته خپل ځان لیونی کړ *mā war ta khpal zān léwanay kar* — I pretended to be mad.

154. Note the following idioms dealing with the use of څومره چه = *sōmra chi* = as much, before

the first clause and ‏دومره‏ = *dōmra* = so much, before the second clause, e. g. :—

‏خومره چه دَ وسَ م کیږری دومره‏
‏کوشش به کوم‏

sōmra chi dā wasā mé kégee, dōmra kōshish ba kawam

I will try my best.

‏خومره چه دَ وَس دَ کیږری دومره‏
‏زر هلته لارشه‏

sōmra chi da wasa dé kégee, dōmra zar halta lārsha,

Go there as soon as you can.

‏خومره چه دَ وسَ م کیدل دومره‏
‏جوارم ورکړل‏

sōmra chi da wasa mé kédal, dōmra jowār mé war kral.

I gave him as much maize as I could afford.

‏خومره چه دَ وسَ م کیدلی دومرۀ‏
‏روپیٔ م ورکړلي‏

sōmra chi da wasa mé kédalé, dōmra rūpai mé war kralé

I gave him as much money as I could afford.

155. When animals and birds are counted use ‏سر‏ = *sara* = Heads, before them as :—

‏شل سرۀ مال‏   *shal sara māl*   twenty head of cattle

‏دیرش سرَ‏   *dérsh sarā*

‏مرغابئ‏   *marghābai*   Thirty geese.

156. In the following idiom "with" the English preposition is not translated as :—

‏تۀ خپل طلب‏   *tuh khpal talab*   What do you do

‏څۀ کوی‏   *sūh kawé*   with your pay ?

157 تا لاش کول = *tālāsh kawal* = to search for.
takes indirect object while لتول = *latawal* = to
search, takes direct object.

ما دَ کتاب تالاش و کړلو *mā dā kitāb tālāsh wo kralo*

or

ما کتاب دَ پاره تالاش و کړلو *mā kitāb da para tālāsh wo kralo*

I searched for the book.

ما کور و لتول لو *mā kōr wo latawalō*   I searched the house.

158. ډک = *dak* = Full, is always governed by
ablative case.

تلاؤ لهُ اوبو نه ډک	*talāw luh obo na dak*	A tank full of water.
بیړی لهُ سړو نه ډکه	*bérai luh saro na daka*	A boat full of men
کمرې لهُ کرسو نه	*kamré luh kursō na daké*	Rooms full of chairs.
ډکی		

159. نه رشتیا = *na rishtiā* = Lit. what I said
is not right and the following is correct, is used
to express "As you were or "I mean."

دَ کور خاوند احمد خان نه رشتیا *da kōr khāwand Ahmad Khan na rishtiā*
محمد خان دَی *Mohmad Khān day*

The owner of the house is Ahmed Khan-as
you were-it is Mohamad Khan.

160.   Adjectives denoting "belonging to" or native of a place, country etc. are formed by adding ‌ي = *ay* as :—

پنجاب *punjāb* Punjab. پنجابیُ *punjābay* from Punjab.

کابل *kābal* Kabul. کابلیُ *kābalay* from Kabul.

پیښور *pekha-* Peshawar. پیښوریُ *pekha-* from war   *wray* Peshawar

161.   Note the following forms :—

سپینه ګیره *spīna gira*	White beard.
سپین ګیریُ *spīn giray*	White bearded.
سره لکئ *sra lakai*	Red tail.
سوُر لکیُ *sūr lakay*	Red tailed.
توره غاړه *tōra ghāra*	Black neck.
تور غاړیُ *tōr ghāray*	Black necked.
سرکوُز *sar kūz*	Head hanging.
سرکوُزیُ *sar kūzay*	Pig.
پیِ مخ *pai makh*	Milk face.
پیِ مخیُ *pai makhay*	Milk faced.

162.   Note the force of repetition of tense in the following examples :—

کۀ لاړو لاړو   *kuh lāro lāro*

If he has gone by his own wish let him go ! I don't care !

كۀ كوي كوي كۀ نۀ كوي نۀ كوي *kuh kawī kawī kuh nuh*
kawī nuh kawī

If he means to do it let him do it, if he does not
mean to do it let him not do it, it makes no
difference to me.

163.   Note the following suffixes :—

در *war*	زرور	*zrawar*	Bold.
	ښكرور	*khkarawar*	Horned (term of abuse).
	بختور	*bakhtawar*	Lucky.
وان *wān*	باغوان	*bāghwān*	Gardener, mali.
	جاله وان	*jālawān*	Th·: owner of the r·..
	كاروان	*kārwān*	Caravan.
چی *chī*	نشانچی	*néshānchī*	Standard bearer.
	توپچی	*tōpchī*	Marksman.
	دندورچی	*dandōrchī*	Halerd, proclaimer.
دان *dān*	زندان	*zandān*	Prison.
	خاندان	*khānadān*	Family.
	نمكدان	*namakdān*	Salt cellar.
دار *dār*	سردار	*sardār*	Indian Officer, leader.
	دوكاندار	*dūkāndār*	Shopkeeper.
	تانړیدار	*tānrédār*	Sub-Inspector of Police.
	دیندار	*dindār*	Pious.
	وفادار	*wafādār*	Faithful.
	زمیندار	*zamīndār*	Farmer.

گاز	gār	خدمتگار	khidmatgār	Servant.
		مدد گار	madadgār	Helper.
		گناهگار	gunāhgār	Sinful, guilty.
داری	dāri	خبرداری	khabardāri	Care.
		لمبرداری	lambardāri	Headman's job. —
		ذو کیداری	saukidāri	Watchman's job.
گر	gar	زر گر	zargar	Goldsmith.
		جا دو گر	jādugar	Juggler.
		کیمیا گر	kimiāgar	Gold aud silver maker
		کاریگر	kārigar	Blacksmith.
کار	kār	زنا کار	zanā kār	Adulterer.
		بد کار	bad kār	Licentious.
		جفا کار	jafākār	Tyrannical.
گی	gī	مهر بانگی	méhrabān gi	Kindness.
		روانگی	rawāngi	Departure.
		پیشگی	péshgi	An advance (of money).
گین	gīn	غمگین	ghamgin	Sorrowful.
		مالگین	mālgin	Saltish or salt mine.
مند or من	mand or man	درد مند	dārdmand	Painful.
		شتۀ مند	shtuhmand	Rich.
		فکر مند	fikarmand	Anxious,
		سود مند	sūdmand	Profitable.

ناک	*nāk*	حرصناک	*harasnāk*	Greedy.
		صبر ناک	*sabar nāk*	Patient.
		شرمناک	*sharam nāk*	Shameful.
ستان	*stān*	گلستان	*gulistān*	Place of flowers.
		و زیرستان	*waziristān*	Waziristan, Country of Waziris.
		کفر ستان	*kufaristān*	Country of unbelievers.
وار	*wār*	آمید وار	*umaidwār*	Hopeful, candidate.
		پیدا وار	*paidāwār*	Produce.
		سزا وار	*sazāwār*	Punished.
ژن	*jhan*	دروغژن	*darōgh jhan*	Liar.
		کبر ژن	*kabar jhan*	Proud.
		غمژن	*ghamjhan*	Full of grief.
زن	*zan*	تورزن	*tūrzan*	Brave.
		لاپزن	*lāpzan*	Boaster.
		لانبوزن	*lānbōzan*	Swimmer.
وال	*wāl*	هیندیوال	*handiwāl*	Mess mate.
		کلیوال	*kaliwāl*	Villager.
		بنیروال	*bunérwāl*	Man of Buner.
		تیراوال	*tirawāl*	Man of Tirah.

164. The following particles are used with adjectives to express quite, very, entirely, absolutely.

تک tak	تک سؤر tak sūr	Quite red.
	تک سپین tak spin	Quite white
	تک شین tak shin	Quite green
تپ tap	تپ تور tap tōr	Very decrepit.
	تپ رُوند tap rūnd or پُه تپو رُوند puh tapo rūnd	Quite blind Stone blind
گرب grab	زور گرب zōr grab	Very old. (applied to a person)
پر par	خر پر khar par	Quite grey, full of dust.
	غور پر ghwar par	Very greasy
پشت pusht	خوشت پشت khusht pusht	Quite wet.
خوشت khusht	اؤند خوشت lūnd khusht	Very wet.
غوټ ghut	غوټ پریکړی ghut prékari	Clear or quite cut off
پټ pat	غټ پټ ghat pat	Very fat.
روغ rōgh	روغ جوړ rōgh jōr	Quite well.
تکنړه takanra	تکنړه غرمه takanra gharma	Blazing noon.
تم tam	تورتم tōr tam	Quite dark.
لغړ laghar	بر بنډ لغړ barband laghar	Stark naked
یخ pakh	یخ پخ yakh pakh	Very cold.
نوزَی nūzāy	نوی نوزَی nāway nūzay	Absolutely-new.
پور pōr	زور پور zōr pōr	Very old. (applied to things worn out)

	شور پور *shōr pōr*		Very greasy
کپر *kapar*	کنډ کپر *kand kapar*		Destroyed
وو،ز *wōg*	کوږ وو،ز *kōg wōg*		Entirely crooked:
چوُړ *chūr*	چپ چوُړ *chap chūr*		Badly shuttered.
وډ *wad*	ګډ وډ *gad wad*		Mixed up.
سمخ *samakh*	سوړ سمخ *sōr samakh*		Very cold.
وور *wōr*	خور وور *khōr wōr*		Scattered.
پنګ *pang*	رنګ پنګ *rang pang*		Smeared (with blood etc.)
جک *jak*	جک جوړ *jak jōr*		Quite well
چنباق *chun-bāq*	چاق چنباق *chāq chunbāq*		Very energetic.
پنر *panr*	چنر پنر *chanr panr*		Noise of birds.
پل *pal*	دل پل *dal pal*		Absolutely crushed.
ګوُم *gūm*	ګم ګوُم *gūm gūm*		Entirely last
تروش *trush*	تنګ تروش *tang trush*		Very Tight.
			„ small.
			„ narrow.

Section 11.

PARTS OF SPEECH.

ADVERBS.

زر *zur*   Soon.

زر زر	zur zur	Quickly.
ولى	walé	Why.
هسى	hasé	Thus.
ناصا په	nāsāpa	By chance.
ناګها نه	nāghāna	
لا	lā	Yet.
خو	kho	But, at least.
سره	sara	Together.
لكه	laka	Like, as.
ورو ورو	vrō vrō	Slowly.
تل	tal	Always.
مُدام	mūdām	
هميشه	hamésha	

ADVERBS OF PLACE.

بهر	bahar	Outside.
چرته	charta	Where.
دلته	dalta or	Here.
دلى	dalé	
هلته	halta	There.
بيرته	biarta	Back.
پورته	pōrta	Above.
هر چرته	harcharta	Everywhere.
دننه	danana	Inside.
نيزدى	nizdé	Near.
بل چرته	bal charta	Some where else.

هيچرته	*hicharta*	No where.
ښکته	*khkatā*	} Below.
لاند	*lāndé*	
لاند باند	*lāndé bāndé*	Upside down.
چاپيره	*chāpéra* or	} Around.
گير چاپيره	*gér chāpéra*	
له لرى نه	*luh laré na*	} From a distance.
دَ ورايه	*da vrāya*	
ورستو	*vrōsto*	Behind.
وراند	*vrāndé*	Before.

THE ADVERBS OF TIME.

آخر	*ākhér*	At last, in the end.
بيا	*biā*	Again.
پخوا	*pakhwā*	Formerly.
اوس	*ōss*	Now.
زر زر	*zar zar*	Quickly.
ورو ورو	*vro vro*	Slowly.
ورمبى	*vrumbay*	Firstly.
وار په وار	*wār puh wār*	In time.
هاله	*hāla*	Then.
كله نه كله	*kala na kala*	Occasionally.
تر كله پورى	*tar kala pōré*	Until when.
كله	*kala*	When.
كله كله	*kala kala*	Sometimes.
په دى شپو	*puh dé shpo vrazo*	
ورځو كښى	*ké*	Now a days.

چرى ـ چرى	*charé charé*	Now and then.
تر اوسَ پورى	*tar osa poré*	Until now.
لا تر اوسَ	*lā tar osa*	Even until now.
بيگاه	*bégāh*	Last night.
پرون	*parūn*	Yesterday.
صبا يا صباله	*sabā or sabāla*	Tomorrow.
بل صبا	*bal sabā*	Day after tomorrow.
سحر	*sahar*	. Morning.
ما خام	*mākhām*	Evening.
نن سحر	*nan sahar*	This morning.
لا بل صبا	*lā bal sabā*	The second day after tomorrow.
نن	*nan*	To-day.
سږ كال	*sag kāl*	This year.
مښى كال	*makhé kāl*	Next year.
پروسكال	*parösa kāl*	Last year.
اورم كال	*oram kāl*	Year before last.
پس	*pas*	After.
هركله	*har kala*	Ever, at any time.
هركله چه	*har kala chi*	Whenever.
مُدام	*mudām*	Always.
و ختى	*wakhti*	Early.
نا وَ خته	*nāwakhta*	Late.
يو ځل	*yau zal*	Once.
دوه ځلَ	*dwa zāla*	Twice.
سو ځلَ	*so zala*	How often ?
ډېرځلَ	*dér zala*	Many times.

THE ADVERBS OF QUANTITY.

ډیر	*dér*	Much.
څومره	*sōmra*	How much, how many.
دومره	*dōmra*	This much.
هرڅومره	*har sōmra*	How ever much.
لږ کو ټي	*lūkūti*	A little.
زیات	*ziāt*	More.
هر	*har*	Every.
څه	*suh*	Some.
هر څو	*har so*	How ever many.
هر څه	*har suh*	Whatever.
هر یو	*har yau*	Everyone.
هر څوک	*har sōk*	Everyone.
تر حد پورې	*tar hada pōré*	To the utmost extent.
تر حد زیات	*tar hada ziāt*	Beyond degree.
له حد زیات	*luh hada ziāt*	„ „
بیحد	*béhada*	Unlimited.

CONJUNCTIONS.

او	*aw*	And.
چه	*chi*	That.
که	*kuh*	If.
ولې چه	*walé chi*	Because.
بلکه	*balké*	More over.
خو	*kho*	But.
ځکه	*zakā*	Therefore.

چه ځکه	zaka chi	Because.
هم	hum	Also.
یا	yā	Or.
سره دَ دی	sara da dé	Not withstanding.

PREPOSITIONS.

See Page No. 14.

INTERJECTIONS.

ای	ay	Oh.
آفرین	āfrin	Bravo.
وای وای	wāi wāi	Oh dear.
توبه	tōba	Fie.
واه واه	wāh wāh	Bravo, Oh (To express extreme surprise).
آخ	akh	Oh (To express extreme surprise).
چښی	chakha	} Get away, (to a dog).
کوری	kuré	
رښتیا	rikhtiā	Indeed.
افسوس	afsōs	
های های	hāi hāi	
وای وای	wāi wāi	Alas.
ارمان ارمان	armān armān	
امان	amān	Mercy.
شاباش	shābāsh	Bravo.

PART II.

PROSE COMPOSITION.

Section 12.

This section of Part II contains sixty short English into Pushtu and Pushtu into English Exercises with Vocabularies, beginning with simple sentences and working upto the standard required for the Higher Standard Examination. The beginner who is taking the Lower Standard Examination is advised to learn the words first and do one or two exercises a day.

VOCABULARY I.

څوک	*sōk*	Who.
نوم	*nūm*	Name.
سړی	*saray*	A man.
ښځه	*khaza*	Woman or wife.
هلک	*halak*	Boy.
جڼۍ	*jinai*	Girl.
ځوی	*zōi*	Son.
لور	*lūr*	Daughter.
ورور	*vrōr*	Brother.
خور	*khōr*	Sister.
چرته	*charta*	Where ?
دلته	*dalta*	Here.
هلته	*halta*	There.

کور	*kōr*	Home, House.
کلّی	*kalay*	Village.
څو يا څومرهٔ	*sō* or *sōmra*	How many or how much.
څو مره لرى	*sōmra laré*	How far.
لرى	*laré*	Far.
نيز دى	*nizdé*	Near.
چاونرِي	*chāwnrai*	Station or Cantonment
نوکر	*naukar*	Servant.
نوکرى	*naukari*	Service.
دُشمن يا دُښمن	*dushman* or *dukhman*	Enemy.
دوست	*dōst*	Friend.
چو تی	*chuti*	Leave.
ولى	*walé*	Why ?
حاضر	*hāzér*	Present.
غير حاضر	*ghair hāzér*	Absent.
نن	*nan*	To day.
پرون	*parūn*	Yesterday.
صبا يا صباله	*sabā* or *sabāla*	To-morrow.
بل صبا	*bal sabā*	Day after to-morrow
بيګاه	*bégah*	Last night.
بيګاله	*bégāla*	To-night.
ماښام	*mākhām*	Evening or p. m.
سحر	*sahar*	Morning or a. m.
غرمه	*gharma*	Noon.
نن سحر	*nan sahar*	This morning.

NOTES :— *(a)* In Pushtù the 2nd person singular is normally used in address i. e., تﮦ = *tuh* = thou, instead of تﺎﺳﻮ = *tāso* = you, and سﺘﺎ = *stā* = they, instead of سﺘﺎﺳﻮ = *stāso* = your.

The 2nd person plural is occasionally used for extreme politeness.

(b) The order of the sentence in Pushtu is usually subject, object, verb.

EXERCISE 1.

1. Who are you ?   2. What is your name ? 3. Who is that man ?   4. Where is your house ?   5. How far is it from the Cantonment ?   6. I am his servant.   7. My name is Ahmad.   8. He is my friend.   9. What is his name ?   10. How many men are on leave ? 11. Why were you absent ?   12. What time is it ?

EXERCISE 2.

1. دﺍ سﺮﻯ ﺧﻮک دﻯ = *dā saray sōk day ?* 2. دَ هﻐﮦ نﻮﻡ ﺻﮦ دﻯ = *da haghuh nūm suh day ?* 3. کﻮرﻮنﮦ ﺉﻰ ﭼﺮﺗﮫ دﻯ = *kōrūna yé charta di ?* 4. سﺘﺎسﻮ کﻮرﻮنﮦ ﺧﻮ مﺮﮦ لﺮﻯ دﻯ = *stāso kōrūna sōmra laré di ?* 5. ﭼﺎﻮﻧﺮﻯ ﺧﻮمﺮﮦ لﺮﻯ دﮦ = *chāwnrai sōmra laré dah ?* 6. دَ ﭼﺎ نﻮکﺮ ﺉﻰ = *da chā naukar yé ?* 7. ﺗﮦ ﺧﻤﺎ نﻮکﺮ نﮫ ﺉﻰ = *tuh zamā naukar nuh yé.*

8. ‏سومره سری غیر حاضر دی‎ = *sōmra sari ghair hāzér di?* 9. ‏پرون زه حاضر نۀ وم‎ = *prūn zuh hāzér nuh wam.* 10. ‏هغه ستا دوست دیٔ کۀ نه‎ = *hagha stā dōst day kuh na ?* 11. ‏صاحب پۀ چوتی باند دیٔ‎ = *sāhib puh chūtai bānde day.* 12. ‏څۀ وخت ؤه‎ = *suh wakht woh ?*.

VOCABULARY II.

Common salutions and expressions used by Pathans.

Q. ‏ستړی مۀ شی‎ *staray muh shé?* May you not get tired ?

A. ‏خوار مۀ شی یا‎ *khwār muh shé`*
or
‏نۀ ستړیٔ مۀ شی‎ *tuh staray muh shé*
[May you not become poor !

Q. ‏پۀ خیر راغلی‎ *puh khér rāghlé ?* You are welcome ?

A. ‏پۀ خیر اوسی‎ *puh khér osé* May you live happily ! (or in peace)

Q. ‏هر کله راشه یا‎ *har kala rāsha?*
or
‏راشه هر کله‎ *rāsha har kala?*
}You are always welcome ?

A. ‏هر کله اوسی‎ *har kala osé* May you live for ever !

Q. ‏ښه چاری‎ *kha chāré ?* Good luck to you ?

A. ‏چار د ښه شه‎ *chār dé kha sha* May your luck be good !

Q. ‏پۀ مښنه د ښه‎ *puh makha dé kha ?* Good bye ?

A. آمین تا سره *āmin tā sara* — Same to you.
(*amin* = so be it).

A. خدای د مل شه *khudāi dé mal sha* — May God be with you.

A. خدای د وبخښه *khudāi dé wo bakha* — May God forgive you.

Q. خدای ته سپارلی یې؟ *khudāi ta spā-ralay yé ?* — You are entrusted to God ?

A. خدای د اباد لره *khudāi dé abād lara* — May God keep you prosperous.

Q. څه حال دی؟ *suh hāl day ?* — How are you ?

A. ښه حال دی د خدای فضل دی *khuh hāl day da khudāi fazal day* — I am all right by the grace of God.

حال *hāl* — Condition.

جوړ *jōr* — Well.

ناجوړ *nā jōr* — Ill.

جک جوړ *jak jōr* — Quite well. (جک = *jak* is only used with جوړ = *jōr*)

تکړه *takra* — Strong.

خوشحال *khushhāl* — Happy.

څنګه *sunga* — How.

فصل *fasal* — Grop.

فصلونه *faslūna* — Crops,

غنم *ghanam* — Wheat.

جوار *jowār* — Maize.

اوربشی *orbashé* — Barley.

پنبه *punba* — Cotton.

شوتل	shautal	Clover.
شولی	shōlé	Rice (Crop).
نری جوار	nari jowār	Charri, cattle fodder.
کال	kāl	Year.
میاشت	miāsht	Month, Moon.
جمعه	juma	Week or Friday.
س.ر کال	sagkāl	This year.
پروسَکال	parōsakāl	Last year.
اورم کال	oram kāl	Year before last.
مښی کال	makhé kāl	Next year.
دولت	daulat	Wealth.
دولت مند	daulatmand	Wealthy.
غریب	gharīb	Poor.
ښه	khuh	Good.
خراپ	hharāp	Bad.
ملک	malak	Head man.
خان	khan	Chief.
فوځ	fauz	Troop, Army.
پلټن	paltan	Regiment.
رساله	risāla	Cavalry.
حوالدار	havāldār	Sergeant (infantry)
دفعدار	dafédār	Sergeant (Cavalry).
سپاهي	spāhi	Soldier.
لیس	lais	Corporal.
لیس نائک	lais naik	Lance Corporal.

EXERCISE 3.

1. May you not get tired, Malak Sahib!
2. How are you? (lit, what condition is)
3. Are you well? 4. Yes, I am quite well.
5. Are you strong? 6. Yes, I am strong.
7. Are you happy? 8. Yes, I am happy.
9. Who is the Khan of this village? 10. Is
he a wealthy man? 11. What is the name of
this village? 12. The name of this village is
Mardan. 13. Are there any troops in Mardan?
14. Yes, there are two Infantry and three
Cavalry Regiments there.

NOTE :—The inflected form of دا = dā This
is :— دې = dé as :—

د دى كلى‎ da dé kali   Of this village.

له دى كلى نه‎ luh dé kali na From this village.

VOCABULARY III.

ځكه‎ zaka	Therefore.	
ځكه چه‎ zaka chi	Because.	
خو - مګر‎ kho, magar,	}	But.
ليكن - ولى‎ lekan, walé	}	
باران‎ bārān	Rain.	
لږ‎ lag	Little.	
ډېر‎ dér	Very, many, much, plenty.	

مُلک یا وطن	*mulk* or *watan*	Country.
ښهر	*khahar*	City.
قحط	*qahat*	Famine.
خلق	*khalq*	People.
ټول	*tōl*	All.
دواړه	*dwāra*	Both.
معلوم	*mālūm*	Known.
ما ته یا رٖا ته	*mā ta* or *rā ta*	
معلوم دیَ	*mālūm day*	I know it.
سور	*sōr*	Rider, Horseman.
عهده	*uhda*	Rank.
عهده دار	*uhda dār*	Non-Commissioned Officer.
پهٔ کښې	*pa ké*	In it.
مزدوری	*mazdūri*	Labour, work, wages.
تنګ	*tang*	Oppressed, worried.
اوس	*oss*	Now.
کهٔ	*kuh*	If or or
ځاي	*zāi*	Place.
کله	*kala*	When ?
کله کله	*kala kala*	Sometimes.

EXERCISE 4.

۱ دَ فصلونو دٖ څهٔ حال دیَ ؟   ۲   سٖر کال فصلونه ښهٔ نهٔ
دیِ ۔ ښکه چه باران لږ وٖو   ۳   کله کله پهٔ باړه کښې اوبهٔ وی او کله
نهٔ وی   ۴   تهٔ عهده داریٔ کهٔ سپاهی ؟   زهٔ دَ رسالیٔ سوریم

ه ۵ دَ دی کلی نوُم در ته معلوم دیَ؟ ۶ تول فوځ اوس پۀ
چاونړي کینس دی ۷ تۀ پۀ نوکرۍ کینس خوشحال یي کۀ نه
۸ دَ کلو خلق دولتمند نۀ وی ۹ بارانونه لری ؤو ختَه پۀ وطن
کینس قحط دی ۱۰ سِتا پۀ پلټن کینس څومره سپاهیان دی
۱۱ دَ هغۀ دوا ره نوکرانو پۀ نوکرۍ کینس تدنگ دی ۱۲ دَ هغَه
خایی نوم ورته معلوم نۀ دی ۱۳ پروسکال دَ غنمو او جوارو فصلونه
خراپ ؤو ۱۴ چاونړۍ لوِده دَه خو پۀ کینس مزدورۍ لرېؤوی -
دَ خان څلور څامن پۀ پۀ فوځ کینس دی -

1. See syntax rule No. 23.
2. Learn the numerals on Page 41.

VOCABULARY IV.

دَ چا	*da chā*	Whose ?
کتاب	*kitāb*	Book.
دا	*dā*	This or these.
کتاب چه	*kitab chi*	The book which.
میز	*méz*	Table.
کرسۍ	*kursai*	Chair.
صاحب چه	*sāhib chi*	The sahib who.
جرنیل صاحب	*jarnail sāhib*	General.
د۔پۀ مینځ کینس	*da-puh mianz ké*	Between, through.
هلک چه نوُم یي	*halak chi nūm yé*	The boy whose name.
تربوُر	*tarbūr*	Cousin.
تڼۀ	*truh*	Uncle.
لارچه	*lār chi*	The road which.

خي	zee	Goes.
گرم	garam	Hot, warm.
گرمي	garmī	Heat.
يخ	yakh	Cold. (adj.)
يخني	yakhni	Cold (noun.)
اوړی	oray	Summer.
مني	manay	Autumn.
ژمی	jhamay	Winter.
سپرلی	sparlay	Spring.
موسم	mōsam	Season.
سيند	sind	River.
خوړ	khwar	Ravine.
غاړه	ghāra	Bank (river)
بيړي	bérai	Boat.
مانږگی	mānrgay	Boat man.
ښکار	khkār	Shooting, Hunting
كب	kab	Fish.
كبان	kabān	Fish (plural.)
يا	yā	or
د كبانو ښكار	da kabāno khkār	Fishing.

چغتی	chaghaté	Snipe	(Sing. چغته	chaghata)
هيلۍ	hilai	Duck	(Sing. هيلي	hilai)
بطی	baté	Geese	(Sing. بطه	bata)
تنزری	tanzari	Partridges	(Sing تنزری	tanzary)
زرکی	zarké	Chikor	(Sing زر که	zarka)
مرزی	marzé	Quails	(Sing مرز	maraz)

سوی *sawé* Hares (Sing سوہ *sawa*)

او سئ *osai* Deer (Sing او سئ *osai*)

اوچ *och* Dry

EXERCISE 5.

1. [1] Have you a book? 2. Yes, I have a book, 3. No, I have not a book. 4. Whose book is this?. 5. It is not my book. 6 The books [2] which are on the table are not mine. 7. The sahib who was here this morning is the General's brother. 8. The country between Peshawar and Kabul is dry and bad. 9. The boy whose name is Ahmad, is my uncle's son. 10. The road which goes through Mardan is not a good one 11. I [3] like Peshawar, but my brother does not like it. 12. Why don't, you like Peshawar?. 13. The heat is great in summer 14. There is little water in this country.

NOTES—1. شته = *shta* = Is there or are there? Look up syntax rule No. 45. 2. چه = *ché* = that (conjunction) makes any interrogation relative i. e. څوک چه = *sōk chi* = He who. 3. خوښ *khwakh* = pleasant or liked See syntax rule No. 28.

VOCABULARY V.

تماکو *tamākū*   Tobacco.

چیلم *chilam*   Pipe.

تیلی	tilay	Match.
هم	hum	Also.
خایښته	khāista	Beautiful or handsome
بدرنگ	badrang	Ugly.
هوښیار	hukhyār	Clever.
کم عقل	kam aqal	Foolish.
وروکی یا warūkay or		
ورکوتی warkōtay		} Small.
لوی	loi	Big or Large.
هسپتال	haspatāl	Hospital.
په خوا زمانه کښی	puh khwā zamāna ké	Formerly.
جبه	jaba	Marsh.
چینه	china	Spring (of water).
توپک	tōpak	Rifle.
کونیز توپک ؟	kūniz tōpak ?	Snider Rifle.
گوریز توپک	gōraiz tōpak	A Martini Henry Rifle.
اوه دزی توپک	owuh dazay tōpak	Lee Metford Rifle.
دری وال توپک	daréwāl tōpak	Pass-made Rifle.
بندری توپک	bandari tōpak	Persian Gulf made Rifle.
چقمقی توپک	chaqmapi tōpak	A flint lock gun.
باتیدار توپک	bātıdar tōpak	A match lock gun.
دَ چرو توپک یا	da charo tōpak or	
چری دار توپک یا	charidār tōpak. or	} A Shot gun.
خکاری توپک	khkāri tōpak	

چرې	*charé*	Shots.
ګولیٔ	*gōlai*	Bullet.
دارؤ	*dārū*	Gun Powder or Medicine.
اوس اوس	*oss oss*	Presently, Recently.
اوسنیَ	*osanay*	Recent.
کارتوٗس	*kārtūs*	Cartridge.
ګټه	*gata*	Packet of 10 Cartridges.
نښه	*nakha*	Mark.
رنګ	*rang*	Colour.
سپیٖن	*spin*	White.

EXERCISE 6.

۱ تا سخه تماکوٗ شته ؟ ۲ ما سخه تماکوٗ نشته او تیلیَ شته
۳ هغهٔ سخه څلور کتابونه دی ؟؟ ؟نهٔ نهٔ دی ۴ تا سخه څومره
روپیٔ دی ۰ څما ترهٔ سخه ډیر دولت وُه ۵ څما یو ورور دیَ هغه
هم په هسپِتال کښ دیَ ۶ ستا څومره څامن دی ؟ ۷ څما
یو آس دی چه رنګ یی سپیٖن دیَ ۸ څما دَ ورور پهٔ ښهر
کښ پنځهٔ کورونه ؤو ۹ څما یو لاس دیَ ۱۰ دا جنیٔ دَ
هلک خور نه ۱۱ هغوی دواړه څائیستهٔ دی ۱۲ دَ هغوی
پلار نهٔ سړیَ وُه او د هغوی مور هوښیاره بنځهٔ ده ۱۳ په خوا
زمانه کښ په دی وطن کښ ښکار وُه مګر اوس نیشته ۱۴ څموږبر
کلیٔ ته نیزدی جبه شته خو ما سخه دَ ښکار ټوپک نشته

VOCABULARY VI.

خوکیدار *saukidār* Watchman.
Chaukidar.

څوکۍ	*saukai*	Post.
جماعت	*jumait*	Mosque.
حجره	*hūjra*	Guest house.
ميلمه	*mélma*	Guest.
ميلما نه	*mélmānuh*	Guests.
غريب	*gharib*	Poor.
دولتمند	*daulatmand*	Rich.
دَ۔طرف ته	*da-taraf ta*	Towards.
طرف۔خوا۔ددو۔پلو	*taraf, khwā,*	
	dada, palau	Side or direction.
نور پریواتهٔ یا قبله	*nwar préwātuh*	
	or *qablā*	West.
قبله	*qabla*	Polite word for west
نور خاته	*nwar khātuh*	East.
سهيل	*suhail*	South.
قطب	*qutab*	North.
لاس	*lās*	Hand.
ښی لاس	*khay lās*	Right hand.
ګس لاس یا	*gas lās* or	} Left hand.
کيڼ لاس	*kinr lās*	
غر	*ghar*	Hill.
اوچت	*ūchat*	High.
مندریَ	*mandray*	Short.
زوړ	*zōr*	Old (Thing or person.
سپين ګيری	*spin giray*	Old, grey bearded man.

نا ست	*nāst*	Sitting	\
ر، لار	*walār*	Standing	Take the Verb
اُودهٔ	*ūduh*	Sleeping	"to be."
ملاست	*mlāst*	Lying	/

EXERCISE 7.

1. This man's house is in the city. 2. This boy's father was my servant. 3. These girls' mother was in the house. 4. When I was in Kohat I had two chaukidars. 5. When I was at home (in the house) my horse was not ill. 6. The khan's house is this side of the Mosque. 7. The guest house is beyond the Malak's house. 8. My uncle had much wealth, but now he is poor. 9. What is your father's name ?. 10. There are many hills towards the west of Peshawar. 11. That is the Afridis' country. 12 Where is your Regiment ? 13. What is your Colonel's name ? 14. The old man was sitting on the chair.

VOCABULARY VII.

خاوند	*khāwand*	Owner.
مالیه	*mālia*	Land Tax.
آبیانه	*abiāna*	Water Tax.
محصول	*mahsool*	Tax on property.
زمکه	*zmaka*	Land or ground.
اوی زمکه	*āvi zmaka*	Irrigated land.

للمه زمکه	lalma zmaka	Unirrigated land.
سا دین	sādin	Ploughed land.
و تره	watra	Land ready for sowing.
شاره زمکه	shāra zmaka	Barren land.
ویجاره زمکه	wijāra zmaka	Waste land.
شولګره	shōlgara	Rice land.
دَ ازغو تار	da azgho tār	Barbed wire.
تار	tār	Wire, telegram, thread.
څینی څینی	ziné ziné	Some.
نه.نه	na-na	Neither-nor.
ژوندی	jhwanday	Alive.
ګينټه	gainta	An hour.
پس	pas	After (time.)
پسی	pasé	After (person.) or business)
روان	rawān	Going on. (in the act of going.)
دروازه	darwāza	Gate.
ور	war	Door.

EXERCISE 8.

۱ دَ دی کور خاوند څوک دی ۲ د هغهٔ ملک نوم څهٔ دی
۳ مالیهیی څوصره ده ۴ کله چه زهٔ په دفتر کښ وم نو نوکرم با هر
ناست وهٔ ۵ ستا پلار ژوندی دی ؟—نهٔ کله هلته وی ۶ دوه ګينټی
پس زهٔ به په دفتر کښ یم ۷ له چاوزوری نه ګیر چاپیره د ازغو تار
دی ۸ یو سړی خان پسی روان دی ۹ قبلی طرف تهٔ دَ ښهر

لویه دروازه ده ١٠ اوس څمۇنر. په پلٹن کښ دوه کرنیلان دی ١١
د اپریدو ملک ٹول غرونه غرونه دی ١٢ ڂینی ڂینی په کښ
ډیر هوڇیار دی ١٣ په دی کلی کښ نۀ حجره شته نۀ جماعت
١٤ زمکه یی ٹوله اوۍ ده ——

SHORT SENTENCES

AND

VOCABULARY VIII.

پوه شوی	*pōh shwé*	Did you understand ?
هو زۀ پوه شم	*ho zuh pōh shwam*	Yes I understood.
پو هیږی	*pōhégé*	Do you understand ?
هو زۀ پو هیږم	*ho zuh pōhégam*	Yes I understand.
بیا و وایه	*biā wo wāya*	Say it again.
ورو ورو و وایه	*vro vro wo wāya*	Say it slowly.
زۀ خبر نۀ یم	*zuh hhabar nuh yam*	I don't know.
دا رښتیا خبره ده	*dā rikhtiā khabara dah*	This is true.
ډیره ښه ده	*déra kha dah*	That is all right.
هوڇیار	*hukhyār*	Intelligent.
سر کار	*sarkār*	Government.
سر کاری	*sarkāri*	Belongs to Govt. (Adj.)
قلا	*qalā*	Fort.
تعلیم	*talim*	Education.

تعلیم یا فته	*talim yāfta*	Educated.
بی تعلیم	*be talim*	Uneducated.
رنگوٹ	*rangūt*	Recruit.
کمزوری	*kamzōray*	Weak.
نوی	*naway*	New.
خټه	*khata*	Mud or muddy.
گران	*garān*	Dear or difficult.
اسان	*asān*	Easy.
ارزان	*arzān*	Cheap.
ژبه	*jhuba*	Tongue or Language.
اور دی	*urdi*	Uniform.
خیرن	*khiran*	Dirty.
پاک	*pāk*	Clean.
رنړی اوبۀ	*ranré obuh*	Clear water.
خړی اوبۀ	*kharé obuh*	Dirty water.
بندوبست	*bāndubast*	Arrangement.
عمر	*umar*	Age.
ژور	*jhawar*	Deep.
پایاؤ	*payāw*	Shallow.
گناه یا قصر	*gunāh* or *qasūr*	Fault.
غزان	*ghuzān* Walnuts. (غز *ghuz* S.)	
بادام	*bādām* Almonds. (S. and P.)	
ذوکی	*khatakay*	Melon.
ایندوانه	*indwāna*	Water Melon.
کیله	*kéla*	Banana.
سمتره	*samtara*	Sweet Orange.

کښ نه ۍک luh-na dak	Full of.
بیشکه béshaka	Certainly.
ګنډ یا شاید gundé or shāyad	Perhaps.
کار kār	Work.
ذمه zema	Responsibility.
ذمهوار zema ẉār	Responsible.
مشر mashar	Older.
کشر kashar	Younger.
پنسن pensan	Pension.
دستور dastūr	Custom.
مغرور maghrūr	Proud.
پټکی patkay	Turban.
ټوپۍ topai	Topi.
کورته kōrta	Shirt.
پر تۆز partūg	Trousers.
پڼی panré	Shoes (F. P.)
خپلی saplai	Grass sandals.
کیرۍ kérai	Leather sandals.
څادر sādar	Sheet.
سینه sina	Chest.
پوره pūra	Complete or up to the standard.
رووند rūnd	Blind.
ګډ gud	Lame.
ګونګ gūng	Dumb.
کونړ kūnr	Deaf.
حمله hamla	An attack.

ده نۀ خبره ښه *kha khabara* It is not a good
     nuh dah   thing.

خبره *khabara*   Word, speech,
           matter.

EXERCISE 9.

1. She is an intelligent woman. 2. Is he your son ? 3. It is a big station. 4. That is the Afridis' Fort and not a Government Post 5. Is it true ? 6. How many educated soldiers are there in your Regiment ? 7. He is ill today. 8. All these recruits are weak. 9. Owing to the rain all the roads are very muddy. 10 Pushtu is not a difficult language. 11. Your uniform is dirty. 12. Whose arrangement is this ? 13. How old are you (what is your age) ? 14. How deep is this river ? 15. Whose fault is this ? 16. How many years' service have you (Thou of how many years servant art) ?.

VOCABULARY IX.

ورځ	*vraz*	Day.
شپه	*shpa*	Night.
نیمه شپه	*nima shpa*	Midnight.
شومه قلاره	*shūma qalāra*	Still night.
قلاره قلاری	*qalāra qalāri*	Quiet.
بادشاه	*bādshāh*	King.
لږ	*lag*	Little.

باغ	*bāgh*	Garden.
ميوه	*méwa*	Fruit.
انار	*anār*	Pomegranates (M.S. & Plu.)
سيوان	*séwān*	Apples (Sing. سيٓو *séw*).
انگور	*angūr*	Grapes (M. Plu.)
شلتا لان	*shaltālān*	Peaches (M.P.) (Sing. شلتالو *shaltālū*)
ناک یا ناشپاتيٕ	*nāk* or *nāshpātai*	Pears.
نارنجان	*nāranjān*	Oranges. (*nāranj* S.)
بيٕہٖيٕ	*behai*	Quinces. (F.S. & P.)
پوړه	*pūra*	Complete.
خبرى	*khabaré*	Conversation (F.P.)
خبر	*khabar*	Message or news.
ترکاری	*tarkāri*	Vegetables.
تيپر	*taipar*	Turnips.
موليٕ	*mūlai*	Radish.
گازرى	*gāzaré*	Carrots.
متر	*matar*	Peas.
الوٓ گان	*alūgān*	Potatoes. (M. P.)
ساگ	*sāg*	Spinach.
زوٓر ور باران	*zōrawar bārān*	Heavy rain.

EXERCISE 10.

يوه ورځ چه زۀ پۀ دفتر کينٕں وم نو زورٖور باران وؤ ۲ پۀ
هندوستان کينٕں يو بادشاه وؤ چه نوٓميٕ اکبروؤ ۳ زۀ پۀ پيٕنتو پوهيږرم
مګر لږو نۀ ۴ ځما نوکر پۀ پيٕنتو نۀ پو هيږريٕ ۵ هغه دَ ونى لاند
پۀ کټ ملاست دىَ ۶ باغ دَ ميوو لۀ ونونو ډک دىَ ۷ ښښه داستاکار

دَى تَهْ ذمه واړيي ۸ څما مشر ورور په رساله کښې جمعدارۀه مهر
اوس پۀ پنسن باند دَى ۹ دا دَ دى ملک دستوُر دى ۱۰ ستا
بقکَى ولَى خيرن دى ۱۱ دَ دى رنگوُپت سينه پوُره نه دَه دا خو
روُند نه دى هغه دوه ځلى دي او دا درى کمزورى دى ۱۲ سيند ژور
نه دى ۱۳ په دى حمله کښې يوه رساله او درى پلتن دى
۱۴ کۀ دا دهغۀ قصوُر وى نو څه خبره نه دَه ۔

VOCABULARY X.

لۀ دى ځاي نه luh dé zāi na	From here.
ځاى zāi	Place.
څومره مُده کيږوى sōmra mūda kégee	How long ago.
څومره مُده پس sōmra mūda pas	How long after.
څومره مُده راسى sōmra mūda rāsé	Since how long.
چُټى chūtī	Leave.
پلن plan	Broad.
اوږد ūgad	Long.
مورچه mōrcha	Trench.
پټى patay	Field.
سوُر sūr	Red.
شين shin	Green.
تور tōr	Black.
زيړ ziar	Yellow.
آبى ābi	Blue.
دَننه danana	Inside.

باهر *bāhar*   Outside.

خپل *khpal*   Own, relative.

خپلوان *khpalwān*   Relations.

کرائیي *karāyeé*   Rent, hire.

څومره لوي *somra loi ?*   How big ?

MISCELLANEOUS COLLOQUIAL SENTENCES I.

Is there anyone there ?	*sōk shta ?*
Who are you ?	*tuh sōk yé ?*
What is your name ?	*stā nūm suh day ?*
What is your father's name ?	*da plār nūm dé suh day ?*
Where is your houe ?	*kōr dé charta day ?*
How far is it from here?	*luh dé ᵶāi na sōmra laré day ?*
Is that your village ?	*dagha stā kallay day ?*
How wide is the trench?	*mōrcha sōmra plana dah ?*
How deep is the river ?	*sind sōmra jhawar day?*
Whose fields are these ?	*dā da chā pati dee ?*
Where is my gun ?	*tōpak mé charta day ?*
This colour is red	*dā sūr rang day.*
Is my servant inside ?	*zamā naukar danana day ?*
Is he a relation of yours ?	*hagha dé khpal day ?*
Are you the owner of this house ?	*tuh da dé kōr khāwand yé ?*
What is the rent of this house ?	*dā dé kōr karāyee sōmra dah ?*

How big is your house ? *stā kōr sōmra loi day ?*

I don't know who is   *zuh khabar nuh yam*
your servant.   *chi stā naukar sōk day.*

VOCABULARY XI.

اسټيشن	*istaishan*	Station.
مور پلار	*mōr plār*	Parents.
مړ	*mar*	Dead.
ژوندی	*jhwanday*	Alive.
څنګه	*sunga*	How.
سپاهی توب	*spāhi tōb.*	Soldiering.
فوځ	*fauz*	Troops, Army.
اباد	*abād*	Populated, cultivated.
ابادي	*abādi*	Population, cultivation.
کپنۍ	*kapnai*	Company.
پښتون	*pukhtūn*	Pathan.
طلب	*talab,*	
تنخواه	*tankhwāh*	Pay.
تغمه	*taghma*	Medal.
لنډه لار	*landa lār*	Short road.
ناجوړتيا	*nājōrtiā*	Sickness.
چرې	*charé*	Ever.
هيچرې	*hicharé*	Never.

EXERCISE 11.

1. What is the name of your village ?   2. In what direction is it ?   3. How far is your village from the Railway Station ?   4. What

is the Railway fare? 5. How many brothers
have you? 6. Are your parents alive? 7.
No, they are both dead. 8. How much land
have you? 9. How are the crops in your
country? 10. Do you like soldiering? 11.
Have you any relations in the Army? 12. Is
there a river near your village? 13. What is
the population of your village? 14. Are you
a private or N.C.O.? 15. How many Pathan
companies are there in your Regiment? 16.
What Regiment are you in? 17. Where is
your Regiment? 18. Who is the Officer
Commanding of your Regiment? 19. What
is your pay? 20. Have you a medal? 21.
Which is the shortest way? 22. Whose
horses are these? 23. I don't like him.

VOCABULARY XII.

چرته	*charta*	Anywhere or where?
څه	*suh*	Any, some, what?
څه قسم	*suh qisam*	What kind of?
تا واده کوی دی	*tā wāduh karay day*	Are you married?
تږی	*tagay*	Thirsty.
تنده	*tanda*	Thirst.
اوږی	*ogay*	Hungry.
لوږه	*lwaga*	Hunger.
کوم	*kum*	Which?

کوم ځای	*kum zāi*	Where, in which place ?
په دی شپو ورځو کښ	*pa dé shpŏ vrazo ké*	Now-a-days.
مُوندلی شی	*múndalay shee*	Can be had, can be obtained, can be received.

بيعه	*baya*	Price	ځنګل	*zangal*	Forest
په کښ	*pa ké*	In it	راسی	*rāsé*	Since
چه په	*chi pa*	In which	لوی	*lōi*	Great
کښ '	*ké*				big, large
لرګی	*largay*	Wood, stick	خدای	*khudāi*	God
			خبر	*khabar*	news
لرګی	*largi*	Wood (Plural)	اکثر	*aksar*	Gene- rally
سکاره '	*skāruh*	Charcoal (M. P.)	قسمت	*qismat*	Luck
ذ کانړی	*da kānri*				
سکاره	*skāruh*	Coal	نصيب	*nasīb*	Fate
خشاک	*khashāk*	Firewood	غله	*ghala*	Grain
کانړی	*kānray*	Stone	دومره	*dōmra*	this much or as much so much
			داسی	*dāsé*	thus, such.

EXERCISE 12.

۱ پۀ کلي کښ د ډيرو ناجوړ تيا ده ؟ ۲ ستا کلي ته نيزدی چرته ښکار مُوندلی شی ؟ ۳ ځۀ قسم ښکار دی ؟ ۴ تا واده کړی دی ؟ ۵ د دی سکارو بيعه څۀ ده ۶ څما اس تږی دی اوبۀ

كوم څائي دى ٧ په دى شپو ورخو كښ پۀ بازار كښ خۀ قسم
ميوه موندلى شى ٨ دلته غله ارزانه ده كۀ ګرانه ٩ افغانستان
ښۀ وطن دى مهر په كښ يخنى ډيره وى ١٠ دَښهر خلق
ښۀ دى ١١ ښهر ته نيز دى دَ لركو يو لوى څنګل دى ١٢
هغه لوى سړى دى ولى هوښيار نه دى ١٣ پښتو اسانه ژبه
ده ١٤ څومره مده راسى تۀ په فوځ كښ يى ١٥ عهده
داران قبول په دفتر كښ دى ١٦ ولى د نن رنګ زبردى ١٧
خدای خبر چه ولى دلته تر كارى دومره ارزانه ده ١٨ دَ دولتمند
سړى دوستان ډير وى ١٩ زۀ غريب يم خكه دوست م نشته ٢٠
اكثر دَ هوښيار سړى قسمت خراب وى—

VOCABULARY XIII.

راشه	*rāsha*	Come !
لارشه	*lārsha*	Go !
كينه	*kéna*	Sit !
څمله	*samla*	Lie down !
(ته) و وايه	*(ta) wo wāya*	Say, speak, tell !
راوړه	*rāwra*	Bring ! (inanimate)
راوله	*rāwala*	Lead ! (animate)
يوسه	*yausa*	Take away ! (animate)
بوزه	*bōza*	Lead away ! (animate)
وبله	*wo bala*	Call !
وليكه	*wō lika*	Write !
ايسار شه	*isār sha*	Wait !
لرى كړه	*laré kar*	Open !
پورى كړه	*pōré kra*	Shut !

کیږده	*kégda*	Place, put !
کړه	*kra*	Do !
شه	*sha*	Become, be !
راوغواړه	*rā wo ghwāra*	Send for ! (thing)
راوبله	*rā wo bala*	Call for ! (person)
ګوره	*gōrā*	Look !
مۀ ویښوه	*muh wikhawa*	Don't wake up !
بل	*bal*	Next or other.
نور	*nōr*	More, or others.
چڼۍ	*chitai*	Letter.
خوراک	*khurāk*	Food.
ډوډۍ	*dōdai*	Bread.
دفتر	*daftar*	Office or landed property.
سايۀس	*sāis*	Syce.
کلف	*kalaf*	Club.
جواب	*jawāb*	An auswer.
موټر	*mōtar*	Motor.
بائيسکل	*bāisekal*	Bicycle.
لينر	*lainr*	Lines.
بيرته	*biarta*	Back.
بيا	*biā*	Again.
دَ سکلو اوبۀ	*da skalo obuh*	Drinking water.
کاغذ	*kāghaz*	Paper.
قلم	*qalam*	Pen.
مشوانړۍ	*mashwānrai*	Ink pot.
سياهی	*syāhi*	Ink.

اخبار	akhbār	Newspaper.
سمدستی	samdasti	At once.
صاف صاف	sāf sāf	Distinctly.
ورو ورو	vro vro	Slowly.
مرمت	muramat	Repair.
سم یا نیغ	sam or négh	Straight.
ګل زیرئ	gul ziarai	Target.
مهربانی ده	mehrabāni dah	Thank you.
ډیره مهربانی ده	déra mehrabāni dah	Thank you very much.
لوکوتی	lūkūti	Little or just.

EXERCISE 13.

1. Come inside, sit on the chair and tell me some thing about your regiment. 2. Call my servant. 3. Tell him to come to the office. 4. Tell the syce to take my horse to the Club and wait for me there. 5. Shut the door. 6. Take this letter to the Adjutant and bring an answer. 7. Take the Sahib's motor to the lines. 8. Bring the bicycle back. 9. Tell my bearer to bring me some water. 10. Is this water fit to drink ? 11. Take these papers at once to the office and then tell the mali to bring water for this field. 12. Speak distinctly and slowly. 13. Send for the jemadar; Why is he not here ? 14. Take my boots for repair.

15. Look straight towards the target. 16. Don't wake me up before 9 o'clock. 17. Please write him another letter. 18. Just call the head man of this village. 19. Bring food for the dogs. 20. Is there any letter for me ?

NOTE :—Wheeled vehicles and irrigation water are treated as moveable objects and take the verbs "*biwal*" and "*rāwastal*".

VOCABULARY XIV.

راكه	*rā kra*	Give me or give us.
وركه	*war kra*	Give him, them, her it.
و ليږه يا	*wo légā* or	} Send.
واستوه	*wāstawa*	
واچوه	*wāchawa*	Put.
مه ايسا ږيږه	*muh isāréga*	Don't wait.
اسپه	*aspa*	Mare.
ميدان	*maidān*	Plain.
يو خوا بل خوا	*yaw khwā bal hhwā*	Hither and thither.
مه ګوره	*ma gōra*	Don't look.
لۀ نه اول يا	*luh-na awal*	} Before in time.
لۀ نه وړمبى	*luh na vrumbay*	
بالكل	*bilkul*	Quite, absolutely.
پنځه نيمى بجى	*pinzanimé bajé*	Half past five.

پاؤ باند پنځهٔ بجی	*pāw bāadé pinzuh bajé*	Quarter past five.
پاؤ کم پنځهٔ بجی	*pāw kam pinzuh bajé*	Quarter to five.
لس ملټَ باند	*las mélata bāndé*	10 minutes past.
لس ملټَ کم	*las mélata kam*	10 minutes to.
درُوند	*drūnd*	Heavy.
سپک	*spak*	Light.

NOTE :—For خهٔ دی = *suh di*, look up Syntax
rule No. 52. For ورته ووایه چه دَننه راشي یا راشه =
warta wo wāya chi danana rāshee or *rāsha*
look up syntax rule No. 16.

EXERCISE 14.

۱   ټول کتا بوُنه راوړه او په میز باند ئی کیږدده   ۲   یوه بله
کرُسیٔ راوره او په برنهٔ کښې ئی واچوه   ۳   ټو لو سپاهیا نو ته
و وایه چه دَننه راشي   ۴   ور ته و وایه چه زر جواب راوړه   ۵   نوکرانو
ته و وایه چه په کُرسو باند نهٔ کیني   ۶   مالی ته و وایه چه
صبا خما دَ باغ دَ پاره اوبهٔ راولي   ۷   میز پوری دوه کرسیٔ هم
کیږ ده   ۸   خما موټر د لته راوله او بائیسکل م کور ته بوزه   ۹   پهٔ
پاؤ باند شپږ بجی را ته نوکر راواستوه   ۱۰   دا چټئ دفتر ته یو سه
خو جواب دَ پاره مهٔ ایسا ږیږوه   ۱۱   ټول اسوُنه او سپی هسپتال
ته بوزه   ۱۲   ما ته سم ګوره یو خوا بل خوا مهٔ ګوره   ۱۳   له دریؤ
ببجو نه اول راشه او ما وینس کره   ۱۴   لهٔ دفتر نه یو بل داسی
کتاب هم راوړه   ۱۵   مهر بانی وکړه دا خبره بیا وکړه   ۱۶   دَ اوبهٔ دَ
سکلو دَ پاره شی دی کهٔ نه   ۱۷   خپل کار وکړه نو دفتر ته راشه   ۱۸

ملک ته سلام ورکړه او ورته و وایه چه صاحب په حُجره کښې ناست
دیَ ۱۹ داخۀ دیِ او دغه څوک دیَ ۲۰ دَ دی کلی مالیه
درنه دَه --

VOCABULARY XV-

اول	awal	First, at first.
بیشکه	béshaka	Certainly.
ما و ویل	mā wo wayal	I said spoke or told.
هیڅ	hiss	Nothing (takes tense in negative.)
داسی	dāsé	So, such or thus.
څۀ	suh	Any thing.
څنګه	sanga	How.
خپل	khpal	Own, (used for reflexive pro.)
جوار	jowār	Maize, Indian Corn.
تخم	tukhum	Seed.
ټا نټی	tānté	Stalks.
مال	māl	Cattle, property.
حکم	hukum	Order.
ګلډانګ سپی	guldāng spay	Bull dog.
شراب	sharāp	Wine.

EXERCIE 15.

1. I beat him, because he beat me first. 2. Certainly he beat me yesterday, but I said nothing. 3. You beat me yesterday and you are beating me again to day. 4. I struck the owner of the house because he had struck all my

dogs. 5. The dog is so ill that he does not eat food. 6. Will you drink any thing ?. 7. I will write a letter to his father, 8. Please write another letter for me. 9. How can I write ?. 10. Tell my servant to keep this dog in his house. 11. We have sown some maize, the grain is very good, but the stalks are so hard that the cattle will not eat them. 12. This man does not obey my orders. 13. We used to keep a bulldog in our house. 14. I wrote a letter to his Colonel at Cherat. 15. The dog bit the man therefore the man beat the dog. 16. I will also send him a message. 17. Can you call my servant ?. 18. I was so ill that I could not drink water. 19. This Darzi cannot sew well so call the Jemadar to arrange for a better one. 20. Don't drink wine.

VOCABULARY XVI.

واښه	*wākhuh*	Grass.
خاي خائيږى يا پته	*zāi zaigay* or *pata*	Address.
خاوند	*khāwand*	Owner.
كله	*kala*	When.
كله كله	*kala kala*	Some times.
سر	*sar*	Head.
پړى يا رسۍ	*paray* or *rasai*	Rope.
ونه	*wana*	Tree.

رو ټۍ	*rōtai*	Bread, food.
مه ورکوه	*muh warkawa*	Don't give him !
ګنډل	*gandal*	To sew, sewing.
خپل ځان	*khpal zān*	Oneself.
په ليکلو کښ	*puh likalō ké*	In writing.
زر	*zar*	Soon.
زر زر	*zar zar*	Quickly.
پخپله	*pakhpala*	Myself, yourself, herself, itself etc.
و يل	*wayal*	To say, speak, tell.
مياشت	*miāsht*	Month, moon.
د دی مياشتی	*da dé miāshté*	On the 20th of this
په شلم تاريخ	*puh shalam tārikh*	month.
ما جب	*mājeb*	Pay.
تپن	*tepan*	Lunch.
غوښه	*ghwakha*	Meat.
پر دی مال	*praday māl*	Others' property.
ګناه	*gunāh*	Sin.
ګنهګار	*gunahgār*	Sinner, guilty.
بی ګناه	*bé gunah*	Not guilty.
موقعه	*moqa*	Chance, spot, opportunity.
موجود	*maujūd*	Present.
غل	*ghal* Thief	(غله *ghluh* Plu.)
ځان	*zān* self.	

EXERCISE 16.

په ٢ بجو اوبۀ نۀ او خوری وانۀ نۀ ځکه دی ناجوړ م اس

اس م ناجوړ دى ځکه نۀ واښۀ خورى او نۀ اوبۀ سكي ۲ پۀ

دی کاغذ باند خپله نامه او دَ پلار نامه او ښای ځائیمَی ولیکه ۳ هغه
ښهٔ نوکر نه وی چه دَ مالک خبره نهٔ مني ۴ کله کله راته چِټي
راليږه ۵ اوس ټول فصلونه کرلی شوی دی ۶ ما په نایي باند
سر خرئیلو پهٔ موقعه موجوُد نه وم ځکه راته معلومه نه ده چا
وهلی دی ۷ ما غل په پټي باند ونی پوزی وترلو او خپل نوکر تهم
ووبل چه روتيي او اوبهٔ مهٔ ورکوه ۸ کوټ کڼلول داسی اسان
کار نهٔ دی هغه خپل ځان لوی کڼي مهر داښه خبره نهٔ ده و
ما درته چِټي لیکله چه ستا خبر راورسیدلو ۱۰ کهٔ ما ورته چِټي
لیکلی نهٔ وی نو هغهٔ به زهٔ بللی نه وم ۱۱ ما ورته تار ولیږربلو او په کښم
و لیکل چه پلار د نا جوړ دی زر راشه ۱۲ هغهٔ راته خبر راولیږربلو
چه زهٔ پخپله هم ناجوړیم او کرنیل صاحب پهٔ چوقټي دی ځکه اوس
هیڅ وبلی نه شم ۱۳ دَ دی میاشتی په شلم تاریخ ماورته یوه چِټي
ولیکله ۱۴ کهٔ څوری څوره که نهٔ څوری مهٔ څوره ۱۵ هغه لهٔ
سر کار نه دوه سوه روپيي ماجب څوری ۱۶ لږیره مهر بانی ده هیڅ
نهٔ څورم ځکه چه ما اوس ټپن څورلی دی ۱۷ څینی څینی
هندوان بالکل غوښه نهٔ څوری ۱۸ پر دی مال څورل ګناه ده ۱۹
دا وروکی ځلک ماله زاکره زهٔ پهٔ خپل کور کښی به یی ساتم ۹۰
ما ورته ولیکل چه ځما دَ کلي مال ټول ناجوړ دی—

VOCABULARY XVII.

 دَ ـپهٔ مینځ کښ *da-puh mianz ké*   Through.

دیوال *déwāl*   Wall.

غیر علاقه *ghair alāqa*   Independent. territory.

رعیت *rait*   British territory, subject.

دَ اور ګاډي	da aur gāday	Train.
کتل	katal	To look, examine.
ګورم	gōram	I examine (present)
زخم یا پرهر	zakham or parhar	Wound.
زخمی یا ژوبل	zakhmi or jhōbal	Wounded.
پۀ وخت	puh wakht	In time
اسمان غوریږي	asmān ghurégee	It is thundering.
غالب ګمان	ghālib gumān day	Probably.
بازان وریدل	bārān warédal	To rain.
واوره وریدل	wāwra warédal	To snow.
واوره	wāwra	Snow, ice.
دازه	dāra	Raid, Raiding party.
دازه مار	dāra mār	Raider.
لۀ ټولونه نیزدي	luh tōlo na nizde	The nearest.
تور	tōr	Black.
دوکان	dukān	Shop.
دوکاندار	dukāndār	Shop keeper.
زۀ ځم	zuh zam	I go.
زۀ راځم	znh rāzam	I come.
کۀ تۀ لارشی	kuh tuh lārshé	If you go.
لواړګی	lwārgay	Landi Kotal.
جم	jam	Jamrud.

داسے	*dāse*	Like this, so, such or thus.
هم پهٔ هغه شپه	*hum puh hagha shpa*	On the same night.
هم پهٔ هغه ورخ یا امرۆزه	*hum puh hagha vraz* or *amrōza*	or On the same day.
لښکر	*lakhkar*	Party of tribesmen.
ګرزېدل	*garzédal*	To walk or wander.
بیرته	*biarta*	Back.
پراؤ	*parāw*	Camp.
رسد یا راسن	*rasad* or *rāsan*	Supplies, rations.
کله چه	*kala chi*	When (Relative).
وختی	*wakhti*	Early or earlier.
نا وخته	*nā wakhta*	Late.
کلیوال	*kaliwāl*	Villagers (S & P).
(ته) نقصان رسېدل	*(ta) nuqsān rasédāl*	To suffer loss.
اوسنی	*osanay*	Recent.
جنګ	*jang*	War or battle.

EXERCISE 17.

1. Where do you live ? I am not living in the village. 2. I am living in Peshawar City, my brother lives in Kohat and after two months we shall live in Cherat. 3. The water of the river flows through my garden. 4. As we reached the wall of the village, the villagers fled towards the mosque. 5. This boy can run

faster than this girl. 6. All the thieves fled towards independent territory. 7. The train arrives at the Station at 2-30 p. m. 8. Don't move, I am going to examine your wound. 9. If you had arrived earlier, you would have seen the king of this country. 10. It is thundering now, it will probably rain tonight. 11. As we saw the raiding party we ran to the nearest village. 12. In the recent war we have suffered a great loss. 13. If you go now you will reach Landi Kotal at 4 p.m. 15. Has your brother arrived from Lahore ? 16. Yes, he arrived before 5 a. m. 17. All my servants cannot live in a small house like this. 18. We arrived there the same night, but the lashkar had run away to the hills. 19. I [1] must go to the office now. 20. When did your regiment arrive in this station ? 21. Has your Colonel arrived back from the camp ?.

VOCABULARY XVIII.

خالی khāli	Empty, only, Saturday.
پروت prōt	Lying.
هشوک hisōk	Nobody (takes tense in negative.)

NOTE:—1. For " must " or " should ", see syntax rules Nos. 21 & 22.

کُوخَه	kūsa	Street.
وِینَے	winé	Blood (Feminine plural.)
سَرہ دَ	sara da	With.
خَهُ داسی یا	suh dāsé or	
داسی	dāsé	So.
هر	har	Every.
وار پَهُ وار	wār puh wār	Turn by turn.
کَثرت	kasrat	Bodily exercise.
فقیر	faqir	Beggar.
شپه او ورځ	shpa aw vraz	Day and night.
شهزاده	shāhzāda	Prince.
شهزادګِي	shāhzādgāi	Princes.
خلاص	khlās	Free, finished.
اسمان پر کیږی	asmān parkégee	It is lightning.
باران به وشی	bārān ba wo shee	It will rain (lit the rain will become.)
وخت پَهُ وخت	wakht puh wakht	Time to time.
پیاده	pyāda	On foot.
خط	khat	Letter,
ګیده یا خیټه	géda or khéta	Stomach.
درد	dard	Pain,
څرب	surb	Fat.
اِتوار	itwār	Sunday.
پیر یا ګل	pir	Monday.
نهی	nahé	Tuesday.
چار شنبه	chārshanba	Wednesday,

پانشنبه	pānshạnba	
یا	or	} Thursday.
دَ زیارت ورځ	da ziārat vraz	
جُمعه	jūma	Friday.
خالی	khāli	Saturday.
دَ اتوار پهٔ ورځ	da itwār pūh vraz	On Sunday.
ځوان	zwān	Youngman or soldier.
مورچه	mōrcha	Breastwork.

EXERCISE 18.

١ نۀ هغه را ورسید او نۀ دَ هغۀ نوکر ٢ چه مُونږ ور ورسیدُو نو کلیَ خالي پروت وُه نۆل خلق تر تښتیدلیَ وُو ٣ نۀ زۀ په خپل و طن کښی اوسم او نۀ ځما ورور ٤ داسی جنگ وُه چه دَ کلي په کُوڅو کښی وینی بهیدلی ٥ پو لۆیټیکل صاحب ته خبر ور کړه چه ځما نو کر سره دَ سلو روپو تښتیدلیَ دیَ ٦ دَ هغۀ کور ته رسیدل څۀ داسی سان کار نۀ وُه ٧ چه وخرَ زیدلو نو زۀ پوه شوم چه ژوندیَ دیَ ٧ دَ کمان افسر صاحب حکم دیَ چه سپاهیان د هر سهر وار په وار دَ کثرت دَ پاره زغلي ٩ فقیر شپه او ورځ په دی غم کښی کړیدلو چه پس لۀ مانه به ځما دَ ځای مالک څوک وی ١٠ یوه ورځ زۀ خپل نوکر سره وگرځیدلم وگرځیدلم ١١ نۀ زۀ رار سیدلیَ نۀ وی نو غل به تښتیدلیَ نۀ وُه ١٢ اسمان غوریږی او پیکیږی باران به وشي ١٣ چه پلڼی ته ور ورسیدرمی نو صوبیدار صاحب ته ځما سلام ورکه ١٤ چه ځما چڼی در ورسیدرمی نو جواب راکړه ١٥ کوټ ماستر صاحب ته و وایه چه واښۀ او نور دَ خوراک ګیزونه پۀ وخت راورسي ١٦ زۀ پوه شوم چه په یوه ګینټه کښی پیاده رسیدلی نۀ شم ١٧ ډیره مهرباني دَه ستا خط رانه په تیراه کښی را رسیدلیَ وُه ١٨

زۀ زغلیدلیَ نۀ شم څکه چه په ځیوه کیس م درد دیَ ۱۹ دَ جیڼن
صاحب پۀ حکم باند ټول ځوانان ځپلو ځپلو مورچوته ییرته وتښتیدل
۲۰ جمعدار صاحب ډیر ځورب دیَځکه سپاهیانو پسی نه شو رسیدلیَ

VOCABULARY XIX.

کټ	*kat*	Bed.
دا هغه سړیَ دیَ	*dā hagha saray day*	This is the man.
سپین	*s̱pin*	White.
صُندق	*sunduq*	Box.
ځیل	*khayāl*	To show, direct.
قالین	*qālin*	Rug.
دری	*darai*	Carpet.
تر-پوری	*tar-poré*	Till, upto.
دوره	*daura*	Tour.
چای	*chāi*	Tea.
پۀ یو ملټ کیس	*puh yaw melat ké*	In a minute.
سرشته دار	*sarishtadar*	Reader (of the court)
کمره یا کوټه	*kamra or kōta*	Room.
ډاګي	*dāgi*	Postman.
آئنده د پاره	*ainda da pāra*	In future.
د-په مخ کیس	*da-pa makh ké*	In the presence of, infront of.
بیعه	*baya*	Price.
مدام.تل.همیشه	*mudām, tal, haméshā*	Always.
څوک نه څوک	*sōk na sōk*	Someone or other.
ځان سره	*zān sarā*	With me, with him etc.

پکار دی چه اصلی پښتون وي	*pakār di chi asli pukhtūn wi*	He must be a real Pathan.
اصلی پښتون	*asli pukhtūn*	Real Pathan.
ضلع	*zela*	District.
کم ذات	*kam zāt*	Low class, menial.
أستکار	*ustakār*	Village workman.
برنده	*baranda*	Vranda.

EXERCISE 19.

1. Bring a bed and put it in the vranda. 2. This is the man who brings horses from Afghanistan. 3. I brought a letter from your Colonel. 4. Tell the syce to bring my white horse to the Club and wait for me if I am not there. 5. Where did you put my gun? I put it under the box. 6. The servants used to bring our food from the city. 7. I will take you to the city and will show you all kinds of carpets. 8. Take away the dogs and don't bring them till the day after tomorrow as I shall be on tour. 9. Bring tea for four men who are coming in a minute. 10. Take my servant to the city and show him my reader's house. 11. [1] He said his name was Ahmad and he said he was a good man. 12. Yesterday my father told me I was a good man. 13. He said his room was smaller than my office. 14. Tell the Postman to bring my letters to the office

in future 15. He brought 20 rupees and put
them before the owner of the house saying that
it was the price of his food. 16. He always
brings someone or other with him. 17. How
can I bring the head-man with me? 18. All
whom you bring in [2] must be real Pathans of the
Peshawar District. 19. Menials and the village
workmen will not do. 20. Can you take my
servant's son with you.?

VOCABULARY XX.

له نن تأريخ نه *luh nan tārikh na*	From this day.
يو ځل *yaw zal*	Once.
دوه ځلَ *dwa zala*	Twice.
درى ځلَ *dré zalā*	Thrice.
داځل *dā zal*	This time.
ويل *wayal*	To say, speak, tell.
ضروری *zarūri*	Important, necessary, urgent.
ضروري ضروري *zarūri zarūri*	Very important ones.
معمولى *māmūli*	Ordinary.
عرضى *arzi*	Petition.
عرضي *arzai*	Petitions.
درخواست *darkhwāst*	Ordinary petition, request.

NOTE :—1. Direct speech.
          2. In syntax rule No. 22.

کچړی	*kacharai*	Court.
جمع کول	*jama kawal*	To collect.
ښۀ غوندی	*khuh ghundé*	Somewhat good.
خرڅ دَ پاره	*khars da pāra*	For sale.
لۀ بَد نصیب	*luh bada nasiba*	Unfortunately.
لۀ ښۀ نصیب	*luh khuh nasiba*	Fortunately.
هره ورځ	*hara vraz*	Every day.
وزګار	*wōzgār*	At leisure.
نا وزګار	*nā wōzgār*	Busy.
مفرور	*mafrūr*	An outlaw.
اِنعام	*inām*	Reward.
مؤندل	*mūndal*	To get, obtain, receive, find.
زۀ مؤمم	*zuh mūmam*	I get, etc. (present).
ټګی	*tagi*	Deceit.
اسان	*asān*	Easy.
رَبړ	*rabar*	Trouble.
لرګی	*largay*	Stick, wood.
لالۀ	*lāla*	To me or for me.
زا بَند ډیر کار دی	*rā bāndé dér kār day*	I have plenty to do.
پۀ دی شپو ورځو کښی	*pa dé shpo vrazo ké*	Now a days.
یوا ځی	*yawāzé*	Alone.
باران کوټ	*bārān kōt*	Overcoat, water proof coat.
بوزبه	*bōnga*	Ransom.

EXERCISE 20.

۱ يو سړيَ يیئ لۀ خذمل نه راوست اوورته يی رو چه لۀ نن تاريخ نه تۀ څمونږ بادشاه يی ۲ به مرزاصاحب څۀ د راوړي دي؟ ما در ته ويلي دي چه ضروري ضروري كاغذونه راوړه او معمولی عرضي او درخواستونه په كچري كښ جمع كوۀ ۳ زۀ به د دَ ملك حجړي له بوزم ۴ نن څويم تاريخ دي . پرون دَ څۀ ورځ وَ ۔ بل صبا دَ پير ورځ ته ۵ ما له يو ښۀ غوندي نوكر راوله ۲ دَ دي وطن خلق لۀ خذمل نه وائنۀ او لرګي راوړي او په ښهر كښ يي خرڅوي ۷ مؤنږو خرځ دَ پاره سكارۀ هم راوړۀ ۸ كۀ تا مفرورڅما بذملیَ ته راوستیَ وی نو ما به ډير لوی انعام دركړیَ وۀ ۹ نوكر ته م و وايه چه څما ټيپن هره ورځ دفتر ته راوړي ښكه چه را باند ډير كار دیَ ۱۰ بی لۀ ټوكيي نه دَ مفروران راوستل اسان كار نۀ دیَ ۱۱ بيا هيچري څما چايئ په دی ميزكينه ږدی ۱۲ څما آس غلو بيولیَ وۀ دَ اپريد و يو ملك لا له پۀ بوذكه راوست ۱۳ ما ته يی رو چه ستا آس م په ډير رپر سره راوستیَ دیَ ۱۴ لږری نوری اوبۀ په ګلاس كښ راوړه ۱۵ پرون مالی دَ دی پقی دَ پاره اوبۀ راوستیَ وی ۱۶ رايی وله چه انعام ورکړوم ۱۷ زۀ څۀ وكړم په دی شپو ورڅو كښ زۀ ډير ناوزګارېم ۱۸ دا كار ما يواڼی كولی نۀ شو ۱۹ څما نوكر ته و وايه چه دفتر ته را پسی باران كوتب م راوړي ۲۰ ټول ټوپكونه راوړه او دَ صاحب پۀ مخ كښ يي و شماره ۔

VOCABULARY XXI.

كرځه ، ـ garza   Turn !

كس لاس	gas lās	Left hand.
ښی لاس	khay lās	Right hand.
پیش کړه	pésh kra	Bring before or produce.
قدم	qadam	Pace.
پوندہ	pūnda	Heel.
سمدستی	samdāsti	At once.
لګول	lagawāl	To fix, apply, and arrange (Flowers etc.)
سنګین	sangin	Bayonet.
مه ځه	muh za	Do not go.
مه راځه	muh rāza	Do not come.
شور	shōr	Noise.
چپ	chup	Silent.
وپستل	wistal	To take out, take off.
وباسم	wō bāsam	I take off (present.)
جامی	jāmé	Clothes.
أدریدل	odrédal	To stand.
نیغ	négh	Straight.
كوږ	kōg	Crooked.
لږ یا لوكوتی	lag or lūkūti	Little or please
ګرمی	garmi	Heat.
یخنی	yakni	Cold.
ناراست	nārāst, sust	Lazy.

MISCELLANEOUS COLLOQUIAL SENTENCES II.

Why did you strike him ?	walé dé hagha wo wahalo

Turn to the right.	*khī lās ta wō garza.*
Bring him before the C. O.	*kamān afsar ta yé pésh kra.*
Turn to the left.	*gus lās ta wo garza.*
Where do you live?	*charta osé?*
When did you arrive here?	*dalé kala rā wo rasédé?*
Keep in step.	*qadam melāo kra.*
Heels together	*pūndé yaū zāi kra.*
Bring him at once	*zar yé rāwala.*
Fix bayonet	*sangin wo lagawa.*
Pull vigorously	*puh zōr sara yé rā wobāsa*
Come here	*dalé rasha* or *dalta rāsha.*
Do not go there	*halta muh za.*
Hurry up	*zar sha.*
Tell the sepoys not to make a noise	*spāhyāno ta wo wāya chi shōr nuh kawee.*
Keep quiet.	*chup sha.*
Take the horse to the house	*ass kōr ta bōza.*
Take off your clothes	*jāmé dé wo bāsa.*
Stand up straight	*négh wodréga.*
Lie down	*sumla.*
Wait a little	*lūkūti sabar wo kra,* or *wār wo kra.*
Take this letter to the Adjutant	*dā chitai jitan sāhib ta yāusa.*

Bring an answer quickly   *zar jawāb rāwra.*

It is very hot today   *nan déra garmi dah*

Owing to the rain it is cold   *da bārān puh sabab yakhni dah.*

You are very lazy   *tuh dér nārāst yé.*

Do not bring all the papers   *tōl kāgazūna muh rāwra.*

Put them in the office   *puh daftar ké yé kégda.*

VOCABULARY XXII.

قصه	*qisa*	Story.
اخستل	*akhistal*	To take or buy. آخلم = *akhlam* I take (present).
خرڅ	*khars kawal*	To sell, spend.
مجرم	*mujrem*	Accused or offender
جرم	*juram*	Crime.
قتل یا خون	*qatal* or *khūn*	Murder.
قاتل یا خونی	*qātél* or *khūni*	Murderer.
وژلَی شوی	*wajhalay*	
سوی یا موی	*shaway saray* or *maray*	Murdered man.
ما خبر کوه	*mā khabar kra*	Let me know
مدرسه	*madrasa*	School.
تیار شه	*tayār sha*	Get ready.
ضروری	*zarūri*	Necessary, urgent.
کار	*kār*	Work.

ناوختۀ	*nā wakhta*	Late.
وختى	*wakhti*	Early.
خما پۀ فكر كينې	*zamā puh fikar ké*	I think, I am afraid, In my opinion.
قريب	*qarib*	About, nearly.
ليدل	*lidal*	To see.
بيرتۀ	*biarta*	Back.
بيا	*bia*	Again.
تږ را تږ	*tag rā tag*	Coming and Going.

EXERCISE 21.

1. When will you go back ? 2. He came inside, sat on the chair and told me to tell him my father's story. 3. When did your brother come from Lahore ? 4. We went to the City but did not see Mahabat Khan's Mosque. 5. The people of the city come to my garden to buy fruit. 6. When you first saw the accused, was he coming to his house or had he arrived there ? 7. Where did you come from ? 8. Let me know wher my servant arrives. 9. I will sit on this chair, you can lie down on that carpet and the village people will come to us. 10. I go at 10 in the morning and come back at 4 p. m. 11. Get ready! We will go to the cantonment at 2-30 p. m. 12. Come to my house every day and do the necessary work. 13. It is very late now, I think you had better

go tomorrow. 14. My servant has gone to
the bazar and will be back in about an hour.
15. Yes, the Khan had come, but I did not see
him. 16. My regiment was in Pindi but it
has now come to Peshawar. 17. Ahmad went
to his house and did not come back again.
18. If he had come, you would have seen him.
19. We used to sit on the bank of that river.
20. I went to the hill without seeing anyone
coming or going.

VOCABULARY XXIII.

راځه چه	*rāza chi*	Let us.
(ته) نقصان رسَول	*(ta) nuqsān rasawal*	To cause damage.
ناراستی	*nārāsti*	Idleness.
نیستی	*nésti*	Poverty.
تخم	*tukhum*	Seed.
(ته) نقصان رسیدل	*(ta) nuqsān rasédal*	To suffer loss,
پریټ	*parait*	Parade
اخبار	*akhbār*	Newspaper.
دَ پهٔ ځای کښ	*da puh zāi ké*	Instead of
وینځل	*winzal*	To wash.
بندول	*bandawal*	To close.
کنجی	*kunji*	Key.
ناظر	*nāzer*	Manager.
کار	*kār*	Work.

ملاحظه کول	mulāheza kawal	To inspect.
ورته به معلومه شي	warta ba malūma shi	He will find.
ضرور	zarūr	Certainly.
معافول (معاف کول)	muāfawal (muāf kawal)	To remit, forgive.
پهٔ یو مخ	puh yau makh	All in one time.
هله یا حمله	hala or hamla	Attack.
نهٔ صرف...بلکه	nuh serf..balké	Not only... but
سیزل یا سوزول	sézal or swazawal	To burn.
سوزیدل	swazédal	To be burnt.
تهٔ شکست ورکول	(ta) shikast warkawal	To defeat.
شکست خوړل	shikast khwaral	To be defeated.
بدرګه	badraga	Escort.
قام	qām	Tribe.
(سره) شپه کول	(sara) shpa kawal	To stay the night with.
وخت رانهٔ وهٔ	wakht rā ta nuh woh	I had no time.
خرڅ دَ پاره	khars da pāra	For sale.
تر اوسَ پوری	tar osa póré	Up to the present. till now.
تیر کول	tér kawal	To pass (time).
هیلئ	hilai	Duck.
جبه	jaba	Marsh.

گَشْت	gasht	Rounds, patrol
دَ چَرو ټوپك	da charō tōpak	Shot gun.
څوكۍ كول	saukai kawal	To guard.
مُلا بانگ مالې	mulā bāng mālé	At dawn.
نښه	nakha	Sign, mark.
نوے	naway	New.
زوړ	zōr	Old.

EXERCISE 22.

۱ راتله چه هغه کلی ته لاړشﺊ او دَ کلی ملک سره دَ رسد
بندوبست وکړﺉ   ۲ صاحب یو خان راغلی دی او تا سره لیدل غواړی
۳ یو کم عقل سړی خپل دښمن ته دومره نقصان نﮥ شی رسولی
لکه چه خپل ځان ته ئی رسوی   ۴ دا رښتیا خبره ده چه ناراستی
دَ نیستۍ تخم دی   ۵ نن دوه ځل ﻮﻫﺭ ته لاړم او راغلم مګر ستا
ورور م و نﮥ لید   ۶ ما هغه دفتر ته زغوښتلو او ورﻨﮥ م تپوس وکړ
چه پرون چه تﮥ پﮥ پرېښه بانډ وی نو چا پوری دَ خندلی وﻮ   ۷ صبا
سحر پﮥ پنځﮥ بجی زﮥ به ښکار له ﻏﻢ ته بﮥ راسره ﺷﻰ کﮥ نﮥ   ۸ پرون
م پﮥ اخبار کښی ولوستل چه ستا سو پلﻦ به کوه'ټ ته ﺷﻰ او بېرته
به نﮥ راﺷﻰ   ۹ کﮥ تﮥ پخپله نﮥ شی راتلی نو ورور دَ پﮥ خپل ځای
کښی راواستوه   ۱۰ قلموﻧﻪ وینښل او دَ دی کمری تولی کُرسۍ او
مېزوﻧﻪ صافول او پنځﮥ بجی دفتر بندول او بیا کنځی ناطر ته ورکول
ستا کار دی   ۱۱ که تحصیلدار دَ فصلونو ملاحظی دَ پاره راﺷﻰ نو
ورﺗﻪ به معلومه ﺷﻰ چه فصلوﻧﻪ ښﮥ نﮥ دی او ضرور به دَ
مالیی معافولو دَ پاره رپوت و کړی   ۱۲ که نول برﻏﯿﺪ
پﮥ یو مخ پﮥ دښمن بانډ هﻣﻠﻪ کړی زوﮯ نو نﮥ صرف

ورته شکستت به ئی ورکوی وُ بلکه دَ هغو کلی به ئی هم سیزلی وُر
۱۳ کۀ زۀ راتلیَ شوی نو پخپله به راغلی وم اودقام بدر کی سره به م
دَ وطن دوره کوی وَه اوشپه به م تاسره کوله مهر وخت راته نه وُه
۱۴ اسۀنه لۀ افغانستان نه راوستلیَ کیدری او پۀ پیښورکښی پۀ
گرانه بیعه خرخیدربی کله کله دا اسۀنه پنجاب ته هم د خرڅ دَ پاره
بیولی کیدری   ۱۵ هغه پاخیدو روان شو ویی و چه صبا به بیا راشم
مهر تراوسَ پوری را نۀ غی   ۱۶ مۀنر دوه دَ چرو تورپکونه خان
سره واخستل او دَ ښکار د پاره روان شۀ خلقو راته و چه پۀ جبو کښی
ډیری هیلی راغلی دی مۀنر تولو ورځ تیره کوه مهر یوه هم ونۀ لیدلیَ
شوه   ۱۷ زۀ خبر درکولو دَ پاره راغلیَ یم چه کۀ نن ستاسو کشت
دَ لاری څوکي کولو دَ پاره لا نۀ رو نو پۀ قلا باند به دَ قطب له دروی
نه حمله وشی   ۱۸ څلوښمښت ترَ څوانان خان سره واخله او لس
لس کس څای په څای په لر کینو تر ملا بازڼ مالی د په خپلو
خپلو څایونو ناست وی   ۱۹ که تر څلوررو بجو دَ دشمن ننه نه وی
نو رانخی د   ۲۰ ته د لکۀ نوکر څما ئی او کار د دَ بل کوی—

NOTE:—1. For *rāza chi* look up syntax
rule No. 30.

2. For the infinitive of purpose see syntax
rule No. 12.

VOCABULARY XXIV.

روان کیدل	*rawān kédal*	To start.
پوری کول	*pōré kawal*	To shut.
ما ور نه تپوس	*mā war na tapōs*	
وکرو	*wɔ kro*	I asked him.
کوم	*kum*	Which.

پس لۀ هغه	*pas luh hagha*	After that, later on, afterwards.
هم پۀ هغه ورځ	*hum puh hagha vraz*	On the very day.
لام	*lām*	Expedition.
جنګ	*jang*	Fight, war, battle.
تیره میاشت	*téra miāsht*	Last month.
تیندک خورل	*tindak khwaral*	To stumble.
خوږ کیدل	*khūg kédal*	To hurt.
ښپه	*khpa*	Foot, leg.
لالتین	*lāltain*	Lamp.
پۀ غلا تلل	*puh ghlā tlal*	To be stolen.
غلا	*ghlā*	Theft.
غل	*ghal*	Thief.
غلۀ	*ghluh*	Thieves
غلا کول	*ghlā kawal*	To Steal.
توره	*tūra*	Sword.
پیشقوزه	*peshqauza*	Killing knife.
توره پۀ لاس	*tūra puh lās*	With a sword in hand.
لختی	*lakhtay*	Water cut.
برتی کول	*barti kawal*	To enlist.
قافیله	*qāfela*	Caravan.
ماشی	*māshay*	A mosquito.
کټمل	*kātmal*	Bug.
ورږه	*vraga*	A flea.
میزری	*mézaray*	Dwarf palm.
بونر	*būnr*	String made of dworf palm.

منجور	*manjawar*	Shrine keeper.
امام	*imām*	Leader in prayer.
سيّد	*sayad*	Descendent of prophet.
ميان	*miān*	Descendent of any religious person.
سپږه	*spaga*	Louce.
پاتی کيدل	*pāté kédal*	To remain.
تير	*tér*	Last.
ميله	*maila*	Fair.
زيارت	*ziārat*	Shrine.
بل کول	*bal kawal*	To light.
مړ کول	*mar kawal*	To put out.

EXERCISE 23.

1. I gave him an order to go to that village
in the plain. 2. He started but an hour later
sent me a message that he could not go. 3
Please shut the door. 4. I asked him what
village he came from (Thou of which village
art?) 5. He said his name was Ahmad but
afterwards said it was Mohammad. 6. He died
on the same night. 7. All the crops have been
harvested. 8. Two of my sons had been
wounded in the Tirah expedition. 9. He
became a Jamadar on the 15th of last month.
10. The Colonel's horse stumbled this morning
but the Sahib was not hurt. 11. We fell off the

motor and I broke my leg (my leg was broken).
12. Light the lamp and do not put it out till
11 o'clock. 13. My house was burgled and all
my clothes were stolen. 14. As we opened the
door of the house I saw a man standing near the
tree with a sword in his hand. 15. The land of
the village is irrigated from this river by a small
water cut. 16. I am glad that the Adjutant
enlisted me on the very day. 17. I cannot shut
the door as I am ill. 18. In the winter and
spring the caravans go on Tuesdays and Fridays ; in the hot weather and rains they only go
on Fridays. 19. The jirga came to the Political
Agent on Sunday last, but as the Sahib was out
on tour, they had to stay in the city for the
night. 20. A fair is held every year at the
shrine of Kaka Sahib at Nowshera.

VOCABULARY XXV.

اوښ	ūkh	Camel.
ساروان	sārwān	Camelman.
ګنی	ganay	Sugar cane.
هيڅ فائده نشته	hiss fāida nishta	There is no use.
شولی	shōlé	Rice (Crop)
زميندار	zamindār	Land owner, farmer.
چلی کار	chalé kār	Cultivator.
مالیه	māliya	Land revenue.
زیات	ziāt	Excessive.

گوره	gura	Brown sugar (gurh)
خرڅول یا خرڅ کول	kharsawal or khars kawal	To sell, spend.
خرڅيدل یا خرڅ کيدل	kharsédal or khars kédal	To be sold, to be spent.
پنبه	punba	Cotton.
علاج	ilāj	Remedy, Cure.
روژه	rōjha	Fast or fasting.
ور	war	Door.
دَ رُوپو تيلي	da rūpo télai	Bag of money
پاتی کيدل	pāté kédal	To remain.
نيمه لار	nima lār	Half way.
کُوز کول	kūz kawal	To take down, take off.
کُوز کيدل	kūz kédal	To get down, dismount.
حجره	hujra	Guest house.
سلام اچول	salām achawal	To say salam to.
پۀ۔باندِ خوَرَول	puh-bāndé khurawal	To cause to eat.
پۀ۔باند سکَول	puh-bāndé skawal	To cause to drink or smoke.
خذمت	khizmāt	Service.
غرق اوده	gharq ūduh	Fast asleep.
هينږهار	henrahār	Neighing of horses.
خبر	khabar	Message or news.
کم	kam	Less, deficient.
دارُو	dārū	Medicine.

پېشنمی یا	*péshnamay*	The time of first
or	or	meal before dawn in
پیشمنی	*péshmany*	month of Ramzan.
گاډی	*gāday*	Cart, car.
دُعا	*dūaā*	Prayer.
مونځ کول	*mūnz kawal*	To pray.
اغوستل	*aghustal*	To wear etc.
اغوندم	*aghundam*	I wear (present.)
پیغمبر	*péghambar*	Prophet.
کوچ کول	*kōch kawal*	To march.
افسوس کول	*afsōs kawal*	To be sorry.
سینتری	*séntri*	Sentry.
پهره	*pehra*	Sentry-go.
ناگهانه	*nāgahāna*	By chance.
ناصاپه	*nāsāpuh*	Suddenly.
چپاؤ	*chapāo*	Surprise attack.
پۀ۔باندې ورختل	*puh-bāndé warkhatal*	To invade.
(سره) مقابله کول	*(sara) muqā-bela kawal*	To withstand.
هم هغسی	*hum haghasé*	Still, in the same manner.
تخت	*takht*	Throne.
فقیر	*faqir*	Beggar.
عبادت	*ibādat*	Worship.
پۀ۔باندې لاس پوری کول	*puh bāndé lās pōré kawal*	To start, commence.
سار فصلونه	*sār faslūna*	Withering crops.

مينه	maina	House.
سترګه	starga	An eye.
سر	sar	Head.
مخ	makh	Face.
خوله	khuluh	Mouth.
مرئ	marai	Throat.
څټ	sat	Back of neck.
تندَی	tanday	Forehead.
غوږ	ghwag	Ear.
وینتۀ	wékhtuh	Hair (M. S. and P.)
لاس	lās	Hand.
ښپه	khpa	Foot or leg.
ګوته	gōta	Finger.
پوزه	pōza	Nose.
زړه	zruh	Heart.
تبز	téz	Fast, sharp.
پۀ بانډ اواز کول	puh-bāndé awāz kawal	To challenge.
(تۀ) اواز کول	(ta) awāz kawal	To call out to.
پۀ بانډ دز کول	puh-bāndé daz kawal	To fire at.
پۀ ټکی	puh taki	Instantly.
ګیر کول	gér kawal	To surround.
مدت راغو ښتل	madat rāghukhtal	To call for help (reinforcements).
تار	tār	Wire, telegram.
شیشه	shisha	Helio.

جنډئ *jandai*   Flag, signalling.

مخبر *mukhber*   Informer, spy.

ضمانت *zamānat*   Security.

ضامن *zāman*   Surety.

منظور کول *manzūr kawal* To sanction.

EXERCISE 24.

١ ساروان نا جوړ شو قافلی پسی ونه رسیدلی شو ٢ اوس
دَ ګنو پهٔ فصل ، کښی هیڅ فائیده نښته ځکه چه مالیه یی ډیره زیاته ده
اوګوره ډیره ارزانه ده ٣ مونږ له پکاردی چه هغه فصلونه وکرو چه ګران
ګران خرڅیږی پکار ؤو چه مونږو سکال پنبه کرلی وی ٤ مونږ یی
ډیر علاج وکړ مګر دَ روژی دَ میاشتی پهٔ دریمه ورځ مړ شو ٥ دَ
دوکان ور ییٔ پوری کړ چه تلو نو دَ رویو تیلئ ورنه هم پهٔ هغه ځای
پاتی شوه ٦ چه نیمی لاری ته ورسیدم نو له ګاډی نه ئی کوز
کړم ځکه چه ځما ټکس خالی تر پیر پوری وُو هلته یوی حجری ته
ورغلم سلام مې وا چاؤه کیڼا ستم دَ حجری خاوند را باند ووډئ وخوروله
چلم ئی را باند وسکولو نو راته ئی ویل چه ما ته نور څهٔ خدمت
وی نو هم زهٔ ورته تیاریم ٧ که دَ کلی خلق غرق ارده نهٔ وی نو
خمونږو دَ اسونو هینوهار به ئی اوریدلی وُه ٨ صاحب که دا انعام
د پهٔ ما پیروز وی نو راته به د دَ داری دَ راتلو خبر راکوی وُه
وَ بادشاه لهٔ تخت نه کوز شو او فقیر ته ئی ووچه راڅه ځما پهٔ ځای
اوس ته که کینه پخپله یی دَ فقیرانو جامی واغوستی پهٔ جماعت کښی
کیناست دَ خدای وک پهٔ عبادت ئی لس پوری کړ ١٠ زهٔ نوزوئ
پسی لهٔ وطن نه راغلیؔ یم مګر اوس خمونږو دَ علاقی برتی بنده ده
١١ ګله چه ووډئ وخورم نو ستا څقی بد ولوم ١٢ که دیڼی
کمشنر صاحب دَ فصلونه ملاحظی کولو دَ پاره راتلیؔ نو تر اوس بد

راغلیَ وّه ارمان دیَ چه یوشل خو ئی ٠ څمونږ دا سار فصلونه لیدلیَ
وی ۱۳ کار را باند دومره زیات دی چه کلم ناکلم م دوه چلی
کاران وسائل او خوا منخوا به وزله مینی هم د اوسیدلو د پاره ورکوم
۱۴ ملک سنگه یوه اسپه دَ چه یو سترګه ئی دَه (یا پۀ یوه سترګۀ رنده
دَه) ولی داسی تیزه ده چه په دری سرَ ئی هم نۀ ورکوی ما خپل
آس پۀ ملک باند پۀ سل روپیَ خرڅ کړ ۱۵ اول سنتری پۀ غل
باند اواز وکړ او بیائی وویشت پۀ ټکی ئی مړ کړ ۱۶ ستا خر
خامن دی لۀ ټولونه مشر څوی د دَ څو کالو دیَ او تۀ دَ څو کالو
نوکر ئی ۱۷ ناګهانه دَ سرکار فوځ پۀ قلا باند حمله وکړه او دَ جرمن
فوځ ئی په کښی ګیر کړ فوځ مدت راغونډلو دَ پاره ټیلیفون ورکړ مګر
دَ سرکار فوځ ټول تارونه پری کړی ؤو بیائی زر شیشه ورکړه او جنډیَ
ئی هم ورته ووهله ۱۸ مؤنږ خپل منخبر ته ویل چه مغ کښی مغ کښی
څه مګر هغه پۀ یوه سترګه مغذور ؤه نۀ شو تلیَ ۱۹ کرنیل صاحب یو
پښتون سړیَ دیَ مُدام پۀ خپلو سپاهیانو ولړ وی ۲۰ که ورشی
او وګوری نو صاحب به راغلیَ وی او ستا ضمانت به ئی منظور
کړی وی

VOCABULARY XXVI.

بی لۀ طلب نه	bé luh talab na	Without pay.
دَشفارس کول	da-shafāras kawal	To recommend.
کمان افسر	kaman afsar	Officer Commanding
(سره) اتفاق کول	(sara) ittefāq kawal or manal	To agree.

هغۀ وليدل	haghuh wo lidal	He saw.
ما ته معلومه شوه	mā ta mālūma shwa	I found out.
خَتل	khatal	To climb.
پوَره كول	pūra kawal	To complete.
سر	sar	Head, top, end.
گَتل	gatal	To win.
بيلل	bélal	To lose.
ها كي	hāki	Hockey.
لوبى كول	lōbé kawal	To play.
لوبه	lōba	Game.
كوت گارت	kōt gārat	Quarter Guard.
تماچه	tamācha	Pistol or revolver.
بدى	badi	Feud.
اورم كال	ōram kāl	Year before last.
پۀ ښۀ شان سره	puh khuh shān sara	Well, satisfactorily.
پورى غاړه	pōré ghāra	Far bank.
راپورى غاړه	rā pōré ghāra	Near bank.
ساتل	sātal	To engage, (servant) keep.
نيول	niwal	To engage (barrister).
كيږى	kégee	Ago, becomes (present of kédal
غوږ ددى	ghwag dé day	Are you listening ?
تيريدل	térédal	To pass by.
اغوستلى وه	aghustalay woh	Was wearing (lit : had worn.)

خاکی یا خر	khāki or khar	Khaki, grey.
ذان پټ کول	zān paṭ kawal	To take cover.
تر بلَ حکمپُوری	tar bala hukma pōré	Till next order.
وادۀ	wāduh	Marriage.
وعدہ کول	wada kawal	To promise.
مال	māl	Cattle.
څرول	sarawal	To graze (transitive.)
ورشو	warsho	Grazing ground.
ګورہ	gora !	Look here !
يو څو	yau so	A few,
دامان	dāmān	Summer pasture ground.
منډۍ	mandai	Market.
ګانړۍ	gānrai	Sugar cane press.

EXERCISE 25.

1. What do you want ? 2. I want ten days leave, without pay. 3. I will recommend you to the Commanding Officer and will send for you if he agrees. 4. The boy fell into the well and saw that he could not climb up. 5. Can you go across the river ? 6. There is no boat, the river is deep so how can I cross ? 7. Can you recognise this man ? Yes he is the man whom I saw in the bazar yesterday. 8. Sultan Mahmud went to Ghazni and left his sardars to complete the necessary work, 9. We found

that the enemy were on the top of the hill. 10. Every. one of the boys got 50/- rupees as a reward for winning the hockey match. 11. A thief was running towards the Guard Room and the sentry shot him dead with a revolver. 12 He had a feud with Mohmands, because they killed his father the year before last. 13. Can you read and write ? 14. I cannot read but in two months I shall be able to read well. 15. Do you see that big tree on the near bank of the river ? That is our camp. 16. Look here, young man I engaged you as Mali on 15/- rupees a month, a few months ago. 17. Do you hear ? 18. I saw a man passing by here wearing a khaki coat. 19. The sepoys will have to dig trenches and take cover till next order. 20. I have heard that the King of Afghanistan is coming to Peshawar.

VOCABULARY XXVI1.

ښۀ ټوپک ویشتل	*khuh tōpak wishtal*	To shoot (well.)
نښه	*nakha*	Mark.
دزکول	*daz kawal*	To fire.
سیلاب	*sélab*	Flood.
نُقصان	*nuqsān*	Loss.
(ته) بد بد کتل	*(ta) bad bad katal*	To stare at.

بی خود	bé khuda	Senseless.
پۀ خود	puh khud	In senses
سترزی غَرَول	stargé gharawal	To open eyes.
سترزی پټی کوه	stargé paté kra	Shut your eyes !
خولۀ وازه کوه	khuluh wāza kra	Open your mouth !
خولۀ پیچی کوه	khuluh piché kra	Shut your mouth !
غوږ کیږده	ghwag kégda	Lit. place ear. } Listen !
پروت	prōt	Lying.
خپل خپلوان	khpal khpalwān	Relations.
گیر چاپیره	gérchāpéra	All round.
پیشکی	péshki	Advance (of money)
پټکَی پۀ سرکول	patkay puh sar kawal	To wear a pagri.
پڼی پۀ ښپو کول	panré puh khpo kawal	To wear shoes.
دستانی پۀ لاس کول	dastāné puh lās kawal	To wear gloves.
سور کیدل	sōr kédal	To mount.
خیر خیریت	khér kheriat	All well.
بالکل	bélkul	Absolutely, entirely
تباه کول یا برباد کول	tabāh kawal or barbād kawal	To ruin.

پۀ‌باند اعتبار کول	*puh-bāndé ittebār kawal*	
پۀ‌باند یقین کول	*puh-bāndé yaqin kawal*	To trust.
پۀ‌باند باور کول	*puh-bāndé bāwar kawal*	
رشتیا	*rishtiā*	Truth.
دروغ	*darōgh*	Lie.
غلط فهمی	*ghalat fahmi*	Misunderstanding.
پۀ کلی باند داره پریوتله	*puh kali bāndé dāra préwatala*	The village was raided.
پۀ کلی باند جرم پریوت	*puh kali bāndé jurm préwat*	The village was fined.
چغه	*chagha*	Pursuit party.
مازدیګر	*māzdigar*	Early evening (between 3 o'clock and sunset).
ماخښین	*māspakhin*	Afternoon.
ما خښتن	*māskhutan*	Night prayer time (between 8 o'clock and midnight.
پۀ لاس راتلل	*puh lās rātlal*	To come in hand, procure.
تحقیقات کول	*tahqiqāt kawal*	To enquire.
تفتیش	*taftish*	Police enquiries.
معلومه شوه	*malūma shwa*	It turned out.
کلیوال	*kaliwāl*	Villager.
غفلت	*ghaflat*	Negligence.

(تئ) لار نيول	*ta lār niwal*	To ambush.
خرا په خبره ده	*kharāpa khabara dah*	It is a bad bussiness.
ډير ځل	*dér zal*	Many times.
د-پرواه كول	*da-parwāh kawal*	To take notice of.
هيڅ پروا نشته	*hés parawāh nishta*	Never mind.
هيڅ باك نشته	*hés bāk nishta*	Never mind.
پهم كول	*paham kawal*	To take care.
سپين سرى ښځه	*spin saré khaza*	White headed woman, old woman.
(پورى) خندل	*pōré khandal*	To laugh at.
لۀ-نه-روان كيدل	*luh-na rawān kédal*	To start, leave, set out from.

EXERCISE 26.

۱ ما دكلى ملك گواهي دپاره ډير ځل راوغوښت مگر رانۀ غیَ ۲ افريديان ډير نۀ توپك ولى هغوىهره ورځ په خپل خپل كلى كيس په نښو باند ليزى كوى ۳ په جنڭ كيس څمونږرو څلور تنَ سپاهيان ووژلَیَ شول ۴ دكور خاوند رو چه ما درى تنَ دارة ماران پيژندلى دى ۵ په سيند كيس سيلاب دىَ ځكه ورنه پوريوتل گران كارديَ ۶ ددى كتاب په لوستلو كيس ستا ځۀ نقصان دىَ ۷ ولى بدبد گورى ۸ لۀ اس نه پريوتم ېپه م ماته شوه بى خودَ شوم چه پۀ خود شوم اوسنرگىم وغړوڼى نوبۀ هسيتال كيس په يو كپ باند پروتوم اوخبل خپلوان رانۀ كير چاپيره ناسترُو اوبى ژرل ۱۰ دااس روپيي پيښكى واخله اونورى بۀ بيادركرم

١١ آزمُوبى ئُى وَسوسه يَئِكَى ئُى پہ سر پرو بوتوُنهئى پہ شپوكول
دستانى یى پہ لاس کوی اوبہ اس سورشہ لپر ١٢ تهُوائى چہ فصلونه
موسَ.رکال شمهٔنه دی پہ باره کښس اوبه کمی دی تسکلو دپاره هم
نهُراخَی مهر پرُوُن خان راغلیَ وَه هغهٔ خو ویل چه ټول خيرخيريت دی
فصلونه بالکل شہ دی اوبه ببری دی ١٣ صاحب موُنَ.ر شهٔ ووايؤ
چه ناپی موپروی نوټول کلَی سو پروی نو ١٤ پہ کلی دا پره پريوته
دوه کوردُنهیی لوُت کول چغهٔ وریسی ووته خو مازدیهر ببرته راغله
ښکه چه دا پره اران پہ لاس ورنه رغلل ١٥ پوس تحقیقات وُپر
معلومه شوه چه دا د کليوالو غفلت دی ښکه ور باندِ دوه زر روپی جُرم
پريوت ١٦ هغه پہ ديرِ ربرِ سره لهٔ کور نه را ووتلو ١٧ ښلوروتنو اپريدو
ورته لار نيولی وَه ټولی جامی ئُی ، تر واخستی ١٨ صوبيدار صاحب
دا دَ دی دارو ديره خراپه خبره ده ۔ ما تهٔ ديرِ ښل پوه کوی ئُی چه
هره شپه دَ خپلی کپنی سره پہ وطن کښس ګشت کوه ۔ مهر تهٔ ښما دَ
خبری هيڅ پروا نهٔ کوی ١٩ سپین سری شنگی تانوه دار پوری
وخندل او تر روانه شوه ٢٠ صاحب که تهٔ راغلیَ نه وی نو زهٔ به ئُی
وژلَی وم ۔

VOCABULARY XXVIII.

ليونَی	léwanay	Mad.
ليونَی سپَی	léwanay spaϳ	Mad dog.
اوچ کول	ūch kawal	To dry.
لوُند	lūnd	Wet.
نور	nwar	Sun, sunshine.
سپوُږمَی	spōgmai	Moon
تروُږمَی	tarōgmai	Moonless.

ستورى	*stōray*	A star.
دير ساعت	*dér sāat*	Much longer, for a long time.
دومره ساعت	*dōmra sāat*	So much longer.
نيول يا گرفتار كول	*niwal* or *géréftār kawal*	To arrest.
پۀ موقعه باند	*puh mōqa bāndé*	On the spot.
پاڅيدل	*pāsédal*	To get up.
هسى تازهيروى	*hasé tā zāhirawee*	They are only pulling your leg !
ټوقى كول	*tōqé kawal*	To joke.
مږه	*maga*	Rat.
ټكره	*tukra*	Piece.
پريږده چه لارشى	*prégda chi lārshee*	Let him go !
چمن	*chaman*	Grass lawn.
كله چه	*kala chi*	As soon as.
اواز	*awāz*	Sound, voice.
بيگل	*bigal*	Bugle.
فوځ	*fauz*	Troops, Army.
(ته) چوټى وركول يا شړل	*ta chuti war-kawal* or *sharal*	To dismiss.
جوارى كول	*jawāri kawal*	To gamble.
جوارگر	*jawārgar*	Gambler.
لۀ نه قرض اخستل	*luh-na qarz akhistal*	To borrow.
ته قرض وركول	*ta qarz war-kawal*	To lend.

خما پۀ هغۀ باند لس روپئی دی	*zamā puh haghuh bāndé las rupai di*	He owes me ten rupees.
دَ هغۀ پۀ ما باند لس روپئی دی	*da haghuh puh mā bāndé las rupai di*	I owe him ten rupees.
بنیا	*bania*	Bunia.
أمید دی	*omaid day*	I hope.
دَ کټ جامی	*da kat jāmé*	Sleeping suit.
فرش	*farsh*	Floor.
شړل	*sharal*	To drive out, turn out.
جرمانه کول	*jarmāna kawal*	To fine.
ویښ کول	*wikh kawal*	To wake up (transitive.)
تر هغۀ وخت پوری	*tar hagha wakhta poré*	Then, till that time
اودۀ کیدل	*úduh kédal*	To sleep.
خوب	*khōb*	Sleep.
خوب لیدل	*khōb lidal*	To dream.
غسل	*ghusal*	Bath.
وینځل	*winzal*	To wash.
ټوله رښتیا خبره	*tōla rikhtia khabara*	The whole truth.

EXERCISE 27.

1. He came out of the door and ordered me to shoot the mad dog 2. Take all the

tables and chairs out of this room and dry them in the sun. 3. The jamadar went into the room and did not stay any longer. 4. Do not laugh at him 5. A boy was sitting on the road-side crying, a man came up on him and asked him why was he weeping. 6. The Police arrested him on the spot ond produced him before the Magistrate. 7. He got up and went out, saying that he would come again tomorrow 8. The old man wrapped the rat in the piece of cloth and took it to the house. 9. Untie the horse and let it go to that grass field. 10. As soon as the horse heard the sound of the bugle he ran towards our troops. 11, I dismissed my servant, because he had lost 200/- rupees in gambling, which he had borrowed from the re-gimental Bania. 12. I hope you did not mind seeing me in my sleeping suit. 13. The Colonel found a sentry sleeping on guard, and shot him dead with his revolver. 14. Jemadar! tell these people that if any one spits on the floor I shall certainly turn him out and fine him five rupees. 15. Wake me at 7 o'clock if I am still asleep. 16. I could not sleep the whole night, because the old man was coughing all the time. 17. The sepoys used to bathe in the spring near the fort. 18. If you had sent for the bearer, he would have told you the whole

truth. 19. Turn to the left. 20. What a
fool you are !

VOCABULARY XXIX

خيني	ziné	From, some.
ورو	vro	Slow.
داک	dāg	Post, mail.
هوائي جهاز	hawāi jehāz	Airship, aeroplane.
پشتو	pukhtu	Modesty, Pushtu.
پشتون	pukhtūn	Modest, Pathan.
پهٔ باند اودرېدل	puh-bāndé odrédal	To take the side of.
سدام پهٔ خپلو سپاهيانو باند ولر وي	mudām puh khpalo spā hiyāno bandé wlār wi	He always takes the side of his soldiers.
تيښته	tékhtā	Flight.
خلاصيدل	khlāsédal	To escape.
معلوميدل	malūmédal	To be seen.
پهٔ پهم سره	puh paham sara	Carefully.
کتل	katal	To look, examine.
ملاحظه کول	mulāhéza kawal	To inspect.
ما ته ياد دی	mā ta yād dee	I remember.
بهانه	bahāna	Pretence.
(ته) تندی تريو کول	(ta) tanday triw kawal	To frown at.
لرل	laral	To have.

دنیا	*dunia*	World. wealth.
آخرت	*ākherat*	The day of judgement.
بدله	*badala*	Revenge.
غضب	*ghazab*	Rage.
پۀ توقو توقو کښی	*puh tōqo tōqo ké*	Jokingly.
قربان دِ شم	*qurbān dé sham*	May I be sacrificed !
بار	*bār*	Load.
قچره	*qachara*	Mule.
پۀ دی حساب سره	*pa dé hisab sara*	At this rate.
نور پریواتۀ	*nwar prewātuh*	Sunset, west.
نور خاتۀ	*nwar khātuh*	Sunrise, East.
دره	*dara*	Valley (over mountain).
غاښی	*ghākhay*	Pass.
پۀ بانډ گمان کول	*puh-bāndé gumān kawal*	To suspect.

EXERCISE 28.

۱ یو مارغۀ دَ بل مارغۀ څښنی لؤر غواړی ولی هغه ترِ دَ مرغانو
دستؤر غواړی ۲ دا سړی ِ پیژنه کله چه زۀ پۀ جذبت کښی
اپریدو و بیولی ڕم نو څما یی ډیر خذمت کړی ۳ وه صاحب تا تۀ
خو معلومه ده چه زۀ پۀ لیکلو لوستلو نۀ پوهیږم نو ستا چقی راتۀ یو
بل سړی ولوسته ۴ که تا توخلی نۀ وی نو نور مرغان به د هم
ویشتلی ڕو مهر بیا هم تۀ ډیر نۀ توریک ولی ۵ که رشتیا وایم نَ

هر چا بدی شم که دروغ وايم نو دَ ملکَ م شرمي ۲ زۀ لرکوټي پۀ
غوبرو درؤند يم ورو خبره نه اورم ۷ اوس ياڼ پۀ هوائي جهاز
کښ ښئ راځي ۸ زۀ پۀ رساله کښ برتي کيدل غوارم دَ رنګووت
افسر دفتر راته وښيه ۹ زۀ پوه شوم چه پۀ ټيښتۀ نۀ خلاصيرم
۱۰ دا آس م پۀ شکل خوښ دمي خو کۀ ښکاربري ۱۱ جرنيل
صاحب راغلو ټول ښيزونه يې پۀ پهم سره وکتل دير خوشحال شۀ چه
تلو نو وي ليکل چه هر شي دير نۀ اوصاف دمي پۀ دريمه مياشت
به بيا ملاحظه کوم ۱۲ ولی چوټی اخلی؟ مدام ستا پلار مږ وي
ستا هير دی ولی ما ته نۀ ياد دی چه دَ تبر اکتوبر پۀ پنهلسم
تاريخ دَ هم پۀ دی بهانه چوټی اخستی وه ۱۳ غوبرونه بۀ
دَ وباسم ۱۴ پښتون له شاباشی ورکوه نو کار به درله پۀ نۀ شان
سره کوي ۱۵ او کۀ تندی دِ ورته تريؤ کړ نو دَ نۀ کار آميد ترمۀ کوه
۱۶ کله سرمي خاندي او کله ژاړی ۱۷ بادشاه دَ غضب جامی
واغوستی په تخت کيناست ۱۸ وزير په ټوقو ټوقو کښ بادشاه ته
ورو چه قربان دَ شم نن يخنی وای چه بيهاله به دَ فرخ داسی
خدمت وکړم چه صبا له به بادشاه او وزيران. دَ خپلو خپلو اسونو
خدمتونه پڅيله کوي ۱۹ نو اوس زرشه دا بارونه له اوښانو نه
کوز کړه پۀ قچرو يی واچوه پۀ دی حساب به تر نور پريواتۀ پوری
له درمي نه و نۀ څوړ ۲۰ تانهدار دَ کور لۀ خاوند نه تپوس وکړ چه
چاړوبل کوی ئی او په چا باند ستا ګمان دمي ـ

VOCABULARY XXX.

پۀ يو کلي کښ *puh yau kali ké* In a certain village.

تر اوسَ پوری *tar osa pōré* Up to the present, so far.

خما ښکار خوښ دى	zamā khkār khwakh day	I am fond of shooting.
پۀ خطا	puh khatā	Accidentally.
لۀ قصدَ	luh qasda	On purpose.
قسم خورل	qasam khwaral	To take oath.
سوګند خورل	saugand khwaral	To take oath.
ايران	Irān	Persia.
سيلاب	sélāb	Flood.
تناؤ	tanāw	Boat rope.
بېړۍ پۀ تناؤ دَه	bérai puh tanāw dah	The boat is pulled by a rope.
چا ئ	chāi	Tea.
پۍ	pai	Milk.
چيني، misri	chini, misri	Sugar.
هګۍ يا ها	hagai or hā	Egg, Eggs.
ها سپينوَل	hā spinawal	To shell an egg.
ختل	khatal	To climb.
دارۀ مار	dāra mār	Raider, dacoit.
شوکه کول	shūka kawal	To loot, rob.
شوکمار	shūkmār	Robber.
خوا و شا	khwā-o-shā	Neighbourhood, vicinity.
ګنړ ځنګل	ganr zangal	Dense jungle.
رنګۍ واښۀ	rangay wākhuh	Thin grass.
وېرېدل	veyarédal	To fear.

كه ستا نصيب به	kuh stā nasib	
وي	khuh wi	If you are lucky.
رنګى باران	rangay bārān	Slight rain.
را ګرزيدل	rā garzédal	To return.
بيرته راتلل	biarta rātlal	To come back.
ساده	sāda	Simple.
غلطى كول	ghalati kawal	To make a mistake.
رسيد	rasid	Receipt.

EXERCISE 29.

1. In a certain village there was a clever boy, who was so clever that his father said that up to the present such a clever boy had never been. 2. He used to read books and newspapers and never played with bad boys. 3. In the city of Peshawar there was a king who had two sons and three daughters. 4. The younger son was fond of shooting. 5. One day he went out shooting to Adam Khel pass and was accidently shot by his own gun. 6. His father took an oath that he would kill all the servants who came with him from Persia. 7. The Kabul river was in flood (in the river of Kabul flood was) and people crossed in a boat which was pulled across by a rope. 8. On the 15th of June of that year I was enlisted as a Jemadar and three years afterwards I became a Subadar. 9. Will you drink tea ? 10. I will eat some

eggs, shell one for me. 11. Put very little sugar in the tea. 12. No, do not put in any milk, I do not like it. 13. Subadar Sahib! take your company and climb the hill. 14. The dacoits appeared to be in great fear of the Indian troops and whenever they heard of any in the vicinity, they at-once moved away to dense jungle or jowar crops. 15. His father died when he was only three years old. 16. When he was very young, he used to drive birds from the field. 17. If you are lucky the raiding gang will probably return on that road this morning. 18. The people of this country are very simple. 19. They are ruined by their Khans and Maliks. 20. You made a great mistake in that you did not take any receipt from him.

VOCABULARY XXXI.

دربار *darbār*		Darbar.
دَ بادشاه پۀ منډو *da bādshāh puh khpo prewat*		Fell at the king's feet.
پۀ ژړا شو *puh jharā sho*		Began to weep.
موسم *mōsam*		Season.
اکثر *aksar*		Generally.
حوالات *hawālāt*		Custody.

لږ ډير	*lag dér*	Somewhat.
ټول کول	*tōl kawal*	To collect.
جمع کول	*jama kawal*	To collect.
حاجت	*hājat*	Need.
حاجتمند	*hājatmand*	Needy.
خنځل ويستل	*zangal wéstal*	To take out weeds.
ورو کی	*wrūkay*	Small.
وارۀ	*wāruh*	Small (M. Plu).
زيات	*ziāt*	More (in comparison)
بی سبب	*bé sababa*	Without reason.
مواجب	*mājéb*	Pay, allowance.
ذمه وار	*zémā wār*	Responsible.
ذمه	*zéma*	Responsibility.
پۀ خوا زمانۀ کښې	*puh khwā zamāna ké*	Formerly.
مشر	*mashar*	Elder.
سپین ګيری	*spin giray*	Grey beard, elder.
پړ	*par*	Loser.
وړ	*war*	Winner.
فريق	*fariq*	Party.
سوره	*swara*	A girl in exchange.
رواج	*rewāj*	Custom.
شاباش	*shābāsh*	Well done.
نمک حلال	*namak halāl*	Loyal.
نمک حرام	*namak harām*	Disloyal.
بال بچ	*bāl bach*	Children, family.
ماشوم	*māshūm*	Child.

زۀ دَ هغۀ دَ لاسَ تذگ یم	zuh da haghuh da lāsa tang yam	I am worried by him.
خَما لاس تذگ دیَ	zamā lās tang day	I have no money.
دَ هغۀ کارجوړ دیَ	da haghuh kār jōr day	He is flourishing.
اوراول	aurawal	To announce, to cause to hear,
سپکوالیَ	spakwālay	An insult, disgrace.
سپک کول	spak kawal	To insult.
مرګ	marg	Death.
سزا	sazā	Punishment.
خپیمانَ کیدل	khpémāna kédal	To repent.
رعیت	rait	Subject (to Govt.)
ارام	arām	Rest.
کوشش	kōshash	Try.
زلزله	zalzala	Earth quake.
لوټی لوټی کول یا	lūté lūté kawal or	To destroy.
بر باد کول	barbād kawal	
لوټه یا غونډه یا	lūta or ghunda,	
تیګه	tiga	Clod of earth.
بهادر	bahādar	Brave.
عمر	umar	Age.
نیت	niat	Intention.
مسافر	musāfar	Traveller.
منت کول	menat kawal	To entreat.

ولی	walé	But, why.
هیڅ فائده ونۀ شوه	hiss fāida wo nuh shwa	No use.
خیال	khyāl	Thought.
خیرخو دی؟	khér kho day	Is all well ? Can I do anything for you ?
نظر	nazar	Sight.
پۀ_باند نظر لریدل	puh-bāndé nazar lagédal	To see.
پۀ_باند مین کیدل	puh-bāndé main kédal	To fall in love.
مسکی کیدل	maskay kédal	To smile.
فائده	fāida	Use, benefit.
پۀ نظر راتلل	puh nazar rātlal	To come into sight.
و فادار	wafādār	Faithful.
بی وفا	béwafā	Faithless.
ویریا	wéryā	Free, gratis.
تنګول	tangawal	To worry.
سوال	swāl	Question.
کانړی مات کول	kānray māt kawal	To declare war, (lit to break stone.)
کانړی کیخودل	kānray kékhodal	To make a truce.

EXERCISE 30.

۱ یوه ورځ یو فقیر پۀ دربار رانغوت دَ بادشاه پۀ غیږو پریوت او پۀ

ژړا شو ۲ غلو دروازه ها ته کړه او ټول مال ئی بوت ۳ دَ کلو

ملکان اکثر پۀ دې موسم کښې پۀ حوالات کښې وي دَ دې
سبب دا دی چه دې فصلونه نۀ نۀ کېږري څکه خلق مالیه نۀ شي
ورکولی او که څۀ لږه ډېره ټوله کړي نو ملک پخپله ورته حاجتمند
وي وئی خوري   ۴ مالي ته م وچه دَ څذَهل وېستو دَ پاره دري
وارۀ واړۀ هلکان وساته ولي چه طلب ئې دَ پنېتو پنتو رویو نه زیاتنۀ
وي   ۵ جرګۍ پولتل صاحب ته وو چه که تۀ بي سبب څموزبر
مواجب بند وې نو آئینده دَ پاره دا آمید مۀ لره چه مونبر به ستا خدمت
وکړو که په لارو شوکي کېږري یا په کلو داري پېوتي نو مونبر ذمهوار
نۀ یؤ او هر رنګ مال چه څمونبر علاقې ته راوستلی شي نو پۀ
بوزڅه به ئی در نۀ کړؤ   ۶ پۀ خوا زمانه کښې به چه دَ پنتو پۀ
سر بدي وشوه نو دَ قام مشرانو به جرګه وکړه او کوم فریق به چه
پوتو نو دَ ور فریق دَ پاره به ي ور باند سوره کېنوه مهر دا رواج
اوس کم دی څکه چه پۀ دې خبره بدي زیاتېږري   ۷ چه دا ئې
واوریدل نو نوکر ئی راوبللو او ورته ئې وو چه شاباش تۀ ډېر نمک
حلال سړی ئی که تۀ مهتي نو ستا بال بچ له به زۀ روټي جامه او
دیرش روپۍ میاشت پنس ورکوم ۷۰ افریدیان چه پۀ بدي کښې تذڅ
شي او یا دَ فصل وخت راشي نو کانړی کېږي دي   ۹ اورزکزیب
دَ هندوانو دَ لس تذڅ شو نو حکم ئی واور اوۀ چه که هر هندوۀ دَ
اسلام سپکوالی وکړ نو دَ مرګ سزا به ورکوی کېږري   ۱۰ بادشاه هغه
دی چه دَ خپل رعیت دَ ازام دَ پاره کوشش کوي   ۱۱ دا دا سی زلزله
وه چه پۀ یو ملک کښې ئی ډېر لوي لوي کم سړي نتتي ما شومان
سپي چرګان ټول دَ خاورو لاند شول   ۱۲ هونبیار سړي هیچری
بهادر نۀ وي   ۱۳ مونبر دعا کوؤ چه نوی بادشاه له خدای لوي
عمر ورکوي او غریب هندوستان ته یی نیت پۀ خیر شي   ۱۴ چه دَ

نهر درواژی ته ورسید نو درواننچی دَ ننه پری نه نود مساپر بير ملت
وكوخو هيئ فائيده و نهٔ شوه خله لاړ دَ سړك خوا ته كيناست
۱۵ درواژه لری شوه او یوه بنله راووته او فقیر ته یی و با نن ولی
مسلی وختی راغلی ۱۶، چه خما نظر ور باند ولرید نو ورباند مین
شوم ۱۷ فقیر راته وكتل او مسكی شو ۱۸ صاحب دا وفادار
سپی كه لاند اوده وه ۱۹ كادی په لس نیمی بجی روانیدوی
۲۰ مامهٔ تذكوه دومره وخت راته نشته چه ستا دَ سوال دَ جواب دركوم-

MISCELLANEOUS COLLOQUIAL SENTENCES III.

Can you recognize this man ?	Dā saray péjhandalay shé ?
Why cannot you recognize him ?	Walé yé nuh pejhané ?
Do you not know his father ?	Tuh da haghuh plār nuh péjhané ?
What is the latest news to-day ?	Nan suh tāza khabar day ?
How old are you ?	Tuh da so kālo yé ?
Are you married ?	Wāduh dé karay day ?
How long have you been in the service.	Da so kālo naukar yé ?
Take this recruit to the hospital and tell the doctor to let me know what is wrong with him.	Dā rangūt haspatāl ta bóza aw dāktar ta wō wāya chi mā khabar kra chi pa duh suh chal shaway day.
That hill is not within the range of our guns.	Dagha ghar zamūng da tōpo da gōlo lāndé nuh rāzee.

Let him write another petition and put it on the Sahib's table.	*War ta wō wāya chi bala arzi wo likee, aw da sāhib puh méz bāndé yé kégdee.*
We did not notice, but there was a big forest on our rear.	*Mūng wo nuh lidalo kho zamūng shā tā yau lōi zangal woh.*
Are the roads good? are supplies obtainable?	*Lāré khé dee? rasad múndalay shi?*
I will dine out to-night.	*Bégāla zamā rōtai bāhar dah.*
Why did you kill this man?	*Walé dé dā saray wō wajhalo.*
Who told you to kill him?	*Chā darta wayali woo chi wō yé wajhna?*
Why did you not take revenge on him?	*Walé dé war na badal wā nuh khistalo.*
Can you shoot well?	*Tuh khuh tōpak wōlé; kuh na?*
I did not see him.	*Mā hagha wō nuh lidalo.*
Did you not see me in the motor yesterday afternoon?	*Parūn māspakhin dé puh mōtar ké wō nuh lidalam?*
I greeted you but you did not answer.	*Mā darta salām wo kro kho tā jawab rā nuh kar.*
Have you heard that the Aka Khel are going to attack the fort?	*Aurédali dé di chi Aka khél puh qalā bāndé hala kawee.*
Go out of my house.	*Zamā da kōra wōza.*

You go and find out somewhere else.	*Lārsha aw bal charta yé malūm kra* or *wo mūma.*
Do not laugh at him.	*War pōré muh khānda.*
The dog barked but when I threw a stone at him, he ran towards the lane.	*Spi woghapal, kho chi puh kānri mé wo wishtalo no da kūsé taraf ta wozghalédalo.*
The thief jumped into the street and got up by the ladder	*Ghal kūsé ta wo dangal aw puh andrapāya bāndé woкhatalo.*
Have you seen him ?	*Tā hagha lidalay day ?*
Why cannot you cross ?	*Walé pōré watalay nuh shé ?*
The Colonel fell off his horse and broke his arm	*Karnail sahib luh ass na préwato aw lās yé māt sho.*
I cannot climb the hill.	*Zuh puh ghar khatalay nuh sham.*
I left the book on the table	*Kitab ra na puh méz pāté sho,*
I left Peshawar on the 20th	*Puh shalam tārikh zuh luh pékhawar na rawān shwam.*
Pull this motor car to that village.	*Dā mōtar dagha kali ta rākāga.*
Whose round was it last night ?	*Bégā da chā gusht woh ?*
I shall stop this custom	*Dā dastūr ba zuh band kram.*
What will the people say ?	*Khalq ba suh wāyee ?*

Why do you not tell me the whole truth ?	*Tōla rishtiā khabara walé nuh kawé ?*
Give me a clean handkerchief.	*Yau pāk rūmāl rākra.*
Thank you for your trouble.	*Zuh stā da rabar da pāra déra shukria adā kawam.*
Every thing is very dear.	*Har shay dér grān day.*
We are paying famine rates.	*Puh mūng bāndé da qahat narkhūna dee.*
Keep it in your house ; I will take it when I come back from the camp.	*Puh khpal kōr ké yé wo sāta chi luh parāw na biarta rāsham, no ba yé wākhlam.*
There will be a big parade tomorrow.	*Sabāla ba yau loi parait wee.*
The General will inspect the Regt.	*Jarnail sāhib ba da paltané mulāhiza kawee.*
It is very cold today, snow will fall on the hills.	*Nan déra yakhnī dah puh ghrūno ba wāwra préwozee.*
Try once more ! I am sure you will do it this time.	*Yau zal biā kōshash wo kra, zamā yaqīn day chi dā zal khuh shān sara ba yé wo kré.*
You mind your business! Who has brought this letter ?	*Tuh khpal kār kawa ! Chā dā chitai rāworé dah ?*
To whom did you take the letter.	*Chā ta dé chitai yaura.*
Can you show me the way to Shahi Bagh ?	*Da shāhi bāgh lār rā ta khayalay shé ?*

I cannot understand what you say.	*Zuh stā puh khabara nuh pōhégam.*
Is there any drinking water near the camp ?	*Parāw ta nizdé da skalō obuh shta ?*
How do you do ?	*Suh hāl day ?*
Does this road lead to Pabbi.	*Dā lār pabo ta talé dah ?*

VOCABULARY XXXII.

زری	*zaray*	Guide.
خطا کول	*khatā kawal*	To miss.
ورک کول	*vrak kawal*	To lose.
پۀ وخت	*puh wakht*	In time.
منل	*manal*	To obey.
الؤخول	*alūzawal*	To blow up to make to fly.
چاودل	*chāudal*	To split, burst.
چرم	*chwam*	(Present.)
فتح مؤندل	*fatah mūndal*	To gain victory.
بری مؤندل	*baray mūndal*	To gain victory.
شکست ورکول	*shikast warkawal*	To defeat.
شکست خوړل	*shikast khwaral*	To be defeated.
شکایت کول	*shekāyat kawal*	To complain.
برابر	*barābar*	Proper, reasonable.
پۀ بیعه اخستل	*puh baya akhistal*	To buy.
شفارس کول	*shafāras kawal*	To recommend.
بار کول	*bār kawal*	To load. (animal).

سپک	*spak*	Light.
درؤند	*drūnd*	Heavy.
پايه	*pāya*	Wheel.
جرم	*jurum*	Crime.
سزا ورکول	*sazā warkawal*	To punish.
سزا موندل	*sazā mūndal*	To be punished.
غوښتل	*ghukhtal*	To ask for.
بيان کول	*biān kawal*	To explain.
ټوله قصه	*tōla qisa*	The whole story.
بد ګڼل	*bad ganral*	To feel offended.
هميشه دَ پاره	*hamésha da pāra*	For good, for always, for ever.
کُه نه وی	*kuh nuh wi*	Otherwise.
هسی نه وی	*hasé nuh wi*	Lest.

EXERCISE 31.

1. If he had come, I would have seen him.
2. If you had sent me a letter, I would have answered it. 3. If you had worked hard, you would have passed the examination. 4. Had they been loyal, the Government would have rewarded them. 5. If our guide had not lost his way, we should have reached the hill in time. 6. Had you accepted it, it would have been all right. 7. If the sentry had fired at the outlaw, he would have certainly killed him 8. If we had not blown up the fort, we could

not have gained the victory. 9. If the enemy
had crossed the river we would have defeated
them. 10. If I had not enlisted in the Army,
I should not have become a Subadar. 11. If
you had not struck him, he would not have com-
plained to the police. 12. If you had charged
(asked for) a reasonable price, I should have
bought it from you. 13. If you had done well,
I would have recommended you to the Colonel
14. If you had loaded it lightly the wheel would
not have broken. 15. If you had not committed this crime, I would not have punished
you 16. If you had asked for ten days leave I
would have certainly given it to you. 17. Had
I seen you in the bazar I would have told you
the whole story. 18. If you had not come he
would have killed me. 19. If the old man had
not laughed, I should not have felt so offended.
20. If I had not felt so offended, I should not
have run away, but I did not mean to run away
for good, otherwise I should not have come back.

VOCABULARY XXXIII.

عدالت	*adālat*	Court.
وختی	*wakhti*	Early.
ناوختہ	*nāwakhta*	Late.
سستی	*susti*	Laziness.
لوکوتی	*lūkūti*	Little.

اسانئ سره	*asānai sara*	Easily.
بی لۀ ربړ نه	*bé lūh rabar na*	Without trouble.
راویښ کیدل	*rāwikh kédal*	To wake up (Intransitive.)
کنډر کول	*kandar kawal*	To burgle.
ارت	*art*	Broad, wide.
لۀ ـنه پۀ لانبو	*luh-na puh*	
پوربوتل	*lānbo pōré-watal*	To swim across.
دولت	*daulat*	Riches.
متل	*matal*	Proverb.
دوکان کول	*dūkān kawal*	To be a shopkeeper.
دَ باد شاه لوړ بۀ م کړی وه	*da bādshāh lūr ba mé karé wah*	I would have married the king's daughter.
مُتیازی کول	*mutyāzé kawal*	To make water, urinate.
معامله	*māméla*	Affair.

EXERCISE 32.

۱ کۀ دَ کور خاوند ور باند را غلیَ وی نو غل بۀ ئی نیولیَ وۀ ۲ کۀ ګرمی زیاته نۀ وی نو زۀ بۀ کشمیر ته تلی نۀ وم ۳ کۀ زۀ ناجوړ شوی نۀ وی نو زۀ بۀ پۀ عدالت کښ حاضر شوی وم ۴ کۀ لار خرابه نۀ وی نو موټر بۀ وختی رسیدلی وو ۵ کۀ دَ کلی خلقو سُستی کړی نۀ وی نو داره ما ران بدئی تول نیولی وو ۶ کۀ تۀ اوَ کوټی وختی راغلیَ وی نو تول انتظام بۀ پۀ وخت شوی وۀ ۷ کۀ اوبۀ ډیرَیَ وی نو فصلونه بۀ ښۀ شوی وو او موټرو بۀ

ما ليه اسانئی سره ورکولی شوه ۸ زۀ درنه دومره لوی يم چه کۀ
زۀ اوښ وی نو تۀ به خروی ۹ کۀ پۀ نيمه شپه کښ راويښ شوی
نۀ وی نو غلو بۀ م پۀ کور کښ کنډر کوی‌وۀ ۱۰ کۀ سيند ارت
نۀ وی نو مۀنر به ورنه پۀ لانبو پوربوتی وو ۱۱ کۀ يو نۀ مرکيدی
نو بل به څۀ خوړل کۀ دولت راسخه نۀ وی نو يو دوست بۀ م هم نۀ وۀ
۱۲ کۀ باران شوی نه وی نو دَ سکلو اوبۀ به هم نۀ وی ۱۳ کۀ
څمۀنر بيوۀنه پۀ غرۀ باند لربيدلی نۀ وی نو دشمن به پۀ پراو باند
حمله کوی‌وۀ ۱۴ کۀ زۀ پښتون نۀ وی نو بۀ م دوکان کوی‌وۀ ۱۵ کۀ
دولت راسخه وی نو بۀ م دَ بادشاه لوړ کوی‌وۀ ۱۶ کۀ زۀ متيازو دَ پاره
باهر وتی نۀ وی نو دا معامله بۀ م ليدلی نۀ وۀ ۱۷ کۀ اپريدی‌م
نيکه قتل کوی نۀ وی نو ورسره بۀ م داسی سخته بدی نۀ وۀ
۱۸ کۀ اڅريزی‌م زده کولی نو اوس به لوی بابو وم ۱۹ کۀ زۀ
لارنۀ شم نوتول مال بۀ م بر بادشی ۲۰ کۀ زۀ پخيله راتللی شوی
نو ډيره نبه بۀ وۀ مګر نۀ شوم راتللی—

VOCABULARY XXXIV.

مرکيدل	*mar kédal*	To die.
لوږه	*lwaga*	Hunger.
هم پۀ هغه معامله کښ	*hum puh hagha māméla ké*	In the same case.
قسم خوړل	*qasam khwaral*	To swear.
له ټولو نه لنډه لار	*la tōlō na landa lār*	The shortest road.
پۀ باند ورختل	*puh-bāndé warkhatal*	To invade.
نوی	*naway*	New.

خرڅ کول	*khars kawal*	To sell, spend.
باَئسکل	*baiskal*	Bicycle.
زۀ تبی نیولیَ یم	*zuh tabé niwalay yam*	I have caught fever
زۀ یخنئی وهلیَ یم	*zuh yakhnai wahalay yam*	I have caught cold.
ځما سر خوږ یږوی	*zamā sar khūgégee*	I have a headache.
پۀ هغۀ باند ننکئ ختلی دی	*puh haghuh bāndé nanakai khatalé di*	He has small pox.
ملګری	*malgaray*	Companion.
بله میاشت	*bala miāsht*	Next month.
تیره میاشت	*téra miāsht*	Last month.
سر	*sar*	Head
سترګه	*starga*	An eye.
پوزه	*pōza*	Nose.
غاښ	*ghākh*	Tooth.
خولۀ	*khuluh*	Mouth.
ژبه	*jhuba*	Tongue, language.
مخ	*makh*	Face.
غوږ	*ghwag*	Ear.
مرئ	*marai*	Throat.
شت	*sat*	Back of neck.
شا	*shā*	Back.
زړه	*zruh*	Heart.
پۍ پوس	*parpus*	Lung.
کناټی	*kunātay*	Buttock.

پتون *patūn*	Thigh.
دودی *dūday*	Hip.
تشی *tashay*	Loin.
خپه *khpa*	Foot, leg.
زنگون *zangūn*	Knee.
گوته *gōta*	Finger.
تلی *talāy*	Sole of foot, palm of hand.

EXERCISE 33.

1. He said he was going to Persia. 2. They said that they were dying of (from) hunger. 3. The Magistrate answered that he was still enquiring into the same case. 4. He asked me what had become of my dog. 5. I asked him if he was prepared to come with me (to go with me) to the city. 6. He swore that he did not see this man with his own eyes. 7. He asked me which was the shortest way to the city. 8. I asked him why was he staying in the hotel. 9. He thought that he also came to the office on the same day. 10. The general concluded that it was difficult for him to invade the country during the winter. 11. He said his son was cleverer than his daughter. 12. The Major himself said that he would take me with him to Afghanistan. 13. He said his son could not ride my black mare. 14. They

replied that they wanted 10 days leave. 15. Did
he say he was new to the country and that he
did not know the custom of the village? 16. Did
you say you were thirsty and that you wanted
to drink some water? 17. He said he would
sell his bicycle. 18. Tell my reader to bring
all the papers. 19. The next day I caught fever,
I therefore told my companion that I could not
go before the 1st, of next month. 20. Every
body seems to have a cold, it is bad weather.
21. You must have written this letter, do you
not remember?

VOCABULARY XXXV.

تيارۀ	*tyāruh*	Darkness.
رڼا	*ranrā*	Light (day.)
رڼا ورځ	*ranrā vraz*	Broad daylight.
دومره لرى	*dōmṛa laré*	So far.
بادشاهي	*bādshāhi*	Kingdom.
خموز.ر فصلونه پۀ باران كېږي	*zāmūng faslūna puh bārān kégee*	Our crops are dependent on the rain fall.
ظلم	*zulum*	Tyranny.
ظالم	*zālém*	Tyrant.
هېرول	*hérawal*	To forget.
باور كول	*bāwar kawal*	To believe.
فيصله كول	*faisala kawal*	To decide, settle.
ماخۀ پوۀ كړ	*mā khuh ṭōh kar*	I made him under-stand well.

يوه پيسه *yawa paisa* Single pice.

كوټه روپيئ *kōta rupi* Bad rupee.

EXERCISE 34.

١ ار دلي جواب راكو چه زۀ ستا نوكر خونۀ يم زۀ دَ سركار نوكريم ٢ بيائي رو چه پۀ تيارۀ كښ ماسپيَ ليدلي نۀ شو ٣ دَ دى علاقي خلق وائي چه مؤنږ جوار كرلي ژوۀ مهر چه اوبۀ كمي وي نو ونۀ شوؙ ٤ كليوالو رو چه تر صبا پورى به مؤنږ دَ ماليئى معافولو دَ پاره ويٻقى كمشنر صاحب ته درخواست وركوؙ ٥ صاحب رو چه زۀ به خلور ورځى پس له دورى نه بيرته راشم ٦ دَ كلو هلكانو رو چه دوه ورو لرى مدرسى ته تلل مؤنږ دپاره ګران كار دى ٧ سليم رو چه زۀ دَ بادشاهي هيڅ پروا نۀ كوم ٨ دَ دى وطن ټول فصلو نه پۀ باران كيږى ٩ ما ته ئى رو چه بيشكه تۀ څما ورورئى مهر ستا ظلم نۀ شم هيرولے ١٠ څويم راته رو چه څما بائسكل ستا له موټر نه ګرندى دى ١١ ملك رو څما دَ كلي خلق داسى هوښيار نۀ دى چه تا وپيژني چه تۀ څمونږ تحصيلدار ئى ١٢ څما لۀ رسيدو نه اول ئى را ته خبر ليدولے ؤ چه پلار د موشوَ دى ١٣ ماورته رو چه زۀ ستا پۀ خبره باور نۀ شم كولى ١٤ خان سلام راليږولى دى او وائي چه صبا به زۀ پخپله ستا ليدلو دَ پاره راشم ١٥ ګل جان پاخيد او وئى رو چه زۀ پۀ جرګه فيصله نۀ كوم ١٦ آستان رو ويل چه ما ټولو هلكانو ته ووبل چه خپل خپل نوم پۀ بورد بلند وليكنى ١٧ رحمت رو چه څما كلى له دى څائى نه سل ميلَ لرى دى ١٨ پۀ كرسيَ باند كيناست او را ته ئى رو چه دپلاقن د څۀ حال دى ١٩ ورتهم رو چه زۀ به ستا پۀ څائي كار كوم ٢٠ ما ښۀ پوه كړ چه كۀ بياد داسى كار وكړ نو يوه پيسه طلب به در نۀ كوم—

VOCABULARY XXXVI.

پۀ غلا تلل	*puh ghalā tlal*	To be stolen.
برنده	*baranda*	Verandah.
مشکل سره	*mushkil sara*	With difficulty.
نیول	*niwal*	To catch, arrest
راضی	*rāzi*	Willing, satisfied.
نوکری کول	*naukari kawal*	To serve.
هیڅوک	*hésōk*	No one.
تاریخ	*tārikh*	Date.
دا	*dā*	The following, this.
بیان	*bayān*	Explanation, statement.
دانه	*dāna*	Grain.
وسله	*wasla*	Arms.
وسله دار سړی	*wasla dār saray*	Armed man.
ما خبر کړه	*mā khabar kra*	Let me know.
تلاؤ	*talāw*	Tank.
دند	*dand*	Pond of water.
لۀ ـنه دک	*luh-na dak*	Full of.
رڼې اوبۀ	*ranré obūh*	Clear water.
خړی اوبۀ	*kharé obuh*	Muddy water.
دَ هغۀ مطلب دا وه	*da haghuh matlab dā woh*	He meant.
هوار کول	*howār kawal*	To level
واښۀ مشین کول	*wākhuh mashin kawal*	To cut grass with a mower.

کوډ کول *gōd kawal*   To weed.

ځنګل ویستل *zangal wistal*   To weed.

وسله کیښودل *wasla
kēkhōdal*   To surrender.

EXERCISE 35.

1. My bicycle has been stolen from the veranda, please inform the Police. 2. 10 days leave was granted to him with great difficulty. 3. The letter was written and sent at once. 4. The doctor was sent for, but we could not understand what he was talking about, as he could not speak Pushtu. 5. The father was killed and the son was arrested. 6. Ask him if he is willing to serve in the Cavalry. 7. No one was seen on the spot. 8. I cannot shoot birds and animals flying and running besides I cannot afford to buy a shot gun. 9. Yesterday the Adjutant called me to the office and I made the following statement. 10. At what time do you feed the horses? 11. If you see any armed man let us know. 12. It is all very well for you to bring up recruits of this type, but they will certainly not be passed by me. 13. Tell all the non-commissioned Officers that the Officer Commanding wants to see them at 10 o'clock outside the office. 14. I saw him running

towards the cantonment. 15. This tank is always full of clear water. 16. The doctor asked me if I had bitten his dog. 17. I laughed when he said this, because he really meant to ask whether his dog had bitten me. 18. When a murder is committed in Lahore, do you make all the Nawabs and Sardars responsible? 19. Tell the mali that while I am away he must cut the grass and take out all weeds. 20. Tell him to make tea and put it on the table at 3-30.

VOCABULARY XXXVII

بونر	*būnr*	Dwarf-palm string for making beds.
میزری	*mézaray*	Dwarf palm.
گذران یا گذاره	*guzrān* or *guzāra*	Living.
(سره) بدنام کیدل	*(sara) badnām kédal*	To get bad name (with).
تبر	*tabar*	Family.
هاله	*halā*	Then.
بدی	*badi*	Feud.
خلاص کول	*khlās kawal*	To finish, settle.
له یو بل نه	*la yāu bal na*	From one another.
یو بل سره	*yau bal sara*	With one another.
خشاک	*khashāk*	Firewood.

جرنده	jranda	Water mill.
ميچن	méchan	Hand mill.
كار روزگار	kār rōzgār	Work etc.
برج	braj	Tower.
يو بل باند	yau bal bānde	On one another.
(پۀ‌باند) دزكول	(puh-bāndé) daz kawal	To fire at.
طرف	taraf	Side. party.
برابر	barābar	Equal.
قام يا قوم	qām	Tribe.
مشر	mashar	Elder.
جوړه يا روغه يا صلح	jōra, rōgha, sula	Peace.
كانړى	kanray	Stone.
برخلاف	barkhélāf	Against.
(پۀ‌باند) دعوى كول	(puh-bāndé) dāwa kawal	To claim, to charge, (against).
مدعى	mudāi	Plaintiff.
مدعاليه	mudālay	Defendant.
سيزل يا ‑سوزول	sézal or swazawal	To burn.
سوزيدل	swazédal	To be burnt.
مقدمه	muqadéma	Case.
ثبوت	sabūt	Proof.
ثابت كول	sābet kawal	To prove.
منكر كيدل	munkar kédal	To deny.
(لۀ‌نه) انكا ركول	(luh-na) inkār kawal	To refuse.

پۀ کانړی باند ویشتل	*puh kānri bāndé wishtal*	To throw a stone at
جګړه کول	*jagara kawal*	To quarrel.
قاضی	*qāzi*	Judge.
ګانړه کول	*gānra kawal*	To mortgage.
خومره چه دَ وس م کیږی دمره کوشش بۀ کوم	*sōmra chi da wasa mé kégee dōmra kōshash ba kawam*	I will try my best.
حق	*haq*	Right.
اسمان شین دی	*asmān shin day*	It is clear (to-day.)
کۀ دِ خوښه وی	*kuh dé khwakha wi*	If you like.
جوړه	*jōpa*	Trading party.
سختی	*sakhti*	Hardship, Evil day.
پۀ کار راتلل	*puh kār rātlal*	To be useful to
طبیب	*tabib*	Doctor, a physician
بیماری یا ناجوړتیا	*bimāri or nājōrtia*	⎫ Disease.
رنځ	*ranz*	⎬
رنځور	*ranzūr*	Patient (in hospital)
پوزی	*puzay*	Matting.

EXERCISE 36.

۱ پۀ ژمی کښ دَ غیر علاقی خلق لرګي اوميزری او پوزی دَ پيښور پۀ ښهر کښ خرڅ دَ پاره راوړی او پۀ دی باند ګزاران کوی

۲ خوکيدار وائی چه پۀ دی طلب باند ښما ګزاره نه کیږی یا م

طلب زيات كړه او يا چوټی راكړه   ۳   د اپريدو دا دستور دی چه
يوه ښځه چا سره بدنامه شي نو ښځتن دا ښځه هم هغه سړي ته
ورو شړي او تر هغه به ئی ورسره بدي وي چه دوه سړي ورنه
ونه وژني   ۴ كله كله دا بدي تر پېړو پوري چلېږي او د يو بل
نه سړي وژني   ۵   ښځي ئی د ځنګل واښه او خشاك راوړي
جرنده كوي د كور ټول كار روزګار كوي او سړي ئی پۀ برجونو كښ
نا ست وي او پۀ يو بل سره بزي كوي   ۶ پۀ بدي كښ ښځي
نۀ ولي   ۷ چه دواړه طرف پۀ قتلاونو كښ برابر شي نو د
قام سپين ګيري را جمع شي جوړه ئی وكړي   ۸ كۀ يو طرف پروي
او بل و پروي نو د لبري مدي د پاره كانړی كيږدي چه كارتوسۀنه
او غله خان ته واچوي نو پۀ مقرر وخت كانړی ئی مات شي
۹ كۀ پۀ روغه كښ چا پۀ يو بل بز وكړ نو ټول قام ور باند را جمع
شي كلي ئی وسيزي   ۱۰ پۀ دي مقدمه كښ ثبوت نۀ وۀ ځكه
تانړه دار هيڅ نۀ شو كولی   ۱۱ مدعي وو چه څلور كال كيږي چه
ما ورته څلولينست روپۍ وركړي دي   ۱۲ مدعا عليه منكر شۀ
او وئی و چه زۀ تا نۀ پيژنم نۀ څوك ئی   ۱۳ ډيری جګړي كولو
پس مؤنړ قاضي ته لاړو   ۱۴ قاضي ورته و چه تا د دي سړي
مال ولي پټ كړي دی   ۱۵ زمكه م كانړه كړه او څوبي له م پر واده
وكړ   ۱۶ څومره چه د وس م كيږي دومره كوشش به وكړم چه ستا
حق ثابت شي   ۱۷ اسمان شين دی ورځ ښه ده جوبي به راشي
۱۸ دوست هغه دی چه پۀ سختئ كښ پكار راشي   ۱۹ چه
غلائي وشوه نو څوكيدارئی وساتلو   ۲۰ طبيب د هغي بيمارۍ علاج
پۀ ښۀ شان سره كولی شي چه ور باند پخپله تيره شوی وي ۔

VOCABULARY XXXVIII.

پایاؤ	*payāw*	Shallow.
پۀ مخ کښ	*puh makh ké*	Further on, in front.
(سره) خبرې کول	*(sara) khabaré kawal*	To converse with. to talk to.
نو	*no*	So, then.
لواړه ژبه کول	*lwāra jhuba kawal*	To speak indistinctly.
ژور	*jhawar*	Deep..
کڼده	*kunda*	Widow.
کنډاؤ	*kandāw*	A gap (in wall etc).
کنډو	*kandū*	Corn bin.
کنده	*kanda*	Abyss.
کڼه	*kand*	A small scale.
کنډۍ	*kundai*	Wooden cup
(ته) طلاق ورکول	*(ta) talāq warkāwal*	To divorce.
زنا	*zanā*	Adultery.
تربور	*tarbūr*	Cousin.
رضا	*razā*	Furlough.
وبا ګډه ده	*wabā gada dah*	Cholera is prevalent.
اجازت	*ijāzat*	Permission.
مینځ	*mianz*	Middle.
سفر	*safar*	Journey.
پۀ مخه راتلل	*puh makha rātlal*	To meet.
لۀ لاس نه	*luh lās na*	By the hand,

گواه یا شاهد	gawāh or shāhad	Witness.
گواهی یا شاهدی	gawāhi or shāhdi	Evidence.
سپينه سپو.ږمۍ	spina spōgmai	Bright moonlight.
لۀ كمرى نه وتل	luh kamré na watal	To leave the room.
كوټه	kōta	Room.
زورور باران	zōrawar bārān	Heavy rain.
سيند ختلى دى	sind khatalay day	The river rose, has risen.
وړل	vral	To carry.
پُل	pul	Bridge.
ګوډر	gūdar	Ferry.
زورور باد	zōrawar bād	Strong wind.
(سره) واقف	sara wāqif	Acquainted (person.)
لۀ-نه واقف	(luh-na) wāqif	Acquainted (language.)
(پۀ-كښ) واقف	(puh-ké) wāqif	Acquainted (country.)
پۀ پهم سره	puh paham sara	Carefully.
زړۀ	zruh	Heart.
پۀ زړۀ سره	puh zruh sara	Attentively.
محاوره	muhāwera	Idiom.
دَ خبرو سړى	da khabaro saray	Converser.
كمۍ	kamay	Scarcity.

ضلع	zela	District.
ویستلی توره	wistalé tūra	Drawn sword.
ستړی	staray	Tired.
اوده کیدل	ūduh kédal	To sleep.
ویشل	wéshal	To divide.

EXERCISE 37.

1. The water is shallow here, but further on it is very deep. 2. How many sepoys are there who wish to speak to me? 3. You speak so fast and indistinctly that I can not understand a word you say. 4. Her husband is dead she is now a widow. 5. I have heard that he has divorced her. 6. Subadar, how many men of your company are on furlough? Have them all recalled at once. 7. Owing to the prevalence of cholera in the city, the people of the city are not allowed to come into the cantonment. 8. In the middle of our journey we met an old man, whom a little boy was leading by the hand. 9. One witness has stated that the night was dark and another that it was bright moonlight. 10. Ahmad Khan left the room where the Deputy Commissioner was sitting. 11. Owing to the heavy rain in Swat, the Kabul river rose and carried away the bridge. 12. I have come to make a report that at 2-30 last night Jan Mohammad killed his own father. 13. How long

before that were you acquainted with him? 14. How long have you been learning Pushtu? 15. If you study the Pushtu idioms attentively and carefully listen to your converser, you will soon be able to speak the language and understand others. 16. Why did you tell me that my father had arrived? 17. On account of scarcity of rain there is little grass in the District. 18. I saw a man running with a drawn sword in his hand. 19. I am tired, I did not sleep last night. 20. Divide the money among these people.

VOCABULARY XXXIX

لۆټ کول	lūt kawal	To loot.
ماشوم	māshūm	Little child.
بهانه	bahāna	Pretence.
پۀ چغه تلل	puh chagha tlal	To pursue.
دَ پاره دَ دی	da pāra da dé	In order to, for this purpose.
را خلاص کول	rā khlās kawal	To release.
بوڼګه	bōnga	Ransom.
دَ دروغو ګواهی	da darōghō gawāhi	False evidence.
نرخ	narkh	Rate.
څرول	sarawal	To graze.
اګر که	agar kuh	Although.
همسايه	hamsāya	Tenant.

همسايه ګان	*hamsāyagān*	Tenants.
ميلمستيا	*mélmastiā*	Hospitality.
ميلمه دوست	*melma dost*	Hospitable.
حج	*haj*	Pilgrimage.
حاجى	*hāji*	Pilgrim.
ورته حاجى صاحب وائى	*warta hāji sāhib wāyee*	He is called pilgrim.
جوړيدل	*jōrédal*	To be made.
معلوميدل	*mālūmédal*	To look like, to seem
كارتوس	*kārtūs*	Cartridge.
پا له اسانه	*pā la asāna*	Easily.
دَ غره لمن	*da ghruh laman*	Skirt of the hill.
زركه	*zarka*	Chikor.
تنزرى	*tanzaray*	Partridge
كرونده	*karwanda*	Newly sown crops.
نهٔ ويشتونكى	*khuh wishtūnkay*	A good shot.
پهٔ لږ ساعت كښى	*puh lag sāat ké*	In a short time.
يوى كول	*yawé kawal*	To plough.
تيريدل	*térédal*	To pass by.
ناگهانه	*nāgahāna*	By chance.
خطا كيدل	*khatā kédal*	To be missed.
عن	*an*	Right-up to, right down to.
لګيدل	*lagédal*	To be hit, to be struck against.
چرګ بانګ مالى	*charg bāng mālé*	At dawn.

ملا بانگ مالی	*mulā bāng mālé*	At·the time of early call to prayer.
گنره يا کنی	*ganra* or *kani*	Otherwise.

EXERCISE 38.

١ پۀ کلی داره پریو ته دَيو هندوؤ کورئی لوټ کړ او يو ماشوم خوئ ئی بوت ٢ دَ کلی خلقو هسی بها نه وکړه چه داړی پسی پۀ چغه تلی يوؤ دپاره د دی چه پۀ کلی جرم پری نۀ وځی ٣ کۀ دا دَچا مسلمان خوئي وی نو کليوالو به ضرور راخلاص کړی وَه مهر اوس دَ دی هلک راخلاصولو دَ پاره يوه لو يه بونه به پکار وی ٥ زۀ به ور باند پۀ عدالت کښی دعوی وکړم او وکيل به ورله ونيسم ٠ کۀ گواهان پکارشی نو پۀ شهر کښی پیر دی ٧ دَ دروغو گواهی ور کولو دپاره پنهَ روپئ نرخ دی ٨ صاحب مؤثر پۀ خپلو غرونوکښی مال خرولو او دَ دوئ دَ قام لس سری راباند راغلل قول مال ئی رانه بوتلو ٩ ١ اُم کۀ موئر هلکان يوؤ خو کۀ ټوپبکونه راسخه وی نو مال ئی را نه نۀ شو بيولی ١٠ هغه مشهوژ سړی دی او ډير همسايه گان لری او ډير ميلمه دوست سړی دی ١١ دوه ځل ئی حج کړی دی دَ څکه ورته خلق حاجی صاحب وائي ١٢ دروغ خو بالکل نۀ وائی ١٣ سپی غاپی گوره چه غل خو نشته ١۴ دَ کوهاټ پۀ دره کښی ډير ښۀ ټو پکونه جوړیری ١٥ چه ماښام شی نو دَغرۀ نه زرکی او تنزری راکوز شی او پۀ کروندو کښی غنم او اوربشی خوری کۀ سړی ښۀ ويشتونکی وی نو پۀ ابر ساعت کښی به دیرش ځلوبينت مرغان ولی ١٦ ما يوی کوله او دی پۀ لار تیریدو ناگهانه يئی راباند ديز وکړ زۀ خطا شوم ولی غوآيئم ولريدو ١٧ چه ماپر ديز وکړ نو عن پۀ سر ولریدو را پريوتۀ او مړ شو ١٨ کۀ هغۀ راباند اول

وز کړی نۀ وی نو زۀ خو لیونی نۀ وم چه ما به ور باند يز کاوۀ
۱۹ چرګ بازۀ مالی روانېدل پکار دي ٗکۀره گاډۍ ته به ونۀ رسی
۲۰ لۀ دی ٗڅایي نه تر لواړګي پوری څومره کرائي لرویٍ—

VOCABULARY XL.

جاهل	*jāhel*	Ignorant.
پره جنبه	*para junba*	Faction feeling.
پۀ خپلو کښ	*pūh khpalo ké*	Among themselves.
وران کېدل	*vrān kédal*	To be ruined, to go wrong.
مسافر	*musāfar*	Traveller.
سلامت	*salāmat*	Safe.
سلامتی	*salāmati*	Safety.
وېره	*vyara*	Fear, danger.
وېرهناک	*vyara nāk*	Dangerous.
لۀ قچری نه بار کوز کول	*luh qacharé na bār kūz kawal*	To unload mule.
گاډۍ تش کول	*gāday tash kawal*	To unload cart.
غوا	*ghwa*	Cow.
غوايۀ	*ghwāyuh*	Bullock (Plural *ghwāyān*.)
پۀ څو د اخستی دی	*puh so dé akhistay day?*	How much did you pay for it?
خیمه یا تنبو	*khéma* or *tanbū*	Tent.
تنبو لګول	*tambū lagawal*	To pitch a tent.

دَ اوبو څوکۍ	*da obo saukai*	Picquet on the water supply.
سخت جرم	*sakht juram*	Serious crime.
مقیزه کول	*matiza kawal*	To elope.
کوشش کول	*kōshash kawal*	To try.
پۀ روپو باندِ فیصله	*puh rūpo bāndé faisala kawal*	To make a money settlement.
ونۀ شو	*wo nuh sho*	Did not become, failed.
بدرګه	*badraga*	Escort.
تاوان ور کول	*tāwān war kawal*	To compensate.
څۀ وشۀ	*suh wo shoo ?*	What happened ?
ژبه دِ وباسه	*jhuba dé wo bāsa*	Put out your tongue.
دارۆ	*dārū*	Medicine or gun powder.
کۀ نۀ وی	*kuh nuh wi*	Otherwise.
تبه به دربائنډ بیا راشی	*taba ba dar bāndé biā rāshee*	You will catch fever again.
چلی کار	*chalé kār*	Cultivator.
دَ زمکی خاوند	*da zmaké khāwand*	Land owner.
شپږمه حصه	*shpagama hisa*	1/6th part.
پیداوار	*paidā war*	Produce.
لر لاندِ	*lag lāndé*	Lower down.

كه زركړې	kuh zar kré	If you make haste.
گړئ	garai	Watch.
گړی ساز	gari sāz	Watch maker.
ځما گړی ورانه ده	zamā garai vrāna dah	My watch has gone wrong.
پۀ چا باند مرمت کول	puh chā bāndé muramat kawal	To have repaired.
پۀ صبانۍ ورځ	puh sabānai vraz	Tomorrow week.
پۀ ننني ورځ	puh nananai vraz	This day week.
پۀ پرونۍ ورځ	puh parūnai vraz	Yesterday week.
لاس تړلی	lās taralay	Hands tied.
رسۍ پۀ غاړه	rasai puh ghāra	With a rope round one's neck.
واښه پۀ خولۍ	wākhuh puh khulé	Grass in one's mouth.
مرېی	mrayay	Slave.
وينځه	winza	Slave girl.
کړکئ	karkai	Window.
جمع کېدل	jama kédal	To be collected, assemble.
انتظار کول	intézār kawal	To wait.
چاندماری	chāndmārai	Musketry, range.
دَ ګولو کار توسونه	da gōlō kārtūsūna	Ball cartridges.
شاخی کار توسونه	shalkhi kārtūsūna	Blank cartridges.

هر سړی د پاره یا *har sari da*
ن هر سړی پۀ سر *para* or *da har*
sari puh sar   For each man.

EXERCISE 39.

1.   They are ignorant people and owing to faction feeling and their fighting among themselves, the country is being ruined. 2. Travellers do not go that way now, all the roads being unsafe. 3. Unload the mules first and then unload the carts. 4. Is this cow for sale, how much do you want for it and how much did you pay for it? 5. if the General pitches his camp on that spot, there is danger that the picquet on the water supply will be attacked from the pass. 6. My brother's son has committed a serious crime. 7. He eloped with a malak's wife and ran away to the hills. 8. We tried to make a money settlement, but failed. 9. If these villagers send their cattle to graze without a proper escort and refuse to send out a pursuit party after them when they are stolen, the Govt. will certainly refuse them compensation. 10. What has happened to the old man who killed Sarfaraz? 11. Put out your tongue; you must take this medicine at once otherwise the fever will recur. 12. The cultivator gets 1/6th of the produce from the land owner. 13. The boatman has gone away but there is a ford lower down and if

you make haste you can cross the river before
sunset. 14. My watch has gone wrong, tell the
bearer to have it repaired. 15. Come tomorrow
week, the office will then be open. 16. He came
in with his hands tied, with rope round his neck
and grass in his mouth and fell at the Deputy
Commissioner's feet and said "I am your slave."
17. Open all the windows while I am sitting
here. 18. At midnight the troops assembled
on the bridge and waited for the next order.
19. Take the recruits to the range tomorrow
and have every thing ready there before the
Adjutant arrives. 20. Take 10 rounds of ball
and 10 rounds of blank for each man.

VOCABULARY XLI.

بلوه	*balwa*	Riot.
ژوبل کیدل	*jhōbal kédal*	To be wounded.
پۀ آخرکښ	*puh ākhér ké*	In the end.
پۀ شروع کښ	*puh shurū ké*	At the beginning.
عمری قید کیدل	*ūmri qéd kédal*	To be sentenced to transportation for life.
پۀ باند دپانسۍ	*puh-bāndé da*	
حکم کیدل	*pānsai hukam kédal*	To be sentenced to death.
إعتبار نۀ دی پکار	*itebār nuh day pakār*	One must not be trusted.
إعتبار	*itébār*	Trust.

ملګرى	malgaray	Companion.
محصول	mahsūl	Toll, custom duty.
سودا ګر	saudāgar	Merchant.
ګټه	gata	Profit.
فائده	fāida	Benefit.
مزدور	mazdūr	Labourer.
مزدورى	mazdūri	Labour, wages.
ګذاره کول	guzāra kawal	To make a living.
زخم يا پرهر	zakhām or parhar	Wound.
نَو يا زوه	naw or zawa	Pus.
خوار	khwār	Poor fellow.
اوږه	uga	Shoulder.
چپ چوړ	chap chúr	Shattered.
اودس ماتى له	audas māti la	
تلل	tlal	To go to make water.
اودس کول	audas kawal	To wash for prayer.
چينه	china	Spring of water.
مونځ کول	munz kawal	To pray,
مانځه دپاره	mānzuh da pāra	For prayer (Oblique.)
خونى	saṅkai	Post.
تار	tār	Wire, telegram.
بارانى زمکه	bārāni zmaka	Unirrigated land.
قيد	qaid	Locked up, imprisonment.
بدن وجود	badan, wajūd	Body.

دَ.دَخاطَر نهٔ تېردل	*da-da khātera nuh térédal*	To displease.
لنگېدل	*langédal*	To give birth to a child.
دَ يو بل ښهٔ ويل	*dā yau bal khuh wayal*	To say good of each other.
خیر خیریت	*khér khériat*	Welfare, all well.
معلوم کېدل	*mālūm kédal*	To be found out.
خیرن	*khiran*	Dirty.
کنزل کول	*kanzal kawal*	To abuse.
لهٔ نه بدل اخستل	*luh-na badal akhistal*	To take revenge.
شرم	*sharam*	Shame.
ښکارېدل	*khkārédal*	To appear.
پردې ژبه	*pradai jhuba*	Foreign language.
زده کول	*zda kawal*	To learn.
ګڼل	*ganral*	To consider.
يو بل وژل	*yau bal wajhal*	To kill each other.
ژوندون	*jhwandūn*	Life.
پیسی اخستل	*paisé akhistal*	To take bribe.
بډي اخستل	*badé akhistal*	To take bribe.

EXERCISE 40.

۱ په دی بلوه کښ دوه سوی قتل شول او پنځه سخت
ژوبل شول ۲ په آخر کښ يو سوی عمری شو او په دوؤ دَ پانسي
حکم وشو ۳ پهٔ ښهٔ پهٔ آس او پهٔ تورهٔ څهٔ اعتبار دی ؟ ۴ دلاری
ماڼری دَ مور مبرؤ وي ۵ په دی موسم کښ ډیر اسونه لهٔ افغانستان

ده راوستلَے کیدرِی اگر چه پۀ لارکښ ورباند ډیر محصول لروِی
مګر بیا هم سودا گر پۀ کښ ډیره ګټه کوِی ۲ غریب خلق پۀ چاوْنِی
کښ مزدورِي کوِی او ورباند ګذاره کوِی ۷ دا ئکتر ورته وو چه مۀ
وِیریدره زخم د کوزم بیا ور نه څه زوه راوتی وَه کۀ نه ۸ یو سرِے
رانه پۀ موټر ولریدد خوار به مُوشی څکه چه او.ره ئی ماته ده
۹ زۀ ودس ماتی دَ پاره لۀ څوکِي نه راووتم اودس ِم ماتکم او پۀ
چینږم اودس وکړ مانئۀ ته اودریدم چه ستا تار راورسید ۱۰ زمکم
ټوله بارانی دَه څکه مدام پۀ مالیه کښ قید یم ۱۱ داسی وویریدم
چه ټول بدن ِم خولی خولی شۀ ۱۲ څلور ورځی شوی دِی
چه غوا م لذ څه شوی دَه څلور سیر پیِ کوِی ۳، پښتانۀ هیچری
دَ یو بل نۀ نۀ وائِی ۴، زۀ ستا خیر خیریت معلومولو دَ پاره
راغلیَ یم ۱۵ پښتوں نۀ دوست دیَ او خطر ناک دشمن دیَ
پۀ شاباش ډیر خوشحالیږِی پښتوں کۀ ډیر غریب وِی خو پۀ وهلو
او کنزلو ورباند خوک کا نۀ شی کولَی ۱۶ پښتوں خپل بدل
هیچری نۀ پریږدِ دی ۱۷ دَ پښتنو تعلیم خوِښ نۀ وِی او دوکان
کول ور ته شرم ښکارِی ۱۹ پښتوں پردیِ ژبه زر زده کولَی شی
۲۰ په ښتو او پۀ زمکه مدام پښتانۀ سره پوبل وژنِی او بیا مقروران
شی مګر پۀ غیر علاقه کښ هم دَ مقرور ژوندوں ګران وِی څکه چه
پریدیان پرپیسی واخلِی او وئ وژنِی—

Miscellaneous Colloquial Sentences IV.

| Does this road go to the city? | Dā lār khahar ta talé dah? |
| He always tells lies. | Hagha mudām darōgh wāyee. |

There will be no parade this evening.	*Nan māzdigar ba parét nuh wee.*
Why do you not come in time?	*Walé puh wakht nuh rāzé?*
It is very cold here in the winter.	*Puh jami ké dalé déra yakhni wee.*
These boys are playing the whole day.	*Dā halakān tōla vraz lōbé kawee.*
If your gun is loaded, unload it.	*Kuh tōpak dé dak wi no khāli* or *tash yé kra.*
Please forgive me this time I shall never do it again.	*Méhrabānī wōkra dā zal mé māf kra, biā ba dāsé kār hicharé wo nuh kram.*
We had five hundred women to cook our food.	*Mūng sara pinzuh sawa khazé wé chi zamūng dōdai ba yé pakhawala.*
How long will it take you to reach there?	*Puh sōmra sāat ké ba halta wo rasé?*
We arrived there a little after midday.	*Mūng halta luh gharmé na lūkūtī vrōsto wōrasédaloo.*
He is quite innocent.	*Hagha bilkul bégunāh day.*
What time will the guard change?	*Gārat ba suh wakht badlégee?*
Show me some other samples.	*Suh nōré namūné rā ta wo khaya.*
Keep your accounts always clear.	*Mudām khpal hésāb sāf sāta.*
Is he a relation of the headman?	*Haghada malak khpal day?*

You are young and strong, why do you not enlist in the army.

Tuh zwān yé aw takra hum yé, walé puh fauz ké nuh barti kégé.

Are the pass made rifles any good ?

Daréwāl tōpakūna suh khuh wee ?

I have forgotten your name.

Sta nūm rā na hér sho.

Have you ever been on active service ?

Tuh charé puh lām talay yé ?

Tell all Indian Officers that I want to see them tomorrow at 4-30 p.m.

Tōlo sardārāno ta wo wāya chi saba puh salōr nimé bajé yé lidal ghwāram.

The ration arrangements were not very good.

Da rāsan intézām bilkul khuh nuh woh.

Have you finished your annual musketry ?

Tā da kāl chāndmārai khlāsa karé dah ?

I get up at five and after a bath and having had my breakfast I go to the office.

Zuh puh pinzuh bajé pāsam aw da ghusal aw hāzérai na pas daftar ta zam.

When did you last go on leave ?

Tér zala tuh kala puh chūtai bāndé talay wé.

I do not remember exactly what clothes the man was wearing.

Mā ta bilkul yād nuh di chi hagha sari sanga jāmé aghustalé wé.

I walked in from Shabkadar this morning.

Nan sahar zuh luh Shabkadar na pyāda rāghlam.

Show me your certificates.

Chitai dé wō khaya.

Take this parcel to the post office and bring a receipt.	*Dā pārsal dākkhāné ta yausa aw rasid rāwra.*
Our ration is free but we can't save any money.	*Zamūng rāsan muft day lékin hiss paisa na shoo bach kawalay.*
Whom do you want to see ?	*Tuh ṣōk lidal ghwāré ?*
The village has two quarters, the upper and the lower ones Sarfarāz is the head man of the upper quarter.	*Puh kalī ké dwa kandi di, bar aw kūz. Sarfarāz da bar kandı malak day.*
The knife and fork are both dirty.	*Churuh aw kānta dwāra khirané di.*
Take this cheque to the treasury and cash it.	*Dā chak khazāné ta yausa aw māt yé kra.*
Bring small change for three rupees.	*Da dréo rūpō māt gud rāwra.*
Do you know where my head clerk lives ?	*Tā ta mālūma dah chi zamā lōi bābū charta ōsee ?*
How many men were absent from rollcall ?	*La géntrai na sōmra sari ghair hāzér woo?*
Why did he go without permission ?	*Walé bé ijāzata lār?*
He said this in my presence "Hide yourself in that thick grass."	*Haghuh dā khabara zamā puh makh ké karé dah, puh hagha ganro wākho ké zān pat kra.*
Where have you been for such a long time ?	*Dōmra dér sat charta wé ?*

Put an anna stamp on this envelope.	*Pa dé lifāfa bāndé da ané tikas wō lagawa.*
When will you fulfil your promise?	*Kala ba khpala wāda pūra kawé ?*
We attacked them with our bayonets, but soon returned.	*Mūng puh khpalo sanginūnō bāndé war bāndé hamla wo kra kho zar rā wo jārwatoo.*
Tell the subedar to be back before sunset.	*Subédār sāhib ta wo wāya chi luh nwar préwātuh na awàl rāshee.*
Put picquets on the hills on all sides, for the camp must be protected.	*Puh tōlō tarafo bāndé puh ghrūno pikatūna wo lagawa, zaka chi parāw sātal pakār dī.*
It appears to me that the enemy has retired.	*Malūmégee chi dushman māt shaway day.*
We halted there for three days.	*Mūng dréo vrazō da pāra halla muqām wo kar.*
Here is the list of 11 bad characters living in your village.	*Dā da yawolaso badmāshānō ferest day chi stā puh kali ké osee.*
For each I require a security of Rs. 500/.	*Da har yau da pāra da pinzo pinzo sawo zamānat ghwāram.*
Does the climate of this country suit you ?	*Da dé mulk ābō hawa dar bāndé rāsta (muafiqa) dah kuh na?*
How many men have been killed in this riot ?	*Pa dé balwa ké sōmra sari wajhalay shawi di ?*

Do they bring horses from Afghanistan ? *Haghui luh Afghānistān na asūna rāwalee?*

Still the merchants make much profit. *Biā hum saudāgar déra gata kawee.*

I came out of the post and went to pray. *Zuh luh saukaī na rā wo watam aw mānzuh la lāram.*

Why do travellers not go that way now ? *Walé musāfar hagha khwā ta os nuh shi tlay ?*

Because all roads are dangerous. *Zaka chi tōlé lāré khatarnāké dī.*

How much did you pay for this horse ? *Dā as dé puh so akhistay day ?*

The elders of the tribe tried to make a money settlement but failed. *Da qām spin giro puh rūpō bāndé da faisalé kōshash wo kar kho wo nuh sho,*

I am a cultivator and live in Yusafzai. I cultivate 10 jaribs of land. *Zuh chalékār yam aw puh yūsufzo ké osam. lās jariba zmaka karam.*

Why did he come with a rope round his neck? *Walé rasaī puh ghāra rāghlo ?*

My village was raided. *Zamā puh kali dāra préwata.*

They carried off Harnam Singh's son. *Da Harnām Singh zōi yé bōtlō.*

How can I give false evidence ? *Sanga da darōghō shahdi war kawalay sham ?*

All the sepoys want to see you. *Tōl spāyān dé lidal ghwāree.*

Why are the people of the city not allowed to come into the cantt?

Walé da khār khalqō ta da chaunrai da rātlo ijāzat nishta ?

The flood has carried away all the bridges on the Kabul river.

Sélāb da kābul puh sind bāndé tōl pulūna woree di.

When I was in the Tirah expedition I was well acquainted with the General.

Chi zuh da Tirah puh lām bāndé wam, no jarnail sara khuh wāqif wam.

Owing to the heavy rain in Swat, the Kabul river is in flood.

Puh Swāt ké da zorā-war bārān puh sabab Da Kabal puh sind ké sélāb rāghalay day.

Where there is no river or canals the women grind their corn with hand mills.

Charta chi sindūna yā nehrūna nuh wi no halta khuzé puh me-chanō oruh kawee.

I have a large family, I therefore have to take to service.

Zamūng lōi tabar ,day zaka naukari kawoo.

Who wrote the letter and sent it back to Delhi ?

Chā chitai wolikala aw Dehli ta yé biarta wo légala ?

Why did the Adjutant call you to the office What did he tell you ?

Walé Ajitan sāhib daftar ta wo balalé suh yé dar ta wo wayal ?

Mind, my dog will bite you.

Paham kawa zamā spay ba dé wo chichi.

He said he would come himself if he wanted to see me.

Hagha wō wé chi kuh zuh dé winam, nō pakhpala ba darsham.

VOCABULARY XLII.

جاسوُس	*jāsūs*	Spy.
مُخبِر	*mukhbér*	Informer.
پټ کول	*pat kawal*	To hide.
خوړ يا ناله	*khwar or nāla*	Ravine.
اګرچه	*agarchi*	Although.
دَ شولو پټی	*da shōlo patay*	Rice field.
توئ	*tōi*	Stream.
دَ غر خوا	*da ghar khwā*	Hill side.
دز کول	*daz kawal*	To fire.
لګيدل	*lagédal*	To be hit.
مقام کول	*muqām kawal*	To halt.
لږ وخت دَ پاره	*lag wakht da pāra*	For a short while.
نړوَل	*narawal*	To knock down (or building).
ذکر کول	*zikar kawal*	To mention.
تازه	*tāza*	Fresh.
درک	*darak*	Trace clue.
چاپ	*chāp*	Foot print.
ظاهره	*zāhéra*	Evidently.
ګډه	*gada*	Sheep.
تلاش کول	*tālāsh kawal*	To look for.
دزی وشوی	*dazé wo shwé*	Shots were fired.
کمر	*kamar*	Cliff, neck (in hill.)
هم پد هغه وخت	*hum puh hagha wakht*	At the same moment.

غائيب كيدل	ghāib kédal	}	To go out of sight.
پناه كيدل	panāh kédal		
روان كيدل	rawān kédal		To start, set out.
نور پريواتهٔ	nwar préwātūh		Sunset.
وريسى كول	warisé kawal	}	To remove.
يو خوانه كول	yau khwā ta kawal		
ټګى	tagi		Trap.
(ته) پهٔ پسوّنى	ta puh psūni ké kénāstal	}	To ambush.
كښى كينا ستل			
(ته) لارنيو ل	ta lār niwal		

EXERCISE 41.

While the force was encamped on a hill near Kaneguram an informer came and told the Political Officer that the Shabi Khels had all their cattle hidden in a nulla about seven miles away to the north. For this he received a handsome reward. Although it was the middle of the day and very hot we started at once for the place. On the way we passed some rice fields which were irrigated from a small stream flowing down the hill side. Near these fields was a tower from which a shot was fired at us as we approached. No one was hit, and the man who fired the shot fled before we could get up to the tower and escaped among the hills

We halted there for a short while and knocked the tower down. Then we went on, and about three o'clock reached the place mentioned by the informer. There were fresh traces of cattle on every side, but evidently their owners had taken them away for we could not find so much as a single sheep. While we were looking about some shots were fired from a neck between two hills, and at the same moment the informer, whom we had brought with us, fled. Many shots were fired after him, but he was soon out of sight. So we started back to camp and going by a different route reached it just before sunset. It was said afterwards that the informer was himself a Shabi Khel, and that he had taken care to have the cattle removed before the troops started, and that the whole thing was a trap. If we had returned by the same route as we went, the tribesmen, who had collected and made an ambush on the road while we were looking for the cattle, would have given us a very bad time.

VOCABULARY XLIII.

له نن تاريخ نه *uh nan tarikh
     na*   From this date.

كنزل كول *kanzal kawal* To abuse.

كمزورى *kamzōray* Weak.

مضبوط	mazbūt	Strong.
ځان	zān	Self.
قوت	quat	Strength.
مغرور	maghrūr	Proud.
په حیرانتیا سره	puh hairāntiā sara	With astonishment.
دلیل	dalil	Reason.
لېونی	léwanay	Mad.
اول	awal	First.
و رومبی	vrūmbay	First.
څنګه چه	sunga chi	As.
هم دغسی	hum dagha sé	The same way.
خبره دا ده	khabara dā dah	The true fact is.
بی ګناه	bé gunah	Innocent.
بی هیڅ	bé hissa	For nothing.

EXERCISE 42.

يوه وز ځ يوی څنګی خپل څښتن ته رووچه لۀ دن تاريخ نۀ پس بيا م نۀ شی وهلۀ ۔ او نۀ راته کنزل کولی شی ۔ څښتن ورته ويل دا خبره د په څۀ خيال و کړه ۔ زۀ درته کمزوری ښکاره شوم او کۀ خپل ځان درته مضبوط ښکاره شوۀ او نۀ د خپل پلار په قوت مغرورۀ شوی چه بیا د نۀ شم وهلی ۔ دی ورته و چه بس ما درنۀ و ويل چه بيا م نۀ شی وهلی ۔ سری بيا ورنه په حیرانتیا سره ټپوس و کړو چه دا خبره ته ٻۀ کوم دليل سره کوی ۔ لېونی خو نۀ ئی چه لونی ئی څنګه چه ۱ اول خما ۖ څښتد وی هم دغسی اوس ئی او څنګه چه زۀ وړومبی ستا څښتن وم ۖ هم دغسی اوس هم يم ۔ نو څنګه د نۀ

شم وهلیَ ۔ ښښی ورته پۀ جواب کښ و ویل چه خبره دا دَه چه هر
څۀ چه ته وائی هغه به منم ۔ نو چه ټولی خبری د ملنم نو تۀ لیونیَ
خو نه ئی چۀ بیﮔناه به م وهی ۔ یا بی هیڅ به راته کنزل کوی ۔
سوی و خندل تر روان شو ۔

YOCABULARY XLIV.

دوۀ جمعی کیږیَ	*dwa jumé kégee*	A fortnight ago.
دَ شپږو اوؤ بجو پۀ مینځ کښ	*da shpagō owo bajō puh mianz ké*	Between 6 and 7 o'clock.
اواز	*awāz*	Voice, noise.
کړ پهار	*krapahār*	Footsteps, sound of feet.
پۀ ترات	*puh trāt*	Galloping.
خلاص راتلل یا پۀ پوره چال راتلل	*khlās rātlal* or *puh pūra chāl rātlal*	To come on at full speed.
سور	*sōr*	Rider.
ظاهره	*zāhéra*	Evidently.
قابو	*qābū*	Control.
آس یې لۀ قابو نه وتلی وُه	*as yé luh qābū na watalay woh*	He lost control of his horse.
راښکل	*rākhkal*	To tug.
سورلیَ	*swarli*	Riding, passenger
رکاب	*rekāb*	Stirrup.
واږی	*wāgé*	Reins.
ګز	*gaz*	Yard.

قدم	*qadam*	Pace.
رغړیدل	*rgharédal*	To roll.
او.ږه	*oga*	Shoulder.
بازیګره	*bāzīgara*	Somersault.
بازیګره اړ ول	*bāzīgara arawal*	To turn a somersault.
خنډل	*sandal*	To brush.
ګرد	*gard*	Dust (flying).
خاوره	*khāwra*	Earth (lying on the ground).
خټه	*khata*	Mud.
جامې	*jāmé*	Clothes.
له ښۀ نصیب	*luh khuh nasiba*	Fortunately.
له بد نصیب	*luh bada nasiba*	Unfortunately.
نرم	*naram*	Soft.
بوس	*būs*	Straw, bussa.
خسڼری	*khasanray*	A straw.
دز	*daz*	A shot (of gun).
دنګل	*dangal*	To bolt.
یاغی کیدل	*yāghi kédal*	To bolt, to run away out of control.
خپل ځان خوزول	*khpal zān khwazawal*	Shake oneself.
یو خوا بل خوا خوا زنګیدو را زنګیدو	*yau khwā bal khwā zangédo rā zangédo*	Swinging from side to side.

EXERCISE 43.

About a fortnight ago when I was walking across the maidan in the early morning between six and seven, I heard the voice of foot steps behind me. Looking round, I saw a horse galloping towards me at full speed. The rider had evidently lost control of his horse, and was leaning back, tugging at the reins and swinging from side to side. His feet were out of the stirrups, and I expected every moment to see him fall. Sure enough he had not gone more than fifty yards or so after passing me when he rolled off and fell on his shoulder, turning a complete somersault. I ran up thinking he might have broken his neck but before I reached him, he was up, and shaking himself began to brush the dust off his clothes Luckily for him he had fallen in a soft place where there was plenty of loose straw and no stones. He told me his horse had taken fright at the firing of a gun and bolted with him.

VOCABULARY XLV.

جولا jōlā	A weaver.
اودل odal	To weave.
لوم owam	I weave (Present.)
پګړۍ یا پټکی pagrai or patkay	Turban.

حُجوہ	*hūjra*	Guest house.
میلمه	*melma*	Guest.
عالم	*ālam*	A learned man.
ادب	*adab*	Respect.
(سره) جوړ تازه	*(sara) jōr tāza*	
کول	*kawal*	To welcome.
مجلس	*majlas*	Assembly, gathering.
دَ-عزت کول	*da-izat kawal*	To respect.
څنګ پۀ څنګ	*sang puh sang*	Side by side, close.
هیڅ یې نۀ ویل	*hiss yé nuh wayal*	Saying nothing.
دَ-یقین کیدل	*da-yaqīn kédal*	To believe.
چپ چاپ	*chap ehāp*	Silent.
آخر	*ākhér*	At last.
پۀ آخر کښ	*puh ākhér ké*	In the end.
دَ میاشتی پۀ آخر	*da miāshté*	
کښ	*puh ākhir ké*	In the end of month.
دَ میاشتی پۀ شروع	*da miāshté*	In the beginning of
کښ	*puh shurū ké*	month.
روژه	*rōjha*	Fast, fasting.
ماتول	*mātawal*	To break.
نور پریواتۀ	*nwar prewātuh*	Sunset, West.
ساعت	*sāat*	Moment.
ناګهانۀ	*nāgahāna*	By chance.
بیا به څۀ چل کیږی؟	*biā ba suh chal kégee?*	What will happen then?

خر *khar*   An ass, donkey.

كتهٔ *kata*   Pack saddle.

زين *zin*   Saddle.

EXERCISE 44.

يو جولا ښی جامی واغوستی سپينه پېړۍ ئی پهٔ سر کړه او
ديو قاضی حجری له ورغَے ۔ قاضی صاحب چه دا ميلمه وليد نو
خيال ئی وکړ چه څوک دَلوئ کور سړی دیَ او عالم هم معلومييږی
نو ډير پهٔ ادب ورته پاڅيد او ډير جوړ تازه ئی ور سره وَړل څکه نور
مجلس هم ډ دهٔ ډير عزت وکړ جولا قاضی صاحب سره څڼی پهٔ
څڼی کيناست هيڅ ئی نهٔ ويل په دی باند نور هم د خلقو يقين
وشهٔ چه ډير هوښيار سړی دیَ نو يو ساعت څو ټول مجلس سره
چپ چاپ ناست وُهٔ هيڅا څهٔ نهٔ ويل آخر يو سړی لهٔ قاضی صاحب
نه تپوس وکړ چه روژه پهٔ څهٔ وخت ماتيږی قاضی جواب ورکړ
چه لهٔ نور پريواتهٔ نه ابو ساعت پس د روژی ماتولو وخت وی ناګها نه
جولا پهٔ کښی ويل قاضی صلحب کهٔ نور ترنيمی شپی پوزی پری
نهٔ وشی نو بيا به څهٔ چل کيږی پهٔ دی باند ټولو وخندل او وئی
ويل چه خر هم هغه دیَ کته ور باند بله دهــــ

VOCABULARY XLVI.

دَ عربو يو ټولۍ *da arabō yau tōlay*   A band of Arabs.

ټولۍ يا داړه *tōlay* or *dāra*   Party, raid.

بندَول *bandawal*   To block.

دَ وطن خلق *da watan khalq*   Inhabitants.

ظلم *zulum*   Tyranny.

بې خبر *bé khabara*   Unwittingly.

(ته) وسله کیښودل	*(ta) wasla kékhódal*	Surrender.
وسله	*wasla*	Weapon.
مغلوب يا لاند	*maghlūb* or *lāndé*	Overpowered.
مورچه	*mōrcha*	Strong hold.
دَ استوږ ئ	*da astōgné*	
ځائی	*zāi*	Fixed residence.
دَ بادشاه مشیر یا	*da bādshāh*	
صلاح کار	*mashir* or *salāh kār*	Counsellor of the king.
مصلحت کول	*maslahat kawal*	To consult.
سره	*sara*	Together.
لری کول یا	*laré kawal* or	
وریسی کول	*warisé kawal*	To remove.
خپګان	*khapgān*	Grievances.
راج	*rāj*	State.
طاقتور	*tāqatwar*	Powerful.
لاند کیدل	*lāndé kédal*	To be subdued.
جاسوس	*jāsūs*	Spy.
مخبر	*mukhbér*	Informer.
موقعی ته کتل	*muqé ta katal*	To watch opportunity.
خالی	*khāli*	Evacuated.
خپل ځان پټ کول	*khpal zān pat kawal*	Conceal oneself.
لوټ	*lūt*	Plunder, loot (noun)
موقعه موندل	*mōqa mūndal*	To get a chance.

پسونی *psūnay*   An ambush.

شوکمار *shūkmār*   A Robber.

شوکه کول *shūka kawal*   To rob.

مر کول یا وژل *mar kawal* or
wajhal   To put to death.

پایه تخت *pāya takht*   Capital.

EXERCISE 45.

A band of Arabs had collected among the mountains and were in the habit of stopping and looting caravans, as they crossed the pass. The inhabitants of the country around were also in great distress because of the tyranny of these bandits, while the Sultan's troops seemed powerless to deal with them, because of the strength of the position they had taken up in the mountains. The Sultan's counsellors were very anxious to deal effectively with the band which was daily becoming more powerful as it was attracting to its banner all the bad characters of the region. They accordingly sent spies to report on the movements of the robbers. Soon after, news came in from a spy that the band had left their strong hold to raid a tribe some distance away. The counsellors seized this opportunity to despatch a regiment of troops to intercept the robbers on their return with the plunder. The operation was completely successful as the thieves fell unwittingly into the ambush. Many of them were killed and the remainder surrendered to the Sultan's troops and were brought into the capital for trial. The Sultan sentenced most of them to death.

VOCABULARY XLVII.

زاکوز کیدل	*rā kūz kédal*	To come down.
خپل خپلوان	*khpal khpalwān*	Relations.
علاج	*ilaj*	Cure, remedy (noun).
دا ښه چل نۀ	*dā khuh chal nuh day*	This is not a good plan.
دى		
سترگى دۀ پټى	*stargé dé paté kree*	He should shut his eyes.
کړى		
خوږر کیدل	*khūg kédal*	To be hurt.
رسول	*rasawal*	To cause to arrive.
مشر	*mashar*	Elder.
پۀ قهر شۀ	*puh qahar shuh*	Became enraged.
ژوندى	*jhwanday*	Alive.
ښيل	*khayal*	To show, direct.
رسۍ	*rasai*	Rope.
سر	*sar*	The end, head.
پاس	*pās*	Up.
را اچول	*rā achawal*	To throw towards me or us.
ملا	*mlā*	Waist.
کلک	*klak*	Hard, tight.
پۀ زور سرۀ	*puh zōr sàra*	With force.

را گذار کول	*rā guzār kawal*	To throw down.
سره دَ راپریوتو	*sara da rāpréwato*	Immediately on falling.
کمبخت	*kam bakhta !*	O you unlucky one !
دخپل لاسَ	*da khpala lāsa*	Intentionally.
اجل	*ajal*	Fixed day for death.
گنره	*ganra*	Otherwise.
خان کندن یا	*zān kandan* or	
ذنکدن	*zankadan*	The point of death.
برج	*braj*	Tower.

EXERCISE 45.

يو جولا پۀ ونه کښی خنتلی وۀ اوبيا نۀ شو راکوزيدیَ نو خپل
ذپلوانُئی راجمع شول پۀ علاجُئی نۀ پوهيدل چه خذمه ئی راکوز کړۀ
چا به ويل راخَيَ چه داونه پری کړۀ نو چه ونه را پريرٌښي نو پڅپله به
تر راکوز شی بل به ويل نه دابنۀ چل نۀ دیَ دَ ونی دَ وني پۀ پريوتو
کښں به سړیَ مړ شي چا به ويل سترگی د ِبقی کوی او راتوپ
د کوی پوه به هم نۀ شي او پۀ زمکه به ودرِیږوی بل ويل نه داهم بنۀ
چل نۀ دیَ اسری به خوَبر شي چا به ويل راخَيَ چه یو پۀ بل
ودرِیږوُ او بل پۀ بل نو پۀ دی شان به خان وز وزسوُو او راکوز به ئی
کړۀ نورو ويل ذا هم بنۀ خبره نۀ دَه چا به ويل راخَيَ چه دَ وني خواته
يو برج جو پر کړۀ چه برج ور ورسی نو پۀ بدئی راکوز کړۀ بل ويل
تر برج تر جو پر ولو به سړیَ دَ لوری او تندی مړشي پۀ دوئ کښں
يو مشر وۀ چه هغه راغیَ نو ورته ديِر پۀ قهر شوُ او ويللُئی چه پۀ
داسی اسان چل باند هم نۀ پو هيږيِ ؟ ورشئ يوه لويه رسي

راو پريي چه رسېئي ئی راورره نو درسېي يو سرئی جولا ته پاس ورگذار کړ
ورته ئی وويل چه ملا پوری ئی کلک وتره چه هغه درسېي سر
ملا پوری، وتپلو نو دی مشر جولا دَ رسېي بل سر پۀ زور سره هکته
راهکلو لاندئی راگذارکړ سپرے سره دَ را پريوتو مېشو دی نورو جولا
گانو ورته و کم بخت دا دکۀ وکړل دخپل لس دَ سپرے ووژلو دۀ ورته
پۀ جواب کښ رو چه اجل ئی ؤه ښکه دۍ شو کنړه ما ډېر خلق پۀ
دی چل سره لۀ کوهی نه راویستلي دی—

VOCABULARY XLVII.

يو خائی کېدل	*yau zāi kédal*	To join.
تحریک یاشور و شر	*tahrik* or	
	shōr-o-shar	Movement.
ظاهره	*zāhéra*	Outwardly.
ځما لۀ وېرى	*zamā luh*	
	veyaré	Through fear of me
پټ	*pat*	Secretly.
پۀ جار	*puh jār*	Openly, publicly
اوزول	*aurawal*	To announce.
اعتبار یا وعده	*itébār* or *wada*	Assurance.
دَ قام مشران	*da qām*	The elders of the
	masharān	tribe.
پۀ باند یا	*puh-bandé* or	Through, by means
پۀ ذریعه دَ	*puh zaria da*	of.
سرحد	*sarhad*	Border.
هله ګله	*hala gula*	Disturbances.
فساد	*fasād*	Mischief.

انگریزي سرکار *angrézi sarkār* BritishGovernment.

لری کول یا رفع *laré kawal* or

کول *rafa kawal* To dispel.

رفع کیدل *rafa kédal* To be dispelled.

دَ پاره دَ دی *da pāra da dé* In order to

رعیت *rait* Subject.

دَ دشمنئی پهٔ نیت *da dushmanai puh niat* With hostile inten-tion.

نیت *niat* Intention.

پهٔ زړه زور تیرَول *puh zruh zōr térawal* or

یا برداشت کول یا *bardāsht kawal* or

صبر کول *sabar kawal* To tolerate.

گمراه *gumrāh* Mis-guided.

بی وجی یا بی *bé waje* or

هِصّه *bé hissa* Unprovoked.

یقین *yaqin'* Belief.

ساتل *sātal* To keep, watch.

منع کول *mana kawal* To prevent.

EXERCISE 47.

You have said my tribesmen can never join in such a movement openly for fear of me. If any one has gone, he must have gone secretly. What I now ask you, in accordance with those assurances of friendship, which you have so readily made, is that you will publicly announce

to the tribesmen throngh your local officers that,
if they cross the borders and join in disturbances
against the British Government, they will incur
your displeasure. (Lit: You will be annoyed from
them). The belief is entertained by many mis-
guided persons that they will not incur your
disapproval by acting in a hostile manner
against Government and this belief can be
dispelled if your officers will keep watch along
the river and at other places in order to prevent
your subjects from crossing the Frontier with
hostile intentions, whether secretly or openly.
I ask you therefore, to issue orders to this effect.
By so doing you may put an end to these
disturbances, which were wholly unprovoked
and cannot be tolerated.

VOCABULARY XLIX.

امزری یا زمری	*amzaray* or *zmaray*	Tiger.
(ته) نصیحت کول	*(ta) nasihat kawal*	To advise.
گوره	*gōra*	Look here.
ځناور	*zanāwar*	Animal.
خبردار	*khabardār*	Beware, be careful.
جګړه خلاصول	*jagara khlāsawal*	To settle dispute.
إنصاف	*insāf*	Justice.
خدائی پاک	*khudāi pak*	Pure God.

طاقت	*tāqat*	Power, strength.
مناسب دى	*munāseb di*	It is befitting.
عاجز	*ājaz*	Poor, needy.
غور	*ghōr*	Justice, care.
پۀ ښۀ شان سره	*puh khuh shān sara*	Satisfactorily.
بيزو	*bīzō*	Monkey.
شکل	*shakal*	Appearance.
اوږد	*ūgad*	Long.
لۀ لرى نه	*luh laré na*	From a distance.
اوږى	*lūgay*	Smoke.
دَ سرى پۀ غوږو ډير بد لږى	*da sarı puh ghwagō dér bad lagee*	One can not bear to hear it.
پۀ باندى صرپه کول	*puh bāndé sarpa kawal*	To spare.
که دلاس دَ کيږى	*kuh da lāsā dé kégee*	If possible.
پۀ باندى لاس برکيدل	*puh-bāndé lās bar kédal*	To get the better of.
مُنصف	*munséf*	Just (Adjective.)
لږ ډير	*lag dér*	Some what.
ملاويدل	*melāwédal*	To resemble.

EXERCISE 48.

يو امزرى خپل ځوى تۀ نصيحت کاوۀ ويل ئى ځوره تۀ بۀ پس لۀ مانه په دى ځنګل کښ دَ ټولو څناورو بادشاه ئى او بادشاه نوم دَ خدائى دى خبردار حه پۀ چا بيځنۀ ظلم ونۀ کړى۔ ډير ځلق به در لۀ دَ جغرو ځلاصولو دپاره راځى ولى تۀ پۀ انصاف سره هرۀ جغره

فیصله کوهٔ چا له چه خدای پاک طاقت ورکوی نو مناسب دی چه
دَ خوارو عاجزو غوٍ پهٔ ننهٔ شان سره کوی مهر یاد لره په دی خذٔهل
کښ یو ښناور دی چه پهٔ دوهٔ ببو کرښی شکل ئی دَ بیزو سره
لر، بیر ملاویدره خلق ورته سپی وائی اکثر ورسنه یو تور اوبرد لرگی
وی هر کله چه مؤنبر خلق ووینی نو دا لرگی راته نیغ ونسی
دَ دی لرگی نه لربزی راوڅی او دَ دی لوربی یو داسی ناکار او
ناښنا اواز وشی چه دسپی پهٔ غوزو بیر بد لربی او دَ دی اواز
پهٔ اوریدو سمدستی سپی زخمی شی پهٔ زمکه راپریوڅی او هوښی
نو ښما خبره واؤره چه په دی ښناور هیچری صر په ونهٔ کوی که ګنهګار
وی که بیګناه خو چه وی وینی او که دَ لاسَ د کیدبی نو وژنهئی
انصاف ورسره مهٔ کوهٔ بچی ورته و ٍبا بانوزه پهٔ ښهٔ بادشاه شوم چه
انصاف ورسره نهٔ کوم امزری ورته ویل بچیّ پهٔ هر ښناور کښ
انصاف شته ولی په دهٔ کښ خوبالکل نشته او دام هم اوریدلی دیٍ ٔ
چه په خپلو وروڼو ئی لاس برشی نو هم ورباند صر په نهٔ کوی نو څکه
ښما نصیحت واوره چه بی انصاف دشمن لهٔ ښان اول وژل
پکار دی —

VOCABULARY L.

بله ورځ	*bala vraz*	The following day.
جامی اغوستل	*jāmé aghustal*	To dress.
زر زر	*zar zar*	Hastily
دَ کبانو ښکار	*da kabānō khkār*	Fishing
ایله ایله رڼا	*ila ila ranra*	Hardly light.
ترڅوڼی	*taraghune*	Dusk.
واقعه	*waqea*	Mishap, adventure.

دوغل	*dōghal*	Pit.
ګرب	*grab*	Hole.
ټوپۍ	*tōpai*	Cap, hat.
لرزیدل	*larzédal*	To shake or shaking, to tremble.
لرزان	*larzān*	Shaking, trembling.
دَ-وار خطا کیدل	*da-wār khaṭā kédal*	To be dismayed.
وار خطا	*wār khaṭā*	Alarmed, dismayed.
اوتر	*autar*	Alarmed, frightened
هډوکی	*hadūkay*	Bone.
کر کر پٔه خندا کیدل	*kar kar puh khandā kédal*	To burst out laughing.
مقام	*muqām*	Halting place.
پراؤ	*parāw*	Camp.
رابر	*rabar*	Adventure.
جست پٔه وخت	*jukht puh wakht* or *puh khuh wakht*	
یا پٔه ښٔه وخت		Just in time.
ښه شروع	*kha shurū*	Satisfactory beginning.
بچ کیدل	*bach kédal*	To be saved.

EXERCISE 49.

The following day my friend and I were up in good time and after dressing hastily mounted our ponies which were in readiness at the door, and started for a twelve miles ride to the river where we were going to fish. It was nearly 3 o'clock when we started. Soon after starting I had a little mishap which might have put an end to my sport for that and many days. In the uncertain light my pony put his foot into a hole and came down with me, throwing me over his head. Luckily my topi saved me and I got up with nothing worse than a shaking. My friend at first was a little alarmed, but when he found there was no bone broken, he burst into a hearty laugh in which I joined. We reached our halting place without any further adventure and just in time to get the best of the early morning. A few minutes afterwards I landed my first mashir, a small one it is true, but a satisfactory beginning.

VOCABULARY LI.

تازه	tāza	Fresh.
مرى	maray	Dead body.
مرى به وشو	maray ba wosho	One would die.
قبر	qabar	Grave.
اديره	adira	Graveyard.
سپرؤدل	sparōdal	To untie, open.
كفن	kafan	Shroud.
را قل كول	rā tōl kawal	To collect, to undress.
كپړه	kapra	Cloth.
گذاره كول	guzāra kawal	To live on
گذران كول	guzrān kawal	

تنڠ کیدل	tang kédal	To be oppressed.
پۀ لاس ورتلل	puh lās wartlal	To come to hand, to find.
ګنړه	ganra	Otherwise.
اسمان	asmān	Sky.
ستورَی	stōray	Star.
مرض	maraz	Illness.
زیاتیدل	ziātédal	To increase.
دارُو	dārū	Medicine.
دَ ـ دمه کیدل	da-dama kédal	To recover from illness.
وصیت کول	wasiyat kawal	To make a will.
وران کار	vran kar	Evil deed.
قیامت	qayāmat	The day of judgement
نیکي	néki	Goodness.
وجه	waja	Reason.
دعا کول	duā kawal	To pray for.
نیک کارُونه	nék kārūna	Good deeds.
نتیجه	natija	Result.
عمل	amal	Act.
بخښل	bakhal	To forgive.
کسب	kasab	Occupation.
پۀ غلا	puh ghla	Secretly.
اولنی	awalanay	The first one, the former.
جوړ	jōr	Accordingly.
وروستنی	vrustonay	The last one, the latter.

خُدای دې ئی وبخښی	*khudāi dé yé wo bakhee*	May God forgive him!
حيادار	*hayādār*	Modest.
شرَمَول	*sharmawal*	To put to shame.
دَ وْرستَنی پهُ نيوو پسی شوَل	*da vrūstoni puh niwo pasé shwal*	They were after arresting the latter.
(ته) دَ اسمان ستوری ښيل	*(ta) da asmān stōri khayal*	To punish severely, (lit. to show the stars of the sky).

EXERCISE 50.

يو سړی وه چهُ تازه مړیَ به وشو نو دَ شپی به ورغی قبر
به ئی دَ دهُ وسپرو دلو دَ مړی نه به ئی کفن راښول کړ کور ته به ئی
راوړ دا دَ کفن کېړه به ئی پهُ يو بل خرڅوله او پهُ دی به ئی گذُران
کاوهُ خلق ور نه ډير تنګ شُو مهر پهُ لاس نهُ ورتلو گنړه دَ اسمان
ستوری به ئی ور ته ښيئلی رؤ يوه ورځ ناجوړ شو مرض ئی ورځ
پهُ ورځ زياتيدهُ پهُ هيڅ دارو ئی ښه نهُ کيده نو پوه شو چه اوسم
آخر وخت دی نو خپل ښوی يی راغوښتلو ورتهُئی وصيت کاوهُ ويلئی
چهُ گوره بچیَ ماډير وران وران کارونه کړی دی خدايـی خبر چه
پهُ قيامت کښ به ښما ښهُ حال وی تهُ خپل مؤنخ اودس کوه
اوبد کارونه مهُ کوه داسی کار کوه چه خلق درنه خوشحالَ شی-او
ستا دَنيکیـی پهُ وجه هم دعا کوی چه کفن کښ (*kakh*) مهر
شو نو ښویـی ئی پهُ زړهُکښ ووَ چه کهُ زهُ ډير نيک کارونه کوم خو
نتيجه به ئی هم ماته رسيدری پلار ته به م ښهُ فائده ونه رسی ښکه
چه هر سړیَ به پهُ خپل عمل خلا صيدری جوړ ماله داسی کار کول
پکاردی چه ور باندم پلار ته خلق دعا کوی او خدايـی ئی وبخښی

نو هاک هم دپلار کسب شروع کړ چه مړۍ به وشو نو د شپۍ به
ورځی قبر به ئی د دۀ وسپرو کفن به ئی ترراتلول کړ او بيا به ئی
ورنه پوزه او غورزو نه. هم پرۍ نول خلقو چه ډاکړ وايد نو ډير خپه
شو ويل ئی اولنۍ کپن کښی (kakh) د خدايي وبخښی ډير
ځنه حيادار سوی وۀ کفن به ئی يولرو ولی مړی خو به ئی نۀ
شرمولو نو و مړبی کپن کښی (kakh) ته به ئی دعا کوله او وک ورستنی
پۀ نيولو پسی شول—

MISCELLANEOUS COLLOQUIAL SENTENCES V.

When did you hear this news?

Dā khabara dé kala aurédalé dah?

It is only a rumour that the Amir of Afghanistan is coming to Peshawar.

Dā khāli yau awāza dah chi da Afghanistān Amir Pékhawar ta rāzee.

The whole of our Regt. deserted from the field of battle.

Da jang luh maidān na zamūng tōla paltan wo takhtédah.

50 of them have been taken prisoners.

Panzōs qaid shwal.

We know nothing of the others. They may have gone towards the enemy.

Da nōrō puh bāb ké hiss khabar nuh yū dushman ta ba takhtédali wi.

Wire the Police and inform the Deputy Commissioner.

Pūlas ta tār war kra aw dipty comishnar khabar kra.

They all will be tried by Court Martial.

Pa kōt marshal bāndé ba da dūi faisala kégee.

Sign this agreement, write your name here.	*Pa dé iqrār nāma bāndé daskhat wō kra, dalta khpal nūm wo lika.*
Do you plead guilty or not guilty ?	*Tuh gunahgār yé kuh bégunāh ?*
Do you want to produce witnesses in your defence ?	*Tuh khpalé safāi da pāra gawāhān pésh kawal ghwāré ?*
Is this your signature ?	*Dā stā daskhat day ?*
Why don't you complain to Govt. against him ?	*Walé war bāndé sarkār ta shikāyat nuh kawé.*
I have seen it with my own eyes.	*Mā puh khpalo stargō lidalay day.*
What enmity is there between you and him?	*Stā aw da haghuh puh mianz ké suh dushmani dah ?*
Can he sing and dance?	*Hagha sandaré wayalay shi aw gadéday shi ?*
Tell the truth and nothing but the truth.	*Rikhtiā rikhtiā khabara kawa.*
This village is of very bad repute.	*Dā kalay dér bad nām day.*
The Regt. will head the list.	*Paltan awal lambar ba shi.*
You will get two months furlough after the grand parade.	*Da lōi parait na pas dar ta da dwao miāshto razā ba milāo shee.*
It is a very disgraceful thing.	*Da déra da sharam khabara dah.*

First take a good aim and then shoot.

Awal khuh zéray wo lagawa aw biā yé wola.

Challenge them first and then shoot.

Awal war bāndé awāz wo kra aw biā yé wola.

We stood our ground for the whole day.

Tōla vraz mūnga muqābila wo kra.

The ascent is difficult on that side, one cannot climb that way.

Puh haghe taraf charāi grāna dah aw saray war bāndé khatalay nuh shee.

It is all descent from Cherat right down to Pabbi.

Luh chirāt na ain tar pabō pōré utrāi dah.

My double barrelled gun has been stolen. I suspect my servant.

Zamā dwa naliz tōpak puh ghlā talay day puh khpal naukar bāndé zamā gumān day.

We surrounded the fort and blocked all the approaches to it.

Mūnga kalā géra kra aw tōlé lāré mo war ta bandé kré.

I am very glad to see you, Sahib.

Sahiba? Zuh stā puh lidalō dér khushāl yam.

You only recently came to Peshawar so I thought I should come to pay my respects to you.

Tuh ōs ōs Pékhawar ta rāghalay yé no fikar mé wo kar chi pakār di chi zuh stā salām wo kram.

I am feeling very cold.

Zama déra yakhni kégee.

It is a pity that you did not tell me this before.

Dā da afsōs khabara dah chi dā hāl tā mā ta awal wo nuh wayalo.

Owing to the Mohmand expedition, no harvesters can be found as they all work as labourers.

Dā Mohmando da lām puh sabab laugari mūndal grān kār day, zaka chi tōl mazdūri kawee.

I cannot drive a tonga as I have never tried.

Zuh tānga nuh sham chalawalay zaka chi hicharé mé kōshash nuh day karay.

He is a great miser and will pay up with great difficulty.

Hagha dér shūm day aw puh déra mushkela sara ba pésé war kree.

This will be settled later on when the sahib comes back from tour.

Vrosto ba dā faisala shee kala chi sāhib luh dauré na biarta rāshee.

Where were you born?

Tuh puh kum zāi ké paida shway wé?

How long has your Regt been in this Station?

Stā paltan pa dé chāwnrai ké kala rāsé dah?

Do you own any land? what revenue do you pay to the Govt?

Stā suh zmaka shta? sōmra mālia sarkār ta war kawé?

Wake me just at 7 if I am still asleep.

Jukht puh owuh bajé mé wikh kra kuh puh hagha wakht zuh ūduh yam.

Bring my breakfast while I am in bed.

Kala chi zuh puh kat ké yam, no zamā hāzéri rāwra.

Take the horse for exercise and saddle it at 5 p. m.	*Ass rōl da pāra bōza aw puh pinzuh bajé māzdigar yé zin kra.*
Do not be late.	*Nāwakhta kawa ma.*
Why did not you bring me some hot water as I told you?	*Chi dar ta mé wo wayal no walé dé suh garmé obuh rā nuh wré?*
All the towels in the house are dirty.	*Puh kōr ké tōl taulyāgān khiran di.*
Bring any one you like.	*Sōk chi dé khwakh wi hagha rāwala.*
Wind this watch as it will stop.	*Dé garai la kunji war kra zaka chi banda ba shi.*
Pump the cycle up I think it is punctured.	*Bāisekal la bād war kra, zamā puh kheyāl ké panchar day.*
Tighten the screws of the wheel.	*Da pāyé dibrai sakhté kra.*
Take the measurement of my foot.	*Zamā da khpé nāp wākhla.*
The leather must be soft.	*Pakār di chi sarman narma wi.*
This room is full of mosquitoes, flit the whole room.	*Dā kamra da māshō na daka dah puh tōla kamra ké da māsko tél charqāo kra.*
I shall dismiss you if you don't prove it.	*Kuh dā khabara sābéta nuh kré, no zuh ba dé nūm kat kram.*
Is there any fishing obtainable here now?	*Oss dalta suh da kabānō khkār mūndalay shi kuh na.*

When the water is clear the fiishermen will come with their nets from Lalpura.

Kala chi obuh ranré shee no machi mārān ba luh lāl ṗūré na sara da jālūno rāshee.

The sky is very clear today.

Nan asmān bilkul or *tak shin day.*

It is getting cooler day by day.

Vraz ṗuh vraz yakhni kégee.

It is cloudy and cold today, it is drizzling.

Nan woriaz dah aw yakhni dah, sāskay dāy.

The rain has stopped now, let us go to the city.

Oss bārān walār day, rāza chi khahar ta lārshoo.

Why did your pony put its foot into the hole?

Walé stā da ass khṗa ṗuh grubi ké lāra.

Because it was dark and he could see nothing.

Zaka chi tyāruh wah aw hiss yé lidalay nuh shwal.

The tiger made a will in favour of his son.

Zmari khṗal zōi ta wasiat wo kro.

Tell your local officer to keep a watch along the river and other places so that the tribesmen may not join the disturbance.

Da khṗal qām masha-rāno ta waya chi da sind ghāré aw nor zāyūno ta khyāl kawee chi da qām khalq ṗuh dé jagara ké shāmel nuh shi.

A weaver had climbed up the tree and could not get down.

Jōla ṗuh wana ké khatalay woh aw biā ra kūzédalay nuh sho.

How did the people bring him down?

Khalqo sanga ra kūz kar?

| They had made a permanent residence on the top of the hill. | *Hagho da ghar puh sar bānde khpal da osédo zāi jōr karay woh.* |

VOCABULARY LII.

و روکی غونډۍ	*warūke ghundai*	Low ridge.
غونډۍ	*ghundai*	Hillock.
لو ره ژوره	*lwarā jhawara*	Low undulation.
ختل	*khatal*	Ascend.
کوزیدل	*kūzédal*	To descer.d.
تنګه تنګۍ	*tanga tangai*	Narrow defile.
قریب قریب	*qarib qarib*	Practically.
حد۔برید	*had, brid*	Limit.
دره	*dara*	Valley.
معمولی	*māmūli*	Precarious kind.
بیا هم	*biā hum*	Even then.
عین تر-پورې	*ain tar-pōré*	Right down till.
لائق	*lāieq*	Fit, worthy, capable.
اباد	*abād*	Cultivated or populated.
ابادی	*abādi*	Cultivation or population.
کلپ	*kalp*	Steep.
اوبهٔ خور	*obuh khwar*	Irrigation.
تل	*tal*	Bed (of the river or well.)
تلیٰ	*talay*	Palm of hand, Sole of foot.

پټ	*pat*	Stealthily.
ګنز ځنګل	*ganr zangal*	Dense Jungle
لوښه	*lūkha*	Reeds.
لوی لوی واښه	*lōi lōi wākhuh*	High grass.
املی	*imli*	Tamarind.
تر اوس پورې	*tar osa pōré*	Still.
غریب خلق	*gharib khalq*	Miserable inhabitant.
ژور	*jhawar*	Deep.
پلن	*plan*	Broad.
اوبه ترزنګون زنګون	*obuh tar zangūn*	
پورې دی	*zangūn pōré di*	The water is knee deep.
ګرزیدل	*garzédal*	To walk, to turn.
وران	*vrān*	Ruined.
زنګون یا	*zangūn* or	} Knee.
ګوده	*gōda*	

EXERCISE 51.

The road now leads over the low ridge on the left, and going over some low undulations, descends to the river through a narrow defile between low hills. This pass is practically the limit of the cultivation of the Mashhad valley; for though there is a little beyond, it is of the most precarious kind. The villagers exist in constant fear from Turkoman raiders; yet under a strong government the whole valley of this

river right down to Akdarhand, is capable of
being kept in the highest state of cultivation, as
there is abundance of water in the river, of which
banks are low enough to admit of its being dist-
ributed for irrigation. The road now goes
along the bed of the river, which is covered with
a dense jungle of tamarind and high grass and
one mile and a half further on passes the old Fort
of Nazarian, where there are still a few miserable
inhabitants. It then crosses the river which is
here only two and a half feet deep and thirty
feet broad, then turns to the left and ascends
the right bank to a ruined fort. It then passes
over an undulation and descends again to the
bed of the river at Inayatabad.

VOCABULARY LIII.

قارغه	*qārghuh*	Crow.
پُه امان	*puh amān*	Peacefully.
سلامتی	*salāmati*	Safety.
سلامت	*salmat*	Safe.
فارسی خوان	*fārsi khwān*	Persian (man.)
پايي	*pai*	Foot ⎫
دست	*dast*	Hand ⎬ Persian.
یا دست مرد	*yā dasté mard*	Either make use of
یا پايي مرد	*yā pai mard*	your hands or feet. (you should fight otherwise run away to save yourself.)

مقابله کول	*muqābéla kawal*	To withstand.
دا بهتره ده	*dā behtara dah*	It is better.
خود	*khud*	Certainly.
تښتیدل	*takhtédal*	To flee.
تـیښته	*tékhta*	Flight.
ادميان	*admian*	Men.
بزُدل	*buzdil*	Coward.
بزدلي	*buzdili*	Cowardice.
دین	*din*	Religion.
مذهب	*mazhab*	Religion.
روا یا حلال	*rawā*, or *halāl*	Lawful.
خصوصاً	*khusūsan*	Especially.
هر کله	*har kala*	When ever.
تیت کیدل	*tit kédal*	To bend down.
لوُنه یا	*lūta* or	
غوندِه	*ghunda*	Clod of earth.
اوچتول	*ūchatawal*	To pick up, lift up.
لستونړی	*lastōnray*	Sleeve.
لۀ لری نه	*luh laré na*	From a distance.
لۀ ورایه	*luh vrāyā*	From a distance.
سیل کول	*sail kawal*	To fly about.
خواه مخواه	*khwāh makhwāh*	Some how or other.

EXERCISE 52.

یو قارغۀ ذبیل څوئ ته نصیحت کاوۀ ویل ئی چه ویره لۀ هرڅیز
نه څه دۀ هر څوک چه ویدیرِی نو مدام به یۀ امان او سلامت وی

فارسی خوان وائي یا دست مرد یا پای مرد او څملوبر دَ خلقو
خو دَ مقابلی طاقت خود نشته نو دا بهتره که چه دشمن ته میدان
پریږدؤ او وتښتؤ ترنه او فرض کوه چه مؤنږ مقابله هم وکړؤ نو خوا
مخواه به مو یا لاس مات شي یا ښپه نو به جنګ کښ څه خیر دی؟
نو بچیّ څما نصیحت واوره هر یو څناور چه درته نیغ شي نو تښته تر
دی تیښتی ته آدمیان بزدلي وائي ، هر څمونږ په مذهب کښ
روا ده خصوصاً لۀ سپو نه ډیر ویریدل پکار دی هر کله چه دی زمکی
ته ڤیت شي نو سمدستی تر الوځه څکه چه دا لۀ زنکی نه کانږی یا
لوڼه را اوچتوي بچي ورته په جواب کښ وو چه با با ؟ که دغه
سپي په لستوڼوي کښ پټ دَ څان سره کانږي راوړی وی نو زۀ
به يئ څۀ وکړم دابه ښۀ وی چه سپي لۀ اړی نه و وینم نو به تر والوځ
پلار ورته و شاباش ؟ تۀ لۀ ماته هوښیار ئی ورځه سیل کوه هر چرته
چه څی سلامت به ئی ––

VOCABULARY LIV.

تَتُو	tatu	Pony.
روان کیدل	rawān kédal	To set out.
نور خاته	nwar khātuh	Day break.
اوبۀ ډکول	obuh dakawal	To draw water.
ګیره	gira	Beard, whiskers.
بریت	brét	Moustache.
ګنړل	ganṛal	To consider.
اوتر	autar	Alarmed.
پس لۀ هغۀ	pas luh hagha	Afterwards.
پیری	péray	Genie.
خاپیري	khāpérai	Fairy.

EXERCISE 53.

I arrived with the Regiment I was attached to all safe at Agra where I bought a pony for eleven rupees and in company with four or five other sepoys, who had got leave also, I set out for my village. I reached my home early one morning before it was light and waited outside till day break. When my mother came out to draw (fill) water, I called to her, but she did not recognise me in the least, for during the four or five years I had been absent, I had grown from a boy into a man. I had also whiskers and a moustache and considered myself a handsome sepoy. My mother seemed so alarmed when I spoke to her, that I also became frightened, but afterwards my father told me that my uncle had written home to say that I had been killed so my mother thought at first that I was a genie.

VOCABULARY LV.

اعتبار	itébar	Trust.
محتاج	muhtāj	Needy.
مشتۀ من	shtuh man	Rich.
دا يوه عامه خبره ده	dā yawa āma khabara dah	This is a common thing.
پردى	praday	Stranger.

خلق ورته نۀ شی کتی	khalq war ta nuh shi katay	The people cannot bear to see him.
شرمیدل	sharmédal	To be ashamed.
حاکم	hākam	Ruler.
سپک کول	spak kawal	To insult.
برباد کول یا تالا کول نورل	barbād kawal or tālā kawal or narawal	To ruin.
کۀ داسی نۀ شی کیدی	kuh dāsé nuh shi kéday	If this is impossible.
کوهی	kūhay	Well (of water.)
ور گذار کول	war gūzār kawal	To throw down.
گذار	gūzar	A blow.
خیر	khér	Well.
د-پۀ سر	da puh sar	Against.
مخبر	mukhber	Informer.
سرۀ زر	sruh zar	Gold.
سپین زر	spin zar	Silver.
زیر	ziar	Brass.
تانبه	tānba	Copper.
مور	mōr	Rich, replete.
مارۀ	māruh	Rich, replete (Plural.)
جور	jōr	Accordingly.
اندر پایه	andrapāya	Ladder.
گټ	gut	Corner.
پهره	péhra	Sentry go.

سنتری اودرول	*sentri ōdrawal*	To post a sentry.
پۀ ډاګ کښې	*puh dāg ké*	
اچول	*achawal*	To post (a letter).
پۀ باند لاس پوری	*puh bāndé lās*	
کول	*pōré kawal*	To start. commence.
کالی	*kāli*	Ornaments.
نغدی روپۍ	*naghdé rupai*	Cash.
پنډ	*pand*	Parcel, bundle.
مالګه	*mālga*	Salt
اوچت پاخیدل	*ūchat pāsédāl*	Get up straight.
نمک حلال	*namak halāl*	Loyal.
نمک حرام	*namak harām*	Disloyal.
نمک	*namak*	Salt (Urdu.)
او ریدل	*aurédal*	To cross over.

EXERCISE 54.

د خلیلو پۀ علاقه کښې پۀ یو کلی کښې یو دولتمند اروۀ چه
خلقو ورباندی د ډیر لوی دولت اعتبار کاوۀ ډیر سړی ښۀ سړی وۀ د خدای
پۀ نمد بهیی غریبانو او محتاجانو له ډیر ښۀ ورکول مګر دغه یو
ګدا ئی وۀ چه شته من وۀ نو ورځ پۀ ورځ بهئی پۀ کلی کښې
دشمنان زیاتیدل او دا یوه عامه خبره ده چه د پیستقو پۀ وطن کښې
څوک دولتمند شی او خدای پاک ورله عزت ورکړی نو د ډیلو پردو
بدی شی او ورته نۀ شی کنی او د هریو داخوښدوی چه دی
خوار شوی بد نام شوی وشرمیدی نو یاخوبی د علاقی د حاکمانو
سپارښ لو ببادوی ئی او کۀ دانه شی ببدی نو پنچله ورته ښۀ
ناښۀ دوهی وکنی پۀ کښې ئی ورکړدا کوی خیر د دی دولتمند

زميندار پهٔ سر ډيرى مخبرۍ غير علاقتى ته لارى چه كهٔ دا وه
پروكوئ نو پهٔ سرو سپينو به مارهٔ شئ جوړ يو شپه دَ پنځهٔ ريشتو
اپريدو يوه داړه چه ورسره دَ كلي بدمعاشان هم يو ځائى شول پهٔ
نيمه شپه پهٔ كلى راننوته اندر پائى يى وتړلى او سم دَ دى زميندار پهٔ
كور ورواوريدل اول خوئى دَ كور ټول سړى او ځوكيدار وتړلو او بيا ئى
دَ كور نظى يو خواته وشړلى او پهره ئى پر ودَروله چه شور ونهٔ كوى
او بيا ئى پهٔ لوټ لاس پورى كړ ټول كالى جامى او نغدى روپئى ئى
راجمع كړلى پنډوونه ئى تړ وتړل چه روانيدل نويو په كښى وړ چه داده
روټنئى راخفى چه ژئ خوړهٔ جوړ تول راجمع شول روټيئ ئى
وخورهٔ پهدى كښى يو مشرهٔ اوچت پاڅيد ويل ئى راځئ چه
ځوهٔ چه دَ دى كور نمک مو وخوړ نو غلا ئى نهٔ كوهٔ كوهٔ آخر مؤنږ كښى خو
هم خهٔ پښتو شته لارل پنډوونه ئى پهٔ ځاى پريښودل—

VOCABULARY LVI.

ميدان	*maidān*	Open ground, plain
خوشى	*khushay*	Deserted, useless.
خالى	*khāli*	Empty.
كوچ	*kōch*	March.
شگه	*shaga*	Sand.
ځاڅكى	*sāskay*	A drop.
موسمى باران	*mōsami bārān*	Periodical rain.
تلاو	*talāw*	Tank.
اوچ	*och*	Dry.
سفر	*safar*	Journey.
زرى	*zaray*	Guide.
زيرى	*zéray*	Good news.

پاؤ باند, یو میل *pāw bānde*
                  yau mil   1¼ mile.

تالاش *talāsh*   Search.

کنودل *kanōdal*   To dig.

مشک *mashk*   Mussak.

دَ مخ کیس صرورت *da ṁakh ke*
                  zarūrat   Future necessity.

EXERCISE 55.

After leaving this place we proceeded twenty three miles and encamped near a well on a piece of open ground in the jungle. Many deserted (empty) villages were met with on the march and the road was, for the most part, over heavy sand, (there was much sand on many parts of the road) without a drop of water near. Periodical rains had failed in this part of the country, the tanks and wells had mostly dried up, which rendered the heat and length of our journey that day all the more distressing. Luckily the guide whom we had brought with us and who had frequently travelled along this road, informed us that at about a mile and quarter distant were a few huts, the inhabitants of which were supplied with water from a spring. We set out immediately in search of it and our great joy found it was not dried up (When we found that it was not dried up we were very much pleased) and

on digging up a little in the sand an abundance
of water flowed out, from which we drank our-
selves and watered our horses and camels and
made the bhisties fill their mussacks for future
necessities.

VOCABULARY LVII

ملاقات	*mulāqāt*	Interview, visit.
لنډ	*land*	Short.
لنډه خلاصول	*landa khlāsawal*	To cut short.
خبره داده	*khabara dā dah*	The true fact is.
عام	*ām*	Common.
ګوته	*guta*	Finger.
بر خلاف	*barkhélāf*	Against.
بر ناحقه	*barnāhaqa*	Without any cause or reason.
نو څۀ چل وشي	*no suh chal woshee*	Then what happens.
لښته	*lakhta*	Stick, cane, power.

EXERCISE 56.

يو زميندار د ډيټي کمشنر صاحب ملاقات د پاره تللی وۀ چه وئی

غوښتو نو پۀ ملاقات کښ تر نه صاحب پُښتنه وکړه چه ماته د پښتنو ټول

حال ووايه چه داخَذه خلق دی دی سړي ورته و چه صاحب

د پښتنو قصی خو ډيری او لوئی لوئی دی نو لنډه ئی خلاصه کړم او

نۀ دا اورېدی قصی درته راشروع کړم صاحب ورته و لنډه ئی وايه ځکه

چه ماته دومره وخت چرته دی چه داسی لوئی لوئی قصی واورم

دۀ ورته و صاحبَ ؟ خبره دَ اده چه پۀ پَښتنو کښں يو سرے لۀ

عامو خلقو نه يوه ګوته اوچت شى نو خلق ئى خوا منخواه برخلاف شى

او چد دوه ګوتى اوچت شى نو خلق ئى بر ناحقه دشمنان شى

او چد درى ګوتى اؤچت شى نو بيا يى وژنى ۔ نۀ ئى پريږردى په

دى باند صاحب ويرِ وخندل او تپوس ئى ترو کړ چه کۀ خلوو ګوتى

او چت شى نو بيا څۀ چل وشى زميندارو بيا سلامت شى دا

څاورمه ګوته ستاسو لخته دَه چه جاله ئى پۀ لاس وراُرئى نو طاقت ئى

پيدا شى او خپل خان پر بچولى شى—

VOCABULARY LVIII.

<div dir="rtl">پۀ باند بحث کول</div>	*puh bāndé bahas kawal*	To discuss.
	or	
<div dir="rtl">خبرو ، اترې کول</div>	*khabaré atare kawal*	
<div dir="rtl">فيصله کول</div>	*faisala kawal*	To decide, to settle.
<div dir="rtl">ټکره</div>	*tukra*	Piece.
<div dir="rtl">دَ حق شفعى دعوى کول</div>	*da haq shufé dawa kawal*	To claim a right? of pre-emption.
<div dir="rtl">جګره</div>	*jagara*	Quarrel.
<div dir="rtl">شريعت</div>	*shariāt*	Mohammedan Law.
<div dir="rtl">کۀ داسى نۀ کوي</div>	*kuh dāsé nuh kawi*	If they refuse to do so.
<div dir="rtl">پۀ باند لښکر کول</div>	*puh-bāndé lakhkar kawal*	To raise an army against.
<div dir="rtl">پۀ باند پۀ زور کول</div>	*puh-bāndé puh zōr kawal*	To compel.
<div dir="rtl">قبضه</div>	*qabza*	Possession.

پښتو	*pukhtu*	Pathan honour.
عرضی	*arzi*	Petition.
دا پښتو کښې پہ دا کار نہ دی پکار	*puh pukhtu ké dā kār nuh day pakār*	The Pathan honour forbids this.
لو کول	*law kawal*	To harvest.
خہ خاص کار	*suh khās kār*	Particular business.
کہ دی کښ ورته	*kuh dé ké war*	Should it be made
خہ خیر وی	*ta suh kher wi*	worth their while.

EXERCISE 57.

The matter was discussed at a full Jirga of all tribes. It will be remembered that the Mondo Khel purchased and forcibly took possession of a piece of land over which the Takhli Khel claimed a right of pre-emption. It was decided that the Mondo Khel should be offered an opportunity of deciding the dispute according to the Mohammadan Law and that if they refused to do so the united tribes should raise an army to compel them. The Mondo Khel said that if they had known that there would have been all this trouble, they would never have taken the land but as they have actually got possession, Pathan honour forbade them withdrawing then. They accordingly sent an application to three tribes asking for their assistance. Had it been worth their while, these tribes would certainly have joined in, as they had finished cutting

their crops and at that time had no particular
business of their own to attend to.

VOCABULARY LIX.

لت	*lat*	Slothful.
ناراستی	*nārāsti*	Laziness.
خوزیدل	*khwazédal*	To move, (intransitive.)
نور	*nwar*	Sunshine.
لاروی	*lāraway*	Traveller.
لۇ کۇټی	*lūkūti*	Little.
مۇنږ سوری ته کړی	*mūng sōri tā krai*	Take us into the shade
بعضی	*bazé*	Some.
ساده	*sāda*	Simple.
خوار	*khwār*	Poor, helpless.
راکۇزیدل	*rā kūzédal*	To come down, dismount.
خدای د و بخښنه	*khudāi dé wo bakha*	May God forgive you !
ثواب	*sawāb*	Reward from God.
ثواب به د وشی	*sawāb ba dé wo shee*	You will get reward from God.
بینت	*baint*	Cane, stick.
بی غیرت	*bé ghairata*	Oh, you shameless one !
دومره نه شرمیږی	*dōmra nuh sharmégé*	Have you not so much shame ?
روغ موټ	*rōgh mōt*	Safe and sound.

بچڙ bachū	My son! (in a sarcastic manner.)
ازار āzār	Curse.
بيره bera	A wild plum.
غلی ghalay	Silent.
خان دَ كوڼ كړ zān dé kūnr kar	You pretended to be deaf.
حد had	Limit.
دۀ له حدَ روبسته duh luh hada wo wista	He has gone beyond the limit.
كم بخت kam bakht	Unlucky.
كوړی شه kuré sha	Get out you beast. (driving away a dog)
له دۀ نه به څوک څۀ la duh na ba sōk suh khér vree خير و ږی	What good is he to people ?
حكومت كول hukūmat kawal	To rule.

EXERCISE 58.

پۀ يو ځای كښې دَ يوی ونی الند درې لقان پراتۀ ؤو ۔ ناراستی
ئی دی دی حد ته رسيدلی وَه ۔ چه دَ ځای نۀ خوزېدل ۔ چه نور به
پر راغی نو دَ لری لاړو ته به ئی دو چه لوكوڼی خو مؤنږ سوری ته
كړئ ۔ بعضی به چه ساده خلق ؤو نو دوئ به ئی سوری ته كړل
يقين به ئی وشو چه څواران به ناجوړ روی ۔ څۀ لۀ ځای نۀ شی
خوزېدی ۔ او چا به در پوری و خندل تر به تير شوی وه ورځ ورباند
يو شور راغی ۔ چه دَ دوئی خوا ته را ناېزدی شو نو يو ورته اواز كړو
چه څوان لوكوڼی دَ دی اسَ را كوژ شه او لرېی اوبۀ راكړه ۔ خدای
دَ وبخښنه ۔ ثواب به دَ وشی ۔ سور چه دا خبره واورېده نو ورته ډير

پَه قهر شو ورغیَ او یو خو بیننونه ئی پر واچول او رئی ویل چه بی
غیرتَ دومره نه شَر میدری چه ما دَ اسر را کوزَ وی او ته پخپله روغ
موټ ئی دَ ځای نَه پا شی چه اوبَه وسکی ۔ هغه بل ور باند
اواز وکړو ویل یی بچو خذمه؟ خما ازار ووهلی که نه ۔ هغه بله ورخ
م درته واز وکړو چه لوکوتی راشه دا بیره راته پَه خولَه کښں واچوه
نو خذمه دَ خان غلی کړ ۔ هغه دریم دی سورته اواز وکړو ویل ئی
صاحبَ یو خوئی نورهم ووهه دَ ناراستی خو هم یو حد وی ۔ دَه لَه
حدَ رویسته ۔ هغه بله ورخ یو سپی راغی خما صنع ئی خقولو ۔
دی کم بخت ورته دَ ناراستی نه دومره نَه ویل چه کوری شه ۔ لَه
دَه نه به خوک خَه خیر و رړی ۔ سور چه دَ دی بل لټه دا خبره
واوریده نو اول خو حیران شَه او بیائی ډیر وخندل ۔ او رئی ویل
چه کَه دا حال وی نو خذمه به دَ هندوستان خلق پَه خپل ملک
بْند حکومت وکړی ۔

VOCABULARY LX.

خانَدان	*khānadān*	Family.
ملا	*mulā*	Priest.
بهادَری	*bahādari*	Adventure, bravery.
تکړه ژوندون	*takra jhwandūn*	Active life.
هغه به لار نیوله	*haghuh ba lār niwala*	He took to the road.
مشهوُر	*mashhūr*	Famous.
داسی چل وشو	*dāsé chal wo sho*	It so happened.
فرض یا کار	*farz* or *kār*	Duty.
پسی کیدل	*pasé kédal*	To hunt down.

نیول	nɪwal	To capture.
مفرور	mafrūr	Outlaw.
انعام	inām	Prize or reward.
نوی اودریدلی	nawé odrédalé	Newly raised (regt.)
د گائد پلتن	da gāid paltan	The Guides Regt.
کوشش کول	kōshash kawal	To try.
تنبو یا خیمه	tanbū or khéma	Tent.
خیال	kheyāl	Thought.
خیال کول	kheyāl kawal	To think.
لار	lār	Path, road.
خور	khwar	Nullah, ravine.
دره	dara	Valley.
غاښی	ghākhay	Pass (on the top of the hill).
دا خاص د گائدو دَ پاره لائق دیَ	dā khās da gāid da pāra lāieq day	He is just the man for the Guides.
چټی یا خط	chitai or khat	Letter, note.
راغوښتل	rāghukhtal	To invite.
پراؤ	parāw	Camp.
معامله	māmela	Matter, affair.
په دی معامله کښی خبری اتری کول	pa dé māmela ké khabaré ataré kawal	} To talk this over.
دَ په سر روپئی منل یا ورکول (یا پیسی)	da-puh sar rufai (or pesé) manal or warkawal	} To put a price on someone's head.

د خبره منل	*da khabara manal*	To accept invitation.
رسوخ ـ اعتبار	*rusūkh* or *itébār*	Reputation.
عزت	*izzat*	Honour.
سرکار	*sarkār*	British govt
لرل	*laral*	To possess, have.
گوره	*gōra*	Look here !
زو رند کول	*zwarand kawal*	To hang.
د خلقو د وراندې	*da khalqo da vrāndé*	Publicly.

EXERCISE 59.

Delawar Khan was a Khatak of good family. He was brought up as a priest, but his love of adventure let him to a more active life. He took to the road and in time he became the most famous robber in the whole of Yusafzai. It happened that one of Sir Harry Lumsden's duties was to hunt down and capture Delawar Khan, who was now an outlaw with a price of two thousand rupees on his head. Many a time did Lumsden and his newly raised 'Corps of Guides' try, but they could not capture Delawar. One day sitting in his tent Sir Harry Lumsden thought that this man must know every path, nullah and pass in the District. He is just the man for the Guides. I will send him a note. A

letter was therefore sent to Delawar Khan invit-
ing him to come into the Camp to talk this
matter over. One day Delawar Khan in answer
to this letter, came up to Lumsden. This man,
with a price on his head, accepted the invitation.
It says much for the reputation for honour which
the British possessed in borderland. Lumsden
said to him, " Look here, Delawar, you are
a fine fellow, but one day I will catch you
and hang you publicly on a tree".

VOCABULARY LXI.

د پۀ سترګو ګوتی	da-puh stargo	To blame (lit. to
منډل	gōté mandal	push fingers into some one's eyes).
شا ر	shār	Barren (land), un- couth, uneducated (person).
وینځه	winza	Slave girl.
بی بی	bi bi	Wife, mistress.
چاودل	chāwdal	To split or burst (Intrans).
چاودی	chāwday	Burst (past part.)
مولی	maulā	God.
شادولا	shādaula	Saint (lit. small headed).
پۀ زور کلی نه	puh zōr kali	It cannot be done
کیږی	nuh kégi	by force.

پۀ سبق کېنول	*puh sabaq kénawal*	To send to school.
مندرسه	*mandrasa*	School.
کېنول	*kénawal*	To make to sit.
نۀ دَ دین شو او نۀ دَسادین شو	*nuh da din sho aw nuh da sādin shō*	He became useless for this world and the next.
زۀ پکه	*zaka paka*	The last brass farthing.
باج کول یا داؤکول	*bāj kawal* or *dāw kawal*	To spend uselessly.
تل توکړه	*tal tūkra*	Land.
صبر	*sabar*	Patience.
(ته) خولۀ چینګول	*(ta) khula chingawal*	To ask for help (lit to grin).
پۀ-باندې زړه کول	*puh-bāndé zruh kawal*	To want to ask but hardly daring to.
(سره) لاس کول	*(sara) lās kawal*	To give a helping hand to.
دَ فکر پۀ تال زنګېدل	*da fikar puh tāl zangédal*	To be undecided.
زنګل یا زنګېدل	*zangal* or *zangédal*	To swing, (intrans.)
تش لاس	*tash lās*	Empty handedness
کۀ رشتیا رابانډ وائی	*kuh rishtiā rā bāndé wāyé*	If I tell you the truth.
کته	*kata*	Pack saddle.
تبخی	*tabakhay*	Chapati cooking pan (Urdu Tawā.)
کټوړی	*katōray*	Copper cup (Urdu Katōra)

كنډول	kandōl	Earthen cup.
څلَی	salay	Heap, grave-mound.
نقل	naqal	Copy.
ننګ	nang	Modesty.
پخوا	pakhwā	Formerly.
ګډورَی	gadūray	Lamb.
پريوتل	prèwatal	To fall.
(ته) لاس وركول	(ta) lās war kawal	To shake hands with, help.
خان خپل خان	zāna khpala zāna	Every one for himself.
ګنره	ganra	Otherwise.
هيندکَی	hindkay	Indian (i. e. non-Pathan.)
يادَول	yādawal	To mention, to talk about.
تل ته کول	tal ta kawal	To defeat.
اغزَی	aghzay	Thorn.
موټی	mūtay	Fist.
ټينګَول	tingawal	To hold firmly.
که خبره پۀ خوی واچوی	kuh khabara pūh zōi wāchawé	If you talk about the son...
دَ پوزی سرئی غوټی شو	da pōzé sar yé ghund sho	He grew up (lit. the tip of his nose became round.)
ته څوک او زۀ	tuh sōk aw zuh sōk	What do I care for you !
څوک		

پَه باند تانړه کیدل *puh bāndé*
tānra kédal

To be quartered on
some one(exceeding
laws of hospitality.)

EXERCISE 60.
(IDIOMATIC)

سوري هر سوري راشي او څما پَه سترګو ګوتی منډی چه خامن در
نه شاړ شوَ دَ وینڅی مات سر وینی او دَ بی بی چاودیَ زړهٔ څوک
نهٔ وینی با با ؟ پَه زور خو کلي نهٔ کیږی دَ جماعت پَه سبقم کینول
دَمَندرسی پَه سبقم کینول چه نهٔ کړی مولي نو څهٔ به وکړی شادولا مشهوره
خبره ده چه نهٔ څی وابه دخلم چه نهٔ څوری څهٔ به دکړم نهٔ دَ دین شوَ
او نهٔ دَ سادین شوَ څما څو چه څهٔ زکه پکهوَه هغهٔ م وربانډ باج کهٔ اوس
دَخلقو زړهٔ دیَ چه دا ټل ټوکړهٔ م ده دام هم وربانډ داؤ کړی ولی
زهٔ څهٔ وکړم کهٔ ګوشت ګران نو صبر ارزان آخر زهٔ خو هم پښتوّن یم
پښتوّده راکس چاته خو خولهٔ نهٔ شم چیدنګولیَ او کهٔ پَه چا باند زړهٔ
وهم کړم نو چه ویی غوارم پَه دی خولی نو څورم بدیی پَه کومه خولی
آخر کهٔ څوک چاسره څهٔ لس وکړی نو خوراکي خو یی نهٔ شی ټوله ورخ
دَ فکر پَه ټل زانګم چه تشه لس تهٔ م دشمن ئی او کهٔ رشتیا رابانډ
وئی نو څما خو هم دغه دَکتی او دَ تبنکی خبره ده اوس خوداسی
وخت راغلیَ دیَ چه که کڼوریَ ورکوی نو کڼویل به پرڅوک در نهٔ کړی
پَه پښتنو لاړل خلی جوړ شول او نقلؤ نهٔ ئی پاتی شول نن خو
پښتو دَ پښتوّن لړه او نذی دَ ، غل لار پخوا به پښتوّن پَه پښتون سر
اینیو او اوس چه څموّنړ مفرور یاغستان ته ورشی نو دَ سلو روپو
کڼوریَ شی پخوا به چه څوک پریوتو نو چا خو به لس ورکړ اوس
خو څان خپلَ څان کهٔ وی در سنه خو خوړه ګنړهٔ مړه خلقو به
هندکیان یادول اوسئی هغوی ټل ته کړی دیَ او کهٔ رشتیا درته

ووايم نو دَ دى زمانى خامن خه دى كه دا دَ دشمن سترګه كښې
اغزى نه وى نو چاله خه كوى بس چه دَ موظى دَ ٢بذهولوشى
نو خى در نه چرګ خو يو مارغه دى چا ونيوۀ دهغۀ دى دمور
زړۀ پۀ خوى او دښوى زړۀ پۀ اوچ ديوال پۀ دنيا كښى هم يو
پلاړ دى چه زړه ئى غواړى چه خوى رانه اوچت شوى او كۀ خبره
په خوى واچوى نو دَليدو نه ئى پۀ نه ليدو خوشخال وى تر هغه
دښوى وى چه لا ئى چرګوړى بازګ نه وى ويلى خو چه دپوزى
سرئى غونډ شى نو بس تۀ خوك او زۀ خوك داخو لا پريوړده چه
ورارۀ م هم راغلى دى پۀ ما ثانوه دى—

Section 13.

The student is advised to learn the following idiomatic sentences carefully before going up for his Examination :—

1. Since I came to this place.	*Kala rāsé chī zuh dé zāi ta rāghalay yam.*
2. Until this is satisfactorily settled, the tribal allowances as well as your own are stopped.	*Tar sō p̄oré chi da dé puh khuh shān sara faisala wō nuh shee, da qām mājéb aw stā khpal dwāra ba band wee.*
3. The ducks are swimming in the water.	*Hilai puh ōbō ké garzi.*
4. Tell the syce to cut some grass for the horse.	*Sāis ta wo wāya chi da āss da p̄āra suh wākhuh wo kree.*

5. We were cutting wood when they attacked us and carried off all our cattle.

Mūng largee wahal chi rā bāndé yé hamla wō kra aw tōl zamūng māl yé bōtlo.

6. I have nothing to do with him.

Zamā war sara hiss gharaz nishta.

7. I owe him five rupees.

Da haghuh rā bāndé pinzuh rūpai dee.

8. Yesterday you said he owes you some money.

Parūn khō tā wo wé chi zama puh haghuh bāndé suh rupai dee.

9. Yes, he owes me five rupees.

Ho zamā war bāndé pinzuh rūpai dee.

10. I can't help it, I will have to send you back to your own country.

Pa dé ké zuh gram nuh yam, zuh ba tā khwā makhwā khpal watan ta biārtā légam.

11. I will try my best to keep you as my own orderly but I do not know whether the colonel will be willing to allow this.

Sōmrā chi mé da wasa kégee, dōmra kōshash ba wo kram chi tā da zān ardali kram, magar zuh khabar nuh yam chī karnail sāhib ba pa dé rāzee shi kuh na.

12. I tried my best to send him to my own regt. but the Colonel did not agree.

Sōmra chi da wasa mé kédalo, dōmrā kōshash mé wō kar chi zuh yé khpalé paltané ta wo légam, magar karnail sāhib wo na manala.

13. This man says you have beaten him, what have you to say for yourself ?

Dā saray wāyee chi zuh dé wahalay yam, puh dé ké stā suh jawāb day ?

14. How far is it to the Mess ? — *Miskōt sōmra laré day?*

15. What is that firing? — *Hagha dazé da suh dee?*

16. What is that noise ? — *Dagha shōr da suh day ?*

17. I will write a letter when I have eaten food. — *Chi rōtai wo khuram nō chitai ba wō likam.*

18. When I had arrived in Kohat I met an old man. — *Kala chi zuh Kohāt ta wo rasédalam nō yau spin giray puh makha rāghlo.*

19. I saw him before he saw me. — *Hagha lā zuh lidalay nuh wam, chi mā hagha wōlid.*

20. If he had killed me he would have been as sorry as I should have been if I had killed him. — *Kuh zuh yé wajhalay way, nō haghuh ba dōmra afsōs karay woh, laka chi da haghuh puh wajhalo (or marg) mā ba karay woh.*

21. I wish I had gone to Kabul. — *Armān day chi zuh Kobāl ta talay way.*

22. I wish I had been married. — *Armān day chi mā wāduh karay way.*

23. I wish I had come before four. — *Armān day chi zuh luh salōrō bajo na awal rāghalay way.*

24. He not only beat me with a stick but if you had not come he would have certainly killed me. — *Zuh yé nuh seraf puh largee bāndé wo wahalam, balké kuh tuh rāghalay nuh way no zuh ba yé wajhalay wam.*

25. What do you do with your pay?

Tuh khpal talab suh kawé?

26. Let alone English I can not speak my own language well.

Angrézi kho prégda chi zuh khpala jhaba hum kha nuh sham wayalay.

27. See if my book is on the table.

Gōra chi zamā kitāb puh méz bāndé kho nishta.

28. See if the sahib is coming.

Gōra chi sāhib kho nuh rāzee.

29. The doctor advised him to drink two seers of milk every day.

Daktar war ta wo wé chi da vrazé dwa séra pai ska.

30. Come to my house every day and bring me some flowers.

Mudām zamā kōr ta rāza aw rā la suh gulūna rāwra.

31. Every kind of shooting can be had in this country.

Pa dé watan ké har rang khkār mundalay shee.

32. My only brother committed a serious crime and became an outlaw.

Zamā khāli yau vrōr woh aw haghuh hum yau sakht juram wō kar aw mafrūr sho.

33. This is the very man whom I wanted to see.

Dā hum hagha saray day chi mā wayal zuh ba yé gōram.

34. We started on the very moment and reached Kabul the same day.

Hum puh hagha sāat mūng rawān shoo aw Kābal ta amrōza wo rasédoo.

35. The thanadar laughed at the old woman

Thānra dār būdai pōré wo khandal aw yé wo

and said "This is the way with you people".

wayal chi dā stāso da khalqō lār dah.

36. Why did you laugh at him ?

Walé dé war pōré wo khandal ?

37. The dog began to bark but no one stirred.

Spay puh ghapā sho magar hésōk wo nuh khwazéd.

38. The sahib is about to come. Just wait he will be here in a moment if you want to see him.

Sāhib rātlūnkay day (or) puh rātlo ké day puh yaw sāat ké ba rāshee kuh yé gōré.

39. I suppose you consider yourself wiser than I am.

Zamā khyal day chi tuh khpal zān luh mā na hukhyār ganré.

40. A little more than three years later this city was again attacked by Aurangzéb.

Luh dréo kālō na lag suh ziāt pas, puh dé khahar bāndé Aurangzéb biā hamla wo kra.

41. He himself did not stay there any longer but left his Sardars to complete the work.

Pakhpala kho dér halta pāté nuh sho magar khpal sardārān yé da kār pūra kawalo da pāra halta prékhōdal.

42. Take either this or that.

Yā dā wākhla yā hagha wākhla.

43. I will take neither.

Zuh yau hum nuh akhlam.

44. Give them five annas each.

War ta pinzuh pinzuh ané war kra.

45. I must have seen this man but I cannot remember now.

Dā saray ba mé lidalay wi, kho os rā ta yād nuh di.

46. Remind me when I go to the Office.

Chi daftar ta lārsham no rā ta yūd kra.

47. I threw a stone at him.

Mā hagha puh kānrī wo wishtalo.

48. When did you meet him?

Kala puh makha daraghay?

49. I met an old man whom a little boy was leading by the hand.

Yau spin giray puh makha rāghlo chi yau warūki halak luh lās na biwalo.

50. I was just missed otherwise my sight would have been destroyed for ever.

Zuh ila bach shwam ganra da ūmar da pāra ba me nazar harbād shaway woh.

51. The old man who had only one eye was telling stories to the boys in the Hujra.

Spin girai chi puh yawa starga kānray woh, halakāno ta puh hūjra ke qesé yé wayalé.

52. The old man's evidence should be accepted as he said he had read the marriage service.

Da spin giri gawāhi dé manzūra shi chi wāyee chi mā yé nikāh taralay day.

53. On the further side of the plain a river had to be crossed twice.

Da mairé puh bala khwā luh yau sind na dwa zala poréwatal woo.

54. He has to go to the office.

Hagha khwā makhwāh daftar ta ba zee.

55. My dog got a thorn stuck in his foot, went lame and would not work.

Zamā da spi puh khpa ke aghzay māt sho. gud sho aw kār yé nuh sho kawalay.

56. I shall pay him out when he comes back.

Chi biarta rāshee no ba war sara poh sham.

57. He was very disconcerted when the stolen property was found in his pocket.

Chi da ghlā māl yé luh jéb na barāmad sho, no dér kacha sho.

58. Needless to say he himself was convinced of his bad habit.

Puh dé ké shak nishta chi hagha pakhpala hum puh khpal bad ādat qāil woh.

59. I had many misfires but even then I shot 125 head of game.

Dér zala mé tōpak ghal sho, kho biā hum mé pinzuh da pāsa shpag shalé marghān wo wishtal.

60. I would have shot many more, but my cartridges were beginning to get wet and would not go off.

Nōr dér ba mé hum wishtali wōo khō kārtūsūna mé puh laundédo rāghlal aw nuh khlāsédal.

61. I have caught cold.

Zuh yakhnai wahalay yam.

62. Who has caught fever?

Sōk tabé niwalay day?

63. The villagers have small pox.

Puh kali wālo bānde nanakai khatali di.

64. My servant has plague.

Zamā puh naukar bānde tāūn lagédalay day.

65. After I came back from the office I had to go to the city.

Luh daftar rātlo na pas zuh khwā makhwah khahar ta lāram.

66. After I finish my work I will have to go to the cantt.

Chi kār khlās kram nō khwā makhwāh ba chawnrai ta zam.

67. Don't fire unless you are fired at.

Kuh dar bāndé daz wo nuh shi no tuh daz muh kawa.

68. Don't fire unless it is absolutely necessary.

Kuh bilkul zarūrat pékh nuh shi no daz muh kawa.

69. Don't allow him to go unless he has a proper pass.

Kuh war sakha barābar pāss nuh wi no tlo ta yé muh prégda (or muh yé prégda chi lārshee).

70. If I were or had been there I would not have let you do this work.

Kuh zuh halta way, no mā ba tuh dé kār kawalo ta prekhay nuh wé.

71. If he is there I shall certainly produce him before the Magistrate.

Kuh hagha halta wi no zarūr ba yé zuh majestarait ta pésh kram.

72. He abused me vilely but I said nothing.

Rā ta yé dér (or bad bad) kanzal wo kral, kho mā hiss wo nuh wayal.

73. The tribe gave 10 hostages and deposited 15 Snider rifles as security.

Qām las tana yarghamal war kralo aw pinzalas kuniz topak yé da zamānat pa taur war kral.

74. Formerly this land had no means of irrigation except rain fall.

Puh khwā zamāna ké dā zamaka bārāni (or lalma) wah.

75. Wait here until I come back from the city.

Tar sō ṗōré chi zuh luh khahar na biarta rā nuh sham dalé isār sha.

76. I sold my horse to him for 50 rupees.

Mā khṗal ass ṗuh haghuh bāndé ṗuh panzōs rūpai khars kar.

77. Never mind I will engage a barrister and prosecute him in the law court.

Hess bāk nishta yau wakil ba wōnisam aw war bāndé ba ṗuh adālat ké dawa wo kram.

78. I have engaged a mali, who really knows his job.

Yau māli mé sātalay day chi waqi ṗuh khṗal kār khuh ṗōhégẹe.

79. Challenge him first and then shoot.

Awal war bāndé awāz wo kra aw biā yé wola.

80. Will you call out to my servant?

Lūkūti zamā naukar ta khō awaz wo kra?

81. My village was raided on the 15th of last month.

Da téré miāshté ṗuh ṗinzalasam tārikh zamā ṗuh kali bāndé dāra ṗréwata.

82. If the stolen property is not found the tribes will be heavily fined.

Kuh da ghlā māl wo nuh mūndalay shi no ṗa qām bāndé ba lōi jurum ṗréwozi.

83. Button your coat.

Da kōt batanūna dé wāchawa.

84. Tie on your putties.

Patai dé wo tara (or tāw kra)

85. Put on your turban.

Patkay dé ṗuh sar kra or wo waha.

86. Put on your shoes.

Panré dé puh khpo kṛa.

87. If you like to start so early you will have to put on your gloves.

Kuh dāsé wākhtī rā-wānégé nō khwā makhwāh ba dastāné puh lās kawé.

88. Do not be angry with me.

Luh mā na muh khapa kéga.

89. I am sorry I did not notice you until you passed on.

Zuh afsōs kawam chi tar hagha wakhta mé wo nuh lidé chi tér shwé.

90. Open your mouth, you must take this medicine at once, otherwise the fever will recur.

Khuluh wāza kra, dā dārū dar la samdasti skal pakār di, kuh nuh wi nō taba ba darbāndé biā rāshee.

91. Shut your mouth after drinking medicine.

Luh dāro skalo na pas khuluh dé piché kra.

92. Open your eyes and look towards me.

Stargé wō gharawa aw zamā taraf ta wo gōra.

93. Shut your eyes and don't open them till I speak to you.

Stargé paté kra aw muh yé gharawa tar sō pōré chi zuh dar sara khabaré wo nuh kram.

94. Open your book and start from where we had got up to

Kitāb dé wo ghwarawa aw tar kuma zāia pōré chi mō lawastay day, luh hagha zāi na shūrū kra.

95. Listen to me.
96. Do you hear?
97. I know what you mean.

Ghwag kégda,
Ghwag dé day?
Sta puh matlab zuh pōhégam.

98. I asked him what village he came from.

Ma war na tapōs wo kar chi da kum kali yé.

99. I have nothing to do with him.

Zamā war sara hiss gharaz nishta.

100. Can not you write with a pencil ?

Tuh puh pensan nuh shé likalay ?

101. I cannot give him any more.

War ta nōr nuh sham warkawalay.

102. In spite of all his good evidence the magistrate had to punish him.

Sara da haghuh da khé gawāhai majestarait war ta khwā makhwāh sazā war kra.

103. I will let you off if you tell me the whole truth.

Kuh tōla khabara rā ta rishtiā rishtiā wō kré nopré ba dé gdam.

104. Let us go to that large village and arrange for grass for our horses.

Rāza chi hagha lōi kali ta lār shōo aw da khpalo asūno da wākho da pāra bandūbast wo kroo.

105. Sahib, I have suffered much injustice.

Sāhiba puh mā bāndé déra be insāfi shawé dah.

106. He must come himself and bring all the books with him.

Pakār di chi pakhpala rāshee aw tōl kitābūna da zān sara rāwree.

107. After three days we found out that the ropes of the tents were missing.

Dré vrazé pas mūng khabar shoo chi da tambwānō rasaɪ vraké di.

108. Put it.

Ké yé gda.

109. Give it to me

Rā yé kra.

110. He has two sons, one takes after his mother and the other takes after his father.

Dwa zāman yé di, yau mōr ta talay day aw bal plār ta tzlay day.

111. I would rather sit in the veranda than out in the field.

Da bahar pati na kho zamā khwakha dah chi puh baranda hé kénam.

112. He lives next door to me.

Hagha rā sara déwāl puh déwāl osee.

113. Next door but one there lives a gambler.

Puh drem kōr ké yau jawārgar osee.

114. Last year the Malik's wife eloped with a Peshawari barber.

Parosakal da malak khaza yau pekhawri nāi sara lāra or *matiza shwa.*

115. I saw him passing by my door.

Mā hagha wo lidalo chi zamā puh dar-wāza térédo.

116. You ought to have gone yesterday.

Tā la parūn tlal pakār woo (or) *pakar woo chi tuh parūn talay way.*

117. I must write to the General about the deficiency of rations.

Da rasan da kami pa bāb ké pakār di chi zuh jarnail sāhib ta wo likam.

118. Wind the watch otherwise it will stop.

Garai la kunji war kra ganra wo ba drégi.

119. May God make you the king of this country!

Khudāi dé da dé mulk bādshāh kra !

120. This made me think that my regt.

Pa dé khābara mé fikar wo kar chi bala

would move on the next day. — *vraz ba paltan mé rawānégee.*

121. Wind your turban round my gun. — *Patkay dé zamā luh tōpak na tāw kra.*

122. I saw him coming. — *Hagha mé wo lido chi rātlo.*

123. I shot him dead with a revolver. — *Hagha mé puh tamācha wo wishto au mar mé kro.*

124. A scorpion stung my toe. — *Yau laram da khpé puh gōta wo chichalam.*

125. He fired at me and hit my finger. — *Rā bāndé yé daz wo kar aw puh gōta yé wo wishtam.*

126. Have my watch repaired. — *Garai mé puh chā muramata kra.*

127. Come on this day week. — *Puh nananai vraz rāsha.*

128. Learn your yesterday's lesson. — *Parūnay sabaq dé yād kra.*

129. Take care not to come by this road again. — *Paham kawa chi biā pa dé lār rā nuh shé.*

130. He may come. — *Gundé hagha rāshee.*